Survival Mom

Survival Mom

How to Prepare Your Family for Everyday Disasters and Worst-Case Scenarios

Lisa Bedford

HarperOne
An Imprint of HarperCollins*Publishers*

HarperOne

SURVIVAL MOM: *How to Prepare Your Family for Everyday Disasters and Worst-Case Scenarios.* Copyright © 2012 by Lisa Bedford. All rights reserved. Printed in the United States of America. No part of this book may be used or reproduced in any manner whatsoever without written permission except in the case of brief quotations embodied in critical articles and reviews. For information address HarperCollins Publishers, 10 East 53rd Street, New York, NY 10022.

HarperCollins books may be purchased for educational, business, or sales promotional use. For information please write: Special Markets Department, HarperCollins Publishers, 10 East 53rd Street, New York, NY 10022.

HarperCollins website: http://www.harpercollins.com

HarperCollins®, ®, and HarperOne™ are trademarks of HarperCollins Publishers.

Book design by Terry McGrath
Illustrations by Lisa Henderling

FIRST EDITION

Library of Congress Cataloging-in-Publication Data is available upon request.

ISBN 978–0–06–208946–5

12 13 14 15 16   RRD(H)   10 9 8 7 6 5 4 3 2 1

Dedicated to the three most important people in my life, Stephen, Olivia, and Andrew.

And thanks, Dad, for always believing I had a book inside me, just waiting to be written.

Contents

What Kind of Survival Mom Are You?

1. **Wandering down Main Street in Disneyland, you find yourself thinking:**
   a. The castle is so pretty. I think I'm going to cry!
   b. We've got sunblock, water bottles, and a packed lunch. We're going to have a great day.
   c. I wonder which kid is going to hit the wall first.
   d. Who is that duck approaching my kid, and WHERE ARE HIS PANTS???
   e. I wouldn't be caught dead at Disneyland. It's a prime terrorist target.

2. **When the electricity goes out, the first thing you do is:**
   a. Call your husband.
   b. Scramble through drawers looking for flashlights and batteries.
   c. Calm the kids, grab your Power's Out Emergency Kit, and begin following the directions on a laminated checklist.
   d. Shut the blinds; fill the bathtubs with water; lock and load.
   e. Head for the bunker. That EMP you've been expecting may have just happened.

3. **You notice that your local Walmart is offering an "Introduction to Handguns" class for women. You immediately think:**
   a. What is this world coming to? Someone is going to get an eye shot out.
   b. I should maybe, probably, learn how to shoot a gun someday.
   c. That's a class I need to take.
   d. I'm glad they finally got my class scheduled. I wonder how many students I'll have this time around.
   e. I'd sign up in a heartbeat if it were "Tactical Urban Sniper Training."

4. **Your idea of food storage is:**
   a. An extra box of Fruit Loops in the cupboard.
   b. Something only Mormons do.
   c. Having at least a month's worth of extra food stashed away. You never know when it might come in handy.
   d. Buckets and barrels, filled with only God knows what because you forgot to label them back in Y2K.
   e. Loading up the bunker with beans, bullets, and Band-Aids.

5. Online, you're known as:

a. CuddleBunny209
b. Momof2CuteKids
c. OneSmartMama
d. WarriorWoman4God
e. LiveFreeOrDie8720

6. You wish your parents had named you:

a. After your grandmother
b. Hillary
c. Something that sounds more presidential
d. Sarah Connor
e. Anything gender neutral

How to Score Your Responses:

Mostly a's: It's time to put on some big-girl panties and take off the rose-colored glasses if you're going to be a Survival Mom.

Mostly b's: Your Survival Mom DNA is starting to show!

Mostly c's: You sound like a sane Survival Mom to me, but then, those would have been my answers, too.

Mostly d's: Are you off your meds again? Seriously. Chill out and listen to some Barry Manilow.

Mostly e's: People think you're crazy, but it's all part of the plan.

From Suburban Mom
to Survival Mom, an Introduction

My transformation from suburban mom to Survival Mom has taken a lifetime. Maybe it began in junior high with my A+ in a desert survival class or with the tales of true survival I read each month in my Nana's copies of *Reader's Digest*. Whenever or wherever the seed was planted, it dug itself into my consciousness and grew deep roots.

By the time I was married and the mother of a toddler, Y2K rolled around. A part of my brain said, "This is much ado about nothing. Y2K+1 will be no more significant than any other day." But something deeper and more primitive spoke up and said, "I'm a mom now. It's my job, my sworn duty, to protect my family." So, I stocked up on toilet paper.

My focus on the basics of survival never disappeared. I began storing blankets beneath the backseat of our Tahoe, and at least one case of water bottles was always stowed in the trunk. My husband began to tease me about my favorite sentence starter, "Just in case …"

Really, survival should be the *last* thing on my mind. I was hardly born to a homesteading or survivalist family. Rather, at an early age my mother taught me the technique of calculating percentage discounts in my head on our frequent trips to the mall.

Last summer when we were hiking at Lake Tahoe on a paved, wheelchair-accessible path (my favorite kind), I noticed that my mother was sporting a brightly colored sequined fanny pack. I was impressed. I knew she read my blog daily and figured that she had paid close attention to my lists of emergency must-haves. If I needed insect repellant or an energy bar, she'd have it. Right? Wrong. Halfway through the hike, she sat on a rock, opened the fancy fanny pack, and pulled out twelve, a *dozen*, different lip glosses. *That* is my survival heritage!

What spurred me into the foreign world of food storage, firearms, and preparedness as a lifestyle was the downturn of the American economy. If my friends could lose jobs and homes, so could we. If nothing else, I'm a realist. Every dormant survival instinct in my body awoke, and I knew that this time was no dress rehearsal as Y2K had

> *I am learning all the time. The tombstone will be my diploma.*
>
> —EARTHA KITT

been. I felt a sense of urgency, as though an F5 tornado was storming toward my house and I only had the briefest of time to prepare. My family's survival and our future well-being were, in large part, in my two French-manicured hands.

At this point, my background as a manic researcher came in handy, and I devoted every spare minute to learning about food dehydration, oxygen absorbers, comparative rifle calibers, and an NRA membership. In no time I could cite the advantages of a gravity-fed well and had Bug Out Bags packed for each member of the family. I was dead serious about being prepared.

Online, I was drawn to survivalist forums, blogs, and websites, but it gradually occurred to me they were all, every single one, designed with men in mind. They were geared toward the survivalist lifestyle that had little in common with my own as a suburban mom. That's when The Survival Mom blog was born. My research, experimenting, and practical applications finally had an outlet and, soon, a worldwide audience.

As though I didn't have enough to do, I developed an original curriculum to teach others about food storage, cooking off the grid, and strategies for getting out of Dodge. Despite my meanderings from one career to another, teaching was always a constant, and I've delighted in sharing my knowledge of survival with others in online webinars and in-person classes.

If the day comes when I am standing in rubble that was once our home and my children look up at me, they will want to know, "Mom, are we going to be okay?" At that moment, I'll know that my transformation into The Survival Mom was worth it.

How to Read This Book

"Once upon a time … the end!"

I remember my dad telling me that story, the shortest story ever told, and then ordering me to get in bed and go to sleep. Most stories and books are linear in nature. There's a beginning, a middle, and an end. This book is not designed to be read in any certain order. It's designed with you in mind, a Survival Mom with unique responsibilities, circumstances, and interests. What may be most important to you will probably be different from every other mom you know.

One thing is certain, though: This book will prod you into a higher level of concern for your family's future. Don't be surprised if you have feelings of panic and of being overwhelmed. Switching from a mind-set and lifestyle of "Life is good and is only going to get better" to "I'm not sure what the future holds anymore or even if there is much of a future" is disquieting, to say the least. Should you sell everything you own and buy a mobile home in Idaho? Do you pretend nothing has changed and call your best friend to schedule a girls' day out, or hunker down with the shades closed and call the doctor for more Prozac?

It's a lot like standing on a shaky bridge. You recognize the peril but aren't sure whether to move forward or go backward. Should you run or take careful, slow steps? The only thing for certain is that staying where you are is the most dangerous position of all.

My recommendation is that you browse through this book, read what catches your eye, and begin making three lists for future actions, To Learn, To Do, and To Buy.

List #1: To Learn

On this list you'll keep track of *skills and knowledge* you realize will be important. A few examples on my own list are: Learn to tie various knots and know when to use them; work on creating recipes from my food-storage ingredients; and push my knitting skills to a higher level and knit a pair of socks.

Interestingly, many items on this list won't cost a dime. If your budget is already strained, and buying even a few extra cans of tuna is a stretch, put more time and energy into learning skills, gaining knowledge, and seeking out other Survival Moms as resources.

List #2: To Do

Here's another list that doesn't have to empty out your bank account. Have you been meaning to compile all your important documents or inventory a garage filled with tools? Do you need to prepare your garden for the spring season?

baby step

Start these three lists right now! Use the form on page 5 or just a piece of paper, get a pen, and begin keeping track of what you need To Learn, To Do, and To Buy. I promise, this book will provide plenty of inspiration!

There are simply dozens of things we intend to do, but they flicker in and out of our minds and are then . . . gone! As you read this book, start adding tasks to a To Do list and keep track of what you accomplish. It's very empowering to see progress, although you will likely never have an empty To Do list!

List #3: To Buy

Ready to shop?

On page 290, you'll find an exhaustive online shopping guide to every product and company mentioned in this book.

Although Lists 1 and 2 will keep you busy, there's really no way around List 3. Stocking up on food, extra toiletries, good quality tools, and other supplies requires money. However, the good news is that a master To Buy list will help set priorities, keep you on budget, and even provide a shopping list when hitting the garage sale circuit.

Without a To Buy list, you may very well find yourself (a) spending money on things you later discover tucked away in a back cupboard or (b) snatching up purchases in a panic. This list helps save money as well as time.

Each chapter contains Instant Survival Tips, Baby Steps, and The Prepared Family, a special section at the end of each chapter with activities involving the whole family. Mini-Glossaries appear in many chapters as well, and there are dozens more tips, including an online shopping guide, in the Extras section.

Even better, you'll find forms at the end of most every chapter for creating your own personalized Family Preparedness Plan. By the time you've finished the book, you'll have a blueprint of specific steps for making your own home and family better prepared. By all means, make copies of the forms in this book, scribble in the margins, highlight important information in your favorite color, and make this book your customized, unique family survival manual.

Family Preparedness Plan— My Three Lists

To Learn

1. _____
2. _____
3. _____
4. _____
5. _____

To Do

1. _____
2. _____
3. _____
4. _____
5. _____

To Buy

1. _____
2. _____
3. _____
4. _____
5. _____

Mini-Glossary

SHTF—HTF=Hits the Fan, and yes, the S stands for exactly what you think it stands for!

TEOTWAWKI—The End of the World as We Know It

Bugging Out—Leaving town quickly in the face of an oncoming disaster

Bug Out Bag (BOB)—Everything you need for basic survival packed in the container of your choice: Army duffel bag, plastic bin, Coach backpack— you name it

CHAPTER 1

Prepare More, Panic Less

Inside every mom is a Survival Mom, whether she knows it or not. Long before we give birth, we worry about our children's survival: their safety, comfort, and happiness. We take every possible measure to prepare for their birth, certain that no other mom has ever been as careful.

These overwhelming feelings of responsibility don't diminish with time. Instead, they intensify as we watch our little ones venture further out into an unpredictable world.

There was a time when a mom's main concerns about her children centered on peer pressure and when Susie should be allowed to shave her legs. Moms of the twenty-first century have those same worries, of course, but the realization has dawned on many of us that the future holds less security and more uncertainty than it did when we were the ages of our children. We feel an instinctive need to focus on the most basic elements of life. To prepare. To survive.

When you think about it, the story of humankind has always been one of survival. Acquiring water and food, a sturdy shelter, and protection from the elements and enemies kept our ancestors busy and out of trouble. Each morning began a day of doing it all over again with no guarantee of a tomorrow.

Survival and self-reliance weren't fads. There was no alternative. To be less prepared than another family made yours more vulnerable, and self-preservation, being the strongest instinct of all, drove these moms into not taking any chances with their offspring.

What Survival Moms worry about

- Will my kids have the same opportunities as I did?
- Will the future be more like *The Jetsons, The Book of Eli,* or *My Name Is Legend*?
- If the bank forecloses on our house, how long will it be before anyone notices we haven't left?
- Might I someday look like those haggard women in photos from the Great Depression?
- Do I have what it takes to be a survivor? Do my kids?

A self-reliant lifestyle and one of preparedness continued well into the twentieth century. I'll bet your great-grandmother—maybe even your grandmother—knew how to preserve food, grow her own produce, and mend everything from socks to jackets. When she canned 40 pounds of peaches, it wasn't because Martha Stewart had proclaimed it the latest trend. Nope. She wanted those extra peaches stashed away because winter storms might kill her entire orchard of peach trees or a swarm of locusts might gorge themselves silly on every single bud next spring.

Her life was unpredictable, and her family was vulnerable to anything and everything Mother Nature might hurl at them. Being prepared wasn't an option; it was a necessity.

The years that followed World War II ushered in a time of incredible, widespread prosperity, drawing more people into cities than ever before and offering an easier lifestyle than any other civilization has ever known. Suddenly, the basics of survival became less of a necessity and almost quaint.

Families no longer needed to grow their own food, not when a terrific Jewish deli was just down the street! Why go through the messiness of canning produce when the grocery store had masses of fresh fruit and veggies available year-round?

City police and fire departments ensured the safety and well-being of residents, and fresh, clean water was only as far away as the twist of a faucet or the flush of a toilet.

Understandably, many of the attitudes of self-reliance and preparedness were lost. They no longer had much value in this newly secure world, and it was into this world *we* were born.

So what happened?

The terrorist attacks on 9/11 were a wake-up call that perhaps our sheltered lives weren't as secure as we thought. In the years that followed, we saw both the buildup and collapse of the real estate market. Retirement funds and investments have plunged in value, unemployment rates continue to rise, and it's hard not to notice that our world is rapidly changing. I know I'm not the only mom who has wondered, "Is anything secure anymore?"

News footage from the dark days of Hurricane Katrina, the 2004 Asian tsunami, Japan's devastating earthquake in 2011, and even everyday natural disasters and severe weather events remind us of our vul-

I am prepared for the worst, but hope for the best.

—BENJAMIN DISRAELI

nerability. Maybe it's not such a good thing that we can watch all these unfold before us on TV and the Internet, up close and personal, because it adds to our worries, even if we live hundreds of miles from any body of water and a tsunami just isn't possible. Ever.

Moms have now come full circle and can appreciate the mind-set and lifestyle of self-reliance and preparedness of our ancestors. Our own world isn't all that secure anymore, and we recognize the need to make our homes and families better prepared for an uncertain future. How many of us have lost sleep, worrying about what the future holds? Don't raise your hand. I know you're out there. Tylenol PM was invented for times like these!

In the midst of all this, there are two things we know for sure. We love our families, and we'll do everything in our power to protect and provide for them.

We're Survival Moms.

INSTANT SURVIVAL TIP

Before another grandma, great-aunt, or elderly friend passes on, what can you learn from her? It only takes one generation for a skill or piece of knowledge to be lost within a family when the next generation no longer has an interest in it or feels it's necessary. Survival Moms know that practical skills have more of a purpose beyond quaint new hobbies. Does this older person in your life know how to can meat, knit socks, or make a killer apple pie? Learn from her before it's too late and you find yourself trying to learn those same skills from a YouTube video.

What Makes a Survival Mom Tick?

Each Survival Mom is unique, but there are a few qualities we have in common.

We're realists—Even in our darkest moments, those days when the fetal position is the only one that makes any sense, we're willing to look life boldly in the eye and accept what is happening. Oh, to be sure, we may drift off into fantasyland every once in a while in an attempt to pretend that life is the way it's always been, but eventually, we slap ourselves back into reality because that's where our family needs us to be.

We're creative—Given enough time, we can make good use out of twenty-two empty tuna cans, a bag of fabric scraps, and a half-used bottle of dog shampoo for the dog that is buried out in the backyard. May he rest in peace.

We never give up—We hope all things, endure all things, and never lose faith, and if we ever start to weaken, we never let on.

We're proactive—Sure, it's fun to worry, fret, and gripe, but in the end, we figure out what needs to be done, and we just do it. We know it's better to prepare on *this* side of a crisis than after the fact.

We're passionate—You don't know militant until you see a Survival Mom defend her kids and her home. She may weigh all of 90 pounds, but I pity the bully who tries to push her kids around or worse. After all these years, Survival Moms haven't evolved all that far from their ancestor, the mother grizzly bear. We'll be prepared for whatever, whenever. We just need a plan, and maybe some chocolate.

Define Your Disaster

Being ready for a crisis requires forethought, planning, and then action. Before you turn that basement into a bomb shelter or stock up on HAZMAT suits, it's important to assess which emergency situations are most likely to happen in your area and in your specific set of circumstances. Tsunamis aren't at the top of the list for desert dwellers, and residents of small rural communities will probably never need to make plans to evacuate highrise apartments.

Until a few years ago, typical disasters in my life involved my nail tech quitting or my husband insisting on a homemade dinner! How times have changed. Now when I consider potential calamities, slightly more serious problems come to mind, like a long-term power outage during the summer or our family business closing its doors. If economic trends continue to spiral downward, a complete collapse of our economy isn't unthinkable, nor is hyperinflation. A drought is more likely than a hurricane where I live, and an earthquake is something I probably will never need to worry about.

In a way, making plans for emergencies is a bit like gambling. You start with the event that has the highest odds first and work your way down from there. Really, should your very first concern be a nuclear attack? Probably not. The odds are much better for a severe weather event, increased crime, or a natural disaster common to your area. Even better odds favor a deep decline in family income and the inability

Most common natural disasters

Floods

Hurricanes

Droughts / water shortages

Earthquakes

Tornadoes

Wildfires

Blizzards

baby step

Plan for a two-week emergency. Assume you have no electricity or phone service.

▪ Stock up on food for two weeks. Be sure this food doesn't require refrigeration or heating.

▪ Store one week's worth of water. That's 1 gallon of water per person per day.

▪ Stock up on extra supplies you use daily, such as shampoo and toilet paper.

▪ Have food and supplies for your pets.

▪ Just in case you have to evacuate, make a plan. Where will you go?

▪ Make it a habit to keep your gasoline tank at least half full.

to pay rent or mortgage payments. For many Survival Moms, a personal financial disaster is at the top of the list.

Caution: you won't be able to prepare for *everything*. This is why it's important to focus on the most probable events first. Once you've done your best preparing for Event #1, begin making plans for Event #2, and what you'll find is that preparedness in one area will overlap onto others. Eventually, you'll have numerous bases covered and can once again sleep through the night. Paradoxically, being prepared is accompanied by peace, not fear.

Here are a few possible disasters to consider. Which ones are most likely to affect you?

▪ Natural disasters—Mother Nature at her worst: wildfires, floods, earthquakes, tornadoes, hurricanes, and more

▪ Extreme weather—"Storm of the Century," ice storms, drought, intense heat waves, blizzards

▪ Personal disasters—loss of job, decreased work hours, illness or injury affecting the ability to work, your mother-in-law moving in

▪ Nuclear events—including, but not limited to, an electromagnetic pulse (EMP), suitcase bombs, and actual mushroom clouds

▪ Terrorist attacks—these could happen anywhere, anytime, although I have to admit that terrorists seem to favor New York City

▪ Social unrest—riots, strikes, large-scale and violent protests

▪ Increased crime rate—home invasions, car-jackings, burglaries

▪ Economic collapse—the devaluation of the dollar, bank closures, hyperinflation, a significant stock market crash

▪ Biological catastrophes—epidemics or pandemics, biological warfare

▪ Utter and complete collapse of civilization—it's happened before, and it can happen again

After thinking it over and talking with my husband, here is the list I wrote for our family.

1. The closing of our family business and subsequent bankruptcy.

2. Losing our home in a foreclosure.

3. A long-term power outage. If it happens in the summer living in Arizona, we're doomed.

4. Economic collapse.

5. A long-term drought.

Once your own list is complete, it will help narrow your focus so you can prepare for the most likely crisis before worrying about the next.

With some planning and preparing, you'll soon realize you have more control than you might think over how these events will affect your family. The key is to identify likely calamities, make appropriate plans, and then take action.

The time to start this process is now. Just because an emergency situation has never happened to you doesn't mean it never will. Bad things happen even in Disneyland! And don't worry that getting better prepared will require you to take drastic, nonsensical measures. You won't be the laughingstock of the neighborhood, I promise! Being ready for unforeseen events is smart, and the steps you'll be taking are common sense, things that millions of other people have done.

The truth is that the interconnectedness that has made our comfortable lives possible is surprisingly fragile. Think of it as an amazing, complex machine. Year after year, the wheels and gears of the machine operate smoothly, and no one ever thinks that it might break down. It only takes a little bit of sand between the wheels, though, to slow the machine down and even bring it to a standstill.

Learn to drink the cup of life as it comes.

—AGNES TURNBULL

||||||||||||||||||||||||||||||||||||||||||||||||||||||||||||||||||||||||||||||||||||||||||||||||||||||||||||||||||||

Just-in-Time Shipping

Back in the day when I clothed my kids in Gymboree from head to toe, the sales clerks could almost always manage to find the size I needed by "checking in the back." Every store has a stockroom in the back where, presumably, massive quantities of extra products are shelved. Well, a couple of years ago I was surprised to find out that this isn't true, Gymboree notwithstanding.

In fact, most stores operate on a system known as "just-in-time shipping." In other words, products arrive *just in time* to be put on the shelves to replace whatever has been purchased. That's why, when a store has a particularly good sale on an item, once it's sold out, it might be out of stock for days or weeks. There are no extras hidden in the back room. Retailers keep their inventories to a bare minimum in order to save money and to not end up with a stockpile of a product that isn't selling.

One impressive feature of this system is that it's run by computers and can actually forecast which products will be needed where and when. For example, when the weather in a certain area takes a turn toward higher temperatures, the system will automatically begin shipping items such as sunblock and beach toys. An oncoming hurricane will trigger the shipment of bottled water, baby formula, and ice. As long as things are running smoothly, this is an amazing system.

Life isn't always a well-greased wheel, however. A major crisis in our country could easily slow the shipping business down to a crawl. It could be a natural disaster affecting the busy ports along the West Coast. Excessively high diesel prices could drive some trucking companies out of business and reduce the amount of goods being shipped via our highways. Whatever the event, the just-in-time shipping strategy may leave American families high and dry in the middle of a major crisis.

The American Trucking Association presents a sobering view of possible consequences of a partial or complete interruption to our nation's trucking business in its report "When Trucks Stop, America Stops." Here is a brief summary of a possible timeline in the event of a truck stoppage.

If I had a formula for bypassing trouble, I would not pass it round. Trouble creates a capacity to handle it.

—OLIVER WENDELL HOLMES

In Less Than 24 Hours

- Delivery of medical supplies to the area affected by a disaster will cease.
- Service stations will begin to run out of fuel.
- U.S. mail and other package delivery will cease.

Within One Day

- Food shortages will begin to develop.
- Without manufacturing components and trucks for product delivery, assembly lines will shut down, putting thousands out of work.

Within Two to Three Days

- Food shortages will escalate, especially in the face of hoarding and consumer panic.
- ATMs will run out of cash, and banks will be unable to process transactions.
- Garbage will start piling up in urban and suburban areas.

Within a Week

- Automobile travel will cease due to lack of fuel. Without autos and buses, many people will not be able to get to work, shop for groceries, or access medical care.
- Hospitals will begin to exhaust oxygen supplies.

This is all from the stoppage of just one part of our society. Preparedness doesn't look so crazy now, does it? Being proactive ahead of time is the key. Simply storing 2 or 3 months of food may make the difference between your family getting daily, nutritious meals and standing in line with hundreds of other hungry people, hoping for a few groceries. Safely storing several gallons of fuel may help you and your family get through the worst of it while no one else can get out on the road.

Just-in-time shipping works well for manufacturers, wholesalers, and retailers, but the system is vulnerable when calamity strikes. Fortunately, we can plan now to take advantage of this knowledge by taking prudent steps to safeguard our families regardless of what is, or isn't, on a store's shelf.

I know God will not give me anything I can't handle. I just wish that He didn't trust me so much.

—MOTHER TERESA

|||||||||||||||||||||||||||||||||||||||||||||||||||||||||||||||||||||||||||||||||||||||||||||||||||||||||||||||||||||||||||||

The Blessing of Options and Time

Hurricane Katrina was a wake-up call for Americans across the country. Who can forget the sight of families stranded on rooftops and bridges, without the most basic essentials for survival? What we did not see, however, were the thousands of families who had planned and prepared ahead. Many of them also lost their homes, but because of their preparedness, they had far more options than those who did not.

I know people in both categories, prepared and unprepared, and have seen firsthand how being prepared can create multiple options.

Family A, for Anonymous— Do you recognize these people?

The thought of preparedness has never occurred to this family. They live from paycheck to paycheck. Even though they realize this is dangerous, they continue to enjoy living beyond their means with frequent vacations and golf games every Saturday morning. At holiday get-togethers, they look great in their latest fashions and expensive vehicles, and their Facebook page is filled with photos of their latest splurges.

However, there's a dark side not seen by many. This family can only make minimal payments on credit cards and they have less than a thousand dollars in savings. Even though severe winter storms are common in their city, they find themselves running out to buy emergency supplies at the last minute every single time. When Dad lost his job last year, the family suddenly found themselves facing a very difficult future.

Within just 2 months, they faced the reality of losing their home in a foreclosure. Their savings account was quickly emptied, and their credit accounts were turned over to collection agencies. Their options are few and dismal:

- Continue staying in their home, enduring calls from creditors and the mortgage company.
- Move in with relatives.
- Apply for government assistance.
- Try to get another job, even if it means earning far less money.
- Sell anything of value to bring in extra money.
- Begin the proceedings to file for bankruptcy.

Family B, for "Boy, are we glad we didn't buy that overpriced Escalade!"

This family has lived the Boy Scout motto, "Be Prepared!" as a way of life. They have always lived below their means and have saved 6 months' worth of living expenses. The only debt they have is their home, and they pay a little extra toward the principal every month. They have focused on stocking up on extra groceries and supplies and have about 3 months' worth in their pantry.

You can't run away from trouble. There ain't no place that far.

—UNCLE REMUS

Over the years, Dad has picked up some carpentry skills, can lay tile, and occasionally gives guitar lessons on the side. Mom has been a stay-at-home mom but was an accountant and a math teacher in the past. If Dad should lose his job, the family's income will take a big hit, but Family B has some interesting options:

- They can live off their savings while Dad takes classes to learn new, marketable skills.

- They have the luxury of time for a relaxed job search.

- The family has the means to relocate to another part of the country that is more desirable or has more jobs available.

- Dad can pick up odd jobs doing carpentry or tile work. Perhaps he can get a subcontractor's license and start a new business.

- By tightening their belts a bit, their 6 months of savings can be stretched to cover 1 or 2 additional months.

- If things got really tight, Mom could become a math tutor or get a job as an accountant or bookkeeper.

Being prepared isn't just about stocking up on massive amounts of food or having a Bug Out Bag parked by the back door. It's also about having practical skills that are always in demand, no matter the condition of the economy. It's knowing how to adapt to sudden changes, like when good times suddenly come to an end. It's a mind-set and a way of life. Peace, confidence, and empowerment come with being prepared, whether it's for a natural disaster, a job loss, or a worst-case scenario.

The #1 Rule of Preparedness

Do your best where you are with what you have.

If you don't have 6 months of living expenses in the bank, acres of lush farmland for vegetable gardens, or a background in homestead living, you're not alone. Don't get discouraged! If you believe that preparedness is important to the welfare of your family, please don't give up now!

A Survival Mom's Story

Andrea Lynch, Ohio

Central Ohio is home to a remarkable Survival Mom, Andrea Lynch, 36, who has adopted the lifestyle and outlook of her grandparents. Raised by a single mom on a poverty-level income, it was the skills and knowledge of Andrea's grandparents, along with her mother's hard work, that allowed her family to survive years of hardship.

Andrea says, "Papaw had grown up poor, too, and was able to teach my family how to grow a big, lush garden that kept us fed. I remember filling a bucket with water from a creek and watering the plants by hand, and we did everything together as a family. We planted and harvested together, and then Mamaw taught us canning and how to juice tomatoes. We made pickled green beans and one of my favorites, summer squash relish."

Andrea's family was able to survive because they had learned how to make do when that was the only option.

Cooking from scratch nearly 100% of the time filled their bellies with hot, wholesome, homegrown food. In fact, Andrea says, "We thought a Pop Tart or Toaster Strudel was an unbelievable luxury!"

So was calling on a plumber, mechanic, or other professional when a problem arose around the house. Although her grandpa was illiterate, he could do just about anything, including taking apart an engine and putting it back together.

As she told me her story, it touched my heart. This grandma and grandpa, both in their 50s, giving their daughter and grandchildren the best they had to offer, old-fashioned skills that many people viewed with disdain. Andrea was blessed with a grandpa who couldn't read a newspaper but was determined that *his* grandkids would never want for life's necessities.

Now, as a mom of two young children, Andrea remembers the lessons she learned every day as a child. Her own children have their own little gardens and fill them with their favorite veggies: carrots, broccoli, spinach, and sugar snap peas. They have been taught by their mother to be stewards of the earth and are learning that lesson well. Andrea makes healthy foods from what she can grow. She makes her own ricotta and mozzarella cheeses and her own cleaning solutions, and she even learned how to do a bit of leatherworking by attending a Renaissance Fair.

Andrea offers this insight to why she has chosen to embrace the ways of her grandparents. "This lifestyle allows us to live more naturally and to have more self-reliance, freedom, and independence. We're not enslaved by convenience products and services that, at first, seem to offer an easier life, but in the long run take away so much of your independence. You end up not even knowing how to grow, preserve, and prepare your own food!"

Her little ones are healthy. They eat whole, organic produce and have a mom who is determined to pass along these skills and attitudes of self-reliance so they will have a better future and can share them with the next generation.

Do your best . . .

Whatever you can accomplish will leave you at a point further down the road than where you are right now. It's just important that you start *now* and do *something*.

You'll accomplish a lot more, and faster, if you and your husband are on the same wavelength. Schedule weekly "Preparedness Powwows" as a couple or a family, if your children are old enough. Each week, discuss a different "What if?" scenario and how you and your family might respond. As you talk, you'll probably come up with a list of supplies you'll need and skills you want to learn. When you know what you don't know, it is just a matter of spending time at the library, doing some research online, and finding people in your circle of friends and acquaintances who already have those skills and can teach them to you. (Keep your To Buy list handy as you visit garage and estate sales and thrift shops. Having a focus will save money and move you toward your goals more quickly.)

. . . where you are . . .

Millions of Americans live in apartments, condos, or mobile homes. If being prepared is your goal, don't let anything stand in your way, especially not your home's square footage.

Vegetables thrive using a Square Foot Gardening approach, and thousands of moms grow veggies and herbs in pots and other containers. With an inexpensive dehydrator, you can easily dehydrate huge amounts of fruits and vegetables that are then easier to store. Eliminate what you don't need, and use that newly found space for the food and supplies you're accumulating. As you de-clutter, you may very well find items you were planning to purchase. Sell your unwanted stuff in a garage sale or donate to a deserving charity. Either way, it won't be your problem anymore!

I know of at least one family who rents a small storage unit for keeping extra garden and hand tools as well as some 55-gallon water barrels and bulkier items. Be creative!

. . . with what you have.

If funds just aren't there for stocking up on food and supplies, use your time to invest in knowledge, research, and learning new skills. You can network online or in real life with others who are like-minded. No two

Get prepared for $5!

What can five bucks get you?

- 15 packages of ramen soup
- 5 lbs. of rice or beans
- 2 packages of baby wipes
- 2 emergency blankets
- 5 light sticks
- 10 cans of tomato soup (on sale)
- 2 or 3 bandannas
- 2 gallons of bleach
- 3–4 boxes of Band-Aids
- 2 jars of grape jam
- 2 jars of peanut butter

families are alike in their needs or circumstances. Only you can determine what is feasible and what can realistically be accomplished. The most important thing is to pace yourself and view preparedness as a way of life.

A Basic Survival Principle: The Rule of Three

This is the rule of redundancy. Have a backup and then a backup to your backup. Old-time survivalists like to say, "Three is two (in case one breaks or is consumed), two is one, and one is none."

One can opener isn't enough. If it breaks, opening cans of soup will be close to impossible. Have a backup can opener and a backup of any other supply, tool, or food that is essential.

When it comes to plans, you can also apply this rule. For example, making up an evacuation plan should include more than one route out of town in case the preferred route is blocked by flood waters or a traffic jam.

Follow the Rule of Three and you can't go wrong!

What Happens Now?

Becoming better prepared for the future isn't a single task or focus. In fact, focusing on just one element—food storage, for example—will leave your family vulnerable in other areas. Preparedness doesn't happen overnight or even in a month or two. Instead, it's a way of life, a new awareness of current events and trends, and a commitment to stay focused on what will help strengthen and ready your family for whatever comes along with a willingness to learn new things.

This book covers all you need to know about the basic necessities of food, water, and shelter, and provides proactive instructions for learning essential skills and gaining knowledge that will be advantageous, no matter what comes down the pike. You'll be reading about how to get your home ready, inside and out, so it becomes the eye of the coming storm, a comfortable, orderly, and secure nook for you and your family. There's lots of common-sense advice that will help your family find some financial stability and connect with others who are like-minded, and because you don't spend *all* your time at home, there's a complete chapter filled with tips and lists for being prepared for emergencies when you're out running errands or on a cross-country family vacation.

Survival is a mom's job, and this book will get you there!

☑ Be rock-solid parents

When flight attendants instruct passengers to put oxygen masks on their own faces before those of their children, it's a logical sequence. Be strong yourself, and you'll be better able to help them. More than ever, our children need us to be rock-solid. We owe it to our kids to be the adults in the family even when childish urges to overspend or disregard commitments and responsibilities tempt us.

If you're not feeling particularly strong, please give yourself permission to take care of *you*. If you need to talk with a counselor about your own fears and feelings of helplessness, make the appointment! When you read a checklist of the symptoms of depression and you can check off most of them, call your doctor! The simple act of journaling can help relieve stress and put concerns into perspective. When Mom and Dad are at a weak point in their lives, children become very vulnerable. Strong parents build strong children.

☑ Talk amongst yourselves

There are conversations children do not need to hear. Has the family down the street lost their home? Is Dad worried about losing his job? Keep those conversations private and between adults only. If it's tough finding a time and place to talk without the kids around, leave the children with a trusted adult, hop in your car, and drive. Literally! Drive 30 or 40 minutes in one direction, turn around and drive back. That's at least an hour of quiet, uninterrupted talking time, and it only costs a few dollars in fuel.

Our kids don't have the same perspective as we do. When my kids heard of a neighbor family who had lost their home, they didn't understand how that could happen. How do you *lose* a house?

☑ Be honest

When questions do arise, answer them honestly with brief, simplified explanations. Kids mostly want and need to hear that they will be okay. Even if your own situation is dire, you can still reassure them by telling them they're loved and that life is still good.

☑ Make family time a priority

My current battle in our home is against screen time, the time any of us spend in front of a television or computer screen. Every minute spent looking at a screen is a minute taken away from family time. Now more than ever, we all need time spent doing things together and talking. Stronger family bonds will help children feel more secure.

The Prepared Family

Reading aloud is one of the best ways I know of building relationships within a family and increasing time together. As a story unfolds, suddenly everyone is experiencing the same adventure together. Books such as *Charlotte's Web* and *James and the Giant Peach* stir up imaginations, but more important, conversations. You'll find more great titles for family read-alouds in the Survival Mom Extras appendix.

Physical exercise and activities don't have to cost a dime, and they provide great bonding time while helping everyone stay in shape. Walks through the neighborhood, bike rides along a dusty trail, or hiking through a forest filled with autumn color provide time to talk, time to observe nature, and a chance to escape from everyday stress.

Focus on the *doing* part of family time. Watching TV or a movie together doesn't count!

☑ Include one-on-one time

Just as important as family time is the time we parents spend with each child individually. My daughter is at her happiest when the two of us are strolling through the aisles of our local craft store. We dream up projects we can do together and then scurry around looking for the supplies, choosing colors, beads, and plumes. My talkative son just wants to be heard. On a trip to a hardware store, he will talk the entire way there and the entire way back. All he needs to know is that Mom or Dad is listening.

If you study your children, you will soon know their deepest needs and desires. Pay careful attention to their begging.

"Mom, please, can't we go to the library?"

"Mom! Watch me hit this ball!"

If you listen, you will soon learn what they need most. Time spent one-on-one can help meet those needs and emphasize their importance to you and the unique place they have in the world.

☑ Emphasize the good

Rising rates of foreclosures, bankruptcies, and job losses can easily overshadow the good that is still in our world. Emphasize the good things that happen on a daily basis. A good report card, a visit from Grandma, or a new pair of shoes help keep our kids focused on positive and uplifting thoughts. There is so much beauty and wonder in the world. Get in the habit of pointing it out. It will be good medicine for everybody!

CHAPTER 2

Survival Begins with Water

". . . and God said, let there be water."

O ops! That's not quite how it goes, but when you're preparing for an emergency or something worse, water had better be your first consideration. It's not uncommon for survivors of a disaster to be found alive and well 2 weeks or more after the original event if they have managed to stay hydrated. However, when water is nowhere to be found, we have less than 3 days to live.

Water storage sounds mundane and almost too elementary to be bothered with. After all, the toilet flushed just fine this morning, and my kids are tired of hearing, "Water is free, and that's what you're going to drink!" We take water for granted, and it's easy to forget that it's the most important thing to consider in your Family Preparedness Plan.

Water isn't just for drinking. Imagine living for more than a few days unable to do laundry, bathe, or prepare any food that requires water or being able to wash dishes. Now, I'm all in favor of ignoring the laundry and dirty dishes, but that's only because around my house we call those "The Kids' Chores." Having mountains of both would be depressing, not to mention unsanitary.

Fortunately, clean water is readily available and inexpensive. Municipal water plants treat water with chlorine and other chemicals to kill pathogens (disease-causing bacteria) that might be present. In fact, they are so careful in their calculations that water leaves the plant carrying more chlorine than is actually necessary.

INSTANT
SURVIVAL TIP

Stock up on paper plates and cups. In an emergency, you won't need to worry about using valuable water washing dishes. Burn those used paper goods in a campfire, sprinkle the ashes in your compost pile, and you've gone green in a big way!

I recommend the WAPI

What could be more low-tech than a tiny plastic tube, a bit of green wax, and several inches of fishing line? Put all that together just right and you have a WAPI, a Water Pasteurization Indicator. When the small plastic tube is dangled into a pot of water, the green wax it contains melts when the water temperature reaches 149 degrees. When this occurs, the water has been pasteurized. The WAPI costs less than $10 and can be purchased at www.sunoven.com.

Chlorine evaporates quickly, and this precaution ensures that any pathogens lurking in the water pipes leading to your home die ugly deaths long before you fill that pretty pitcher with water and lemon slices. If you're going to store water for emergencies and your water comes from a water treatment plant, there's no need to do anything else to the water before storage. Just fill your containers and cap tightly.

But it's important to remember tainted water can make you and your family extremely sick, so in addition to storing the clean water now, it's important to know how to purify water, should the need arise, *and* have the necessary supplies on hand. In fact, the best strategy is to have at least two different methods for purifying water. It's the "backup to your backup" principle in action.

Before boiling your water, bleaching it, or doing anything else to purify it, start with sanitized containers. Swish a bit of my Survival Mom's All-Purpose Sanitizer (see recipe on page 37) around the inside of the container and then fill with clean water. Avoid reusing milk and fruit juice containers. Milk protein and fruit sugars aren't easily removed and provide a friendly atmosphere for future bacterial growth.

Here are four easy ways to make sure your drinking water is ready to drink.

Boiling water—Health experts agree that this is the safest way to purify water, but not everyone agrees on the length of boiling time required. Some websites and books recommend anywhere from 1 to 10 minutes. The correct length of time? One minute, at the most.

See, pasteurization is the process that kills microorganisms that cause diseases and occurs at just 149 degrees Fahrenheit. Water has to reach 212 degrees Fahrenheit in order to boil, so if you're boiling water to purify it, the 212 degrees is overkill. The use of a WAPI will identify when the correct temperature has been reached; otherwise, boiling is a helpful visual cue.

In order to preserve time, energy, and fuel, bring water to a boil to ensure it reaches the temperature required for pasteurization. Remove from the heat source, cool, and drink.

There are downsides to the boiling method, as effective as it is. Heating water to a boiling point isn't quick if you need clean water in a hurry. In a power outage, you may not be able to boil water or you may be in a location where fuel isn't available for building a fire. However, if you have them, a portable camp stove or even a solar cooker can bring water to the pasteurization level, giving you all the pure water you need.

Bleach—Use bleach that has no additives, such as scents, phosphates, or soap. Add eight drops, or ⅛ teaspoon, per gallon if the water is clear. Otherwise, follow the directions in the chart below. Once the bleach has been added, stir it thoroughly and allow it to sit for 30 minutes.

Water Amount	Cloudy Water	Clear Water
1 quart	4 drops	2 drops
1 gallon	16 drops	8 drops
5 gallons	1 teaspoon	½ teaspoon
55 gallons	4 tablespoons	2 tablespoons

Bleach loses its effectiveness with time, so keep an eye on the expiration dates of each bottle. If you end up with bleach that is long past its peak, pour a cup or two down each sink in the house, allow to sit for a few minutes to kill off any lurking bacteria and odors, and then rinse the drain with water. If you store a small amount of bleach in a Bug Out Bag or other emergency kit, be sure to store it in an airtight container that is leakproof. To be on the safe side, place the small container of bleach inside two Ziploc bags.

Calcium hypochlorite—This is an excellent alternative to bleach, as long as you use pure granular calcium hypochlorite because it has a shelf life of many years. You probably know calcium hypochlorite by its more common name, pool shock. Before you rush out to stock up

The Red Cross method

The American Red Cross uses both boiling and bleach to purify water. Here is its official procedure.

1. If water is cloudy or contains particles, filter using a piece of cloth or a coffee filter to remove solid particles.

2. Bring water to a rolling boil for about one full minute.

3. Let it cool at least 30 minutes. Water must be cool or the next step in adding chlorine bleach will be useless.

4. Add the required amount of liquid chlorine bleach according to the table on the left.

5. Let stand 30 minutes. If the water does not have a chlorine smell, repeat Step 4. Otherwise, it is safe to drink.

on pool shock, though, make sure that what you're buying doesn't contain stabilizers. The only active ingredient should be calcium hypochlorite and the product should be approved by the National Sanitary Foundation (NSF). I recommend Cal-Shock 65.

How is this product used to purify water? It's a simple two-step process. First, add one heaping teaspoon of granular calcium hypochlorite to 2 gallons of water. This mixture is basically homemade bleach and could also be used for household cleaning and laundry. The safest level of chlorine in drinking water is around 2 ppm. I highly recommend having a pool test kit on hand to ensure any water purified with this method doesn't contain too much chlorine (it could cause diarrhea) or too little.

Then, to purify water, add 1¼ teaspoons of this new bleach solution to 1 gallon of water (1 part solution to 100 parts water) and allow the mixture to sit for at least 30 minutes before drinking. If the smell of chlorine is too strong, pour the water from one container into another several times to allow the chlorine to dissipate.

One pound of calcium hypochlorite can purify thousands of gallons of water. You definitely get your money's worth with this product. Just be very careful around its fumes and store it in a cool, dry location in an airtight container.

UV light—For years, hospitals and water treatment plants have used ultraviolet (UV) light to purify water. Now, a company called SteriPEN brings the same technology in portable form to families.

This product uses a small dose of UV rays to kill waterborne microbes in 90 seconds when you simply stir a liter of water with its wand. The lighted wand is on a timer, so it's a foolproof system. Although there is one version of the SteriPEN that is powered with a hand crank, all the others are battery powered and require a backup supply of new batteries. Another downside is that this product is designed to purify small amounts of water at a time.

Two additional methods—Water purification tablets are often packed along with camping and hiking gear and emergency bags. Potable Aqua is one popular brand name. The tablets are lightweight and easy to pack but shouldn't be used by pregnant women or anyone allergic to iodine, and they shouldn't be used for more than 6 weeks. Follow the package directions exactly if you use this method.

baby step

Merely two 2-liter water bottles per day, per person, is sufficient water storage. Fill fourteen of these to have enough water for one person to last a week. Repeat this step for each family member until your water storage is complete!

Finally, one more system that is handy to have on hand for purifying small amounts of water is a portable filtration device. Katadyn and Berkey are two of the bestselling names in the water purification business and they both offer small, portable devices ideal for storing in a backpack or emergency kit. Prices are reasonable enough to have more than one around the house and in each emergency bag.

How Do I Store All This Water?

Filter first, purify second

If you notice debris in your water, or if it's cloudy, use a filter before purifying. Inexpensive coffee filters are a good choice, as are multiple layers of cheesecloth and even clean T-shirt fabric. Commercial filters, such as SteriPEN's FitsAllFilter, can be purchased online.

The general rule of thumb for water storage is to plan on 1 gallon per day per person, minimum. A family of four would need to store 28 gallons for a week's worth of water. However, if you live in areas that are hot and humid during the summer months, it would be a wise idea to store twice this amount. Our bodies lose about 2 to 3 quarts of water per day through sweat, breathing, and urine, so it's better to err on the side of too much water than too little.

It's also better to err on the side of safe storage where leaks can't ruin carpets, boxes of photographs, or anything else of value. Make sure each bottle is capped tightly, and if possible, store water containers off the ground. Ask yourself, "If these water containers leaked, would it ruin my life?" Okay, maybe not your *life*, but flooring and furniture are nearly as important!

As your water storage increases, you'll discover the unfortunate fact that water weighs a lot—over 8 pounds per gallon! Carrying a case of water from the car into the house one day, my daughter remarked, "Why don't they make dehydrated water?"

I guess it takes a kid to come up with a truly revolutionary concept. "Just add water to this pouch, and you have . . . water!" I can see the TV commercials and celebrity endorsements now!

Water is a very important part of being prepared for emergencies, big or small, and I recommend using a system of three layers to ensure you have the right amounts of water in the right-size containers.

Layer #1

Your first layer of water storage should consist mostly of smaller containers that are easily portable. I recommend using clean 2-liter soda bottles, or bottles in a similar size. In just a few minutes these can be rinsed out with warm water with just a drop of soap (add a drop of bleach for better sanitation), rinsed, and refilled. Commercial water bottles in 2- to 5-gallon sizes are also excellent choices. Even Mylar bags, properly sealed, can store water indefinitely.

Don't worry about adding any extra bleach to your tap water if it comes from a municipal water treatment plant. If you're storing well water or water from another source, though, treat it with bleach, using the measurements in the chart on page 23.

Larger bottles will come in handy for flushing toilets, rinsing dishes, and for sponge baths—much easier than emptying out a dozen or so 16.9-ounce bottles!

Store these water containers in closets, cabinets, or under beds. Dark places are best since sunlight can degrade the plastic. Never reuse gallon milk containers: because they are biodegradable, they aren't designed for long-term storage, and they don't have tight-fitting caps.

I discovered a huge upside to storing these bottles beneath my kids' beds one day when my daughter came to me complaining that she could no longer "clean" her room. Her favorite technique, after all, was shoving everything under the bed and pronouncing the room *clean*!

Layer #2

Since Survival Moms are constantly on the go, it just makes sense to have a good supply of water in portable, lightweight containers. The second layer of your water storage should be commercially bottled water. Cases of smaller water bottles are easy to stack and store, and the smaller-size bottles are handy for tossing in a backpack or diaper

You already have stored water!

Don't forget the water in your hot water heater and in the tops of your toilet tanks, unless the tanks contain a toilet bowl cleaner. All this water could account for 40 gallons or more. Never use water from car radiators, water boilers, or waterbeds.

bag. Watch for sales and coupons to make this layer of your water storage easy on your budget.

Avoid storing these in the garage, as heat can cause the plastic to degrade more quickly.

Some water safety experts believe that bottled water produced by companies such as Dasani, Aquafina, and Costco are preferable to smaller store brands. Typically, store brands don't have the same level of quality control as these better-known brands.

Layer #3

Large, commercially produced water drums add a final layer to water storage. These typically hold 30 to 55 gallons and come in lots of different shapes and varieties. Some retailers sell water tanks that hold hundreds of gallons. Consider them, depending on your space, budget, and needs.

Not surprisingly, these larger containers are somewhat expensive, quite bulky, and incredibly heavy when filled. It's possible to find recycled drums that once held liquids such as soy sauce, but these will need to be thoroughly cleaned and sanitized. If you live near "horse people," ask them where they get their barrels for animal water, feed, and barrel races. Used 55-gallon water barrels or drums can be found for less than $20 each.

Storing one or more drums outdoors is a good way to have a water supply for animals and your garden. If possible, keep these outdoor drums in the shade or covered. Fill them using the garden hose and be sure to

Pets need water, too!

Figure on storing 1 ounce of water per day for every pound your dog or cat weighs. Water for larger animals can include well water and water stored in large barrels.

add bleach at a ratio of 1 teaspoon of bleach per gallon of water, or according to the chart on page 23. Additional chlorine (bleach) is important with water stored outdoors, as it can help reduce the growth of algae. Just make sure you place the barrels exactly where you want them, long term, because you *will not be able to move them* once they're filled!

When water is stored outdoors, be aware that it may freeze during the winter. Get ready for the winter by leaving a few inches at the top of each container to allow for expansion. If your winters are cold enough to freeze 55 gallons of water, have a Plan B for providing water for your animals, and be sure you have an ample supply stored indoors for your own use.

Another wintertime option is to store water in smaller buckets that will be lightweight enough to bring inside and allow to thaw.

Large water barrels are also essential in storing rainfall. Be sure to place a screen over the opening of the barrel to keep out leaves and other debris. If mosquitoes are a problem in your area, add a tablespoon or so of oil or liquid soap to the water to kill insect eggs.

This water will absolutely have to be filtered and purified before drinking. To be on the safe side, use a combination of both boiling and bleach or calcium hypochlorite. Running the water through a Berkey filter will also filter out just about anything and everything undesirable.

Not everything that is faced can be changed, but nothing can be changed until it is faced.

—JAMES BALDWIN

If You Have a Faucet, Why Store Water?

It has been decades since American moms had to trot down to the stream or an outdoor well to bring in water for washing up and drinking. It's nearly impossible to imagine a return of those days, but the floods of New England in the spring of 2010 found families lining up for bottled water and boiling what came out of their taps to make sure it was safe to drink. Paradoxically, severe floods can overwhelm city water plants with more of the wet stuff than these plants can treat. Hurricanes, earthquakes, and frozen pipes can all cause a temporary disruption to a family's water supply.

A major disruption in our power grid would cripple city water systems, which rely on electricity. These systems have backup generators,

What about swimming pool water?

One of my friends confided in me that she was prepared to sit by her pool with a shotgun and guard her water if need be. Her comment made me curious. Just how safe is pool water for drinking? Well, she can save her shotgun shells because the answer is, not at all!

Water treatment plants add chlorine to our drinking water, so it isn't the chlorine in our pools that presents a problem. Chlorine evaporates so quickly that stabilizers must be added, and it's the stabilizer that is unhealthy. Stabilizers don't dissipate or evaporate. They stay in the water, increasing in volume with each addition of new chlorine. The only way to reduce the amount of stabilizer in your pool water is to drain the pool, partially or completely, and then refill it with fresh water.

Alan Martindale, water quality supervisor for the city of Mesa, says there are four very important reasons not to consume swimming pool water, other than a gulp or two by accident when splashed in the face by your toddler.

- High total dissolved solids (mineral content such as chloride, sulfate, calcium, and magnesium) can cause a laxative effect, not a good problem to have in an emergency!

- Treatment chemicals are not safe for long-term ingestion. Pool chlorine is often stabilized with cyanuric acid, a derivative of cyanide.

- Chlorine-resistant critters such as Giardia and Crypto (typically from pets) can be present, as well as skin particles, skin oils, hair, and other yucky stuff left behind by swimmers.

- Boiling pool water will only increase the concentration of chemicals and total dissolved solids.

Additionally, a power outage will shut down your pool's pump and filtration system, leading to the growth of algae and other microbes within a few short days. Mosquitoes and their eggs will take over your pool and backyard in no time at all. To prevent this, begin testing the water for chlorine. It needs to be kept up to at least 1.0 ppm. To maintain proper levels, use either liquid or granular chlorine. If your pool supply store stocks the granular tri-chlor, this would be an excellent choice. Treat your pool with 3–4 pounds of granular chlorine, or its liquid equivalent, and then check the chlorine level the next day. Adjust the amount of chlorine by testing your water every 2 days. Keeping mosquitoes in check is important to the health of your entire neighborhood.

Unfortunately, that reservoir in your backyard, known as your swimming pool, won't be of any use if you're planning on drinking the water. Instead, plan on that water as a backup (yes, another layer!) for doing laundry, flushing toilets, and washing the dog!

The water bladder alternative

A water bladder may work out better for your needs than barrels. These bladders are like very, very large, rugged balloons. They can be stored in bathtubs or on any flat surface. They take up a lot of room—and the water will not be potable—but their size and shape may be a better alternative for some.

but in dire circumstances it would be a matter of time before they ran out of fuel.

So, just because water came out of your faucet today, don't get too cocky. Water is so easy to store that you might as well take this simple precaution. You know, just in case.

A Modern-Day Drought

Librarian Beth Felosi remembers the driest days of Atlanta's drought in 2007. Lake Lanier is the main water source for a city that houses half a million people. At the height of the drought, the low level of the lake set a new record. Beth told me: "At the time of the drought I worked near Lake Lanier, and every day there was a sign that I would pass by telling what the level of the lake was. Every day it would be lower and lower and lower. It was an odd feeling." She kept hoping and praying for rain, as residents were given stricter guidelines about water usage.

All outdoor watering, such as irrigating the garden and even washing the car, was banned. Residents were encouraged to shorten shower times, as well as use their dishwashers and washing machines less frequently. If a severe drought happens again, Beth is ready:

"I've installed two rain barrels that I use for the garden and other plants around the house. I've cut back on showers and how often I use the dishwasher. I also have been stocking up on bottled water. It doesn't hurt to have extra for any reason."

What's her advice for anyone facing a similar challenge? "Don't let local news reports terrify you. Listen to what they have to say and try to cut back on how much water you use, but don't live in constant fear that you are going to turn on the tap and find no water. If you do, you'll go crazy."

Color Codes for Water

Did you know that water comes in more than one color? Black water is water from sewage sources that contain human waste. Gray water is the water that drains from your dishwasher, sinks, bathtub, and washing machine; it's never safe to drink, but it can be recycled and put to use to water landscaping, thus freeing up stored water for other uses. However, like so many other things in life, this is a bit easier said than done.

The most rudimentary system to direct gray water to a lawn or a garden is with a simple garden hose connected to the drain line of your washing machine. However, Buzz Boettcher of Gray Water Recycling Systems says this isn't the smartest move to make. Your lawn will end up with piles of lint and residue from soap and dirty laundry. This may not give you the lush greenery you're hoping for.

Filtering systems are sold commercially, and some are basic enough for a DIY installation. Others are more complex, require trained technicians for installation, and can cost thousands of dollars. These will provide the best-quality water for recycling in gardens; in fact, schools and even beauty salons use these systems to recycle their water. The Internet has dozens of plans for DIY systems. Buzz cautions against reusing any water coming from the kitchen sink or dishwasher, as it's impossible to tell what food byproducts and bacteria may still exist in the water. Laundry water could be safely reused for irrigation if it hasn't been used to wash underwear and doesn't contain bleach.

You may not be interested in an official gray water recycling system but still want to conserve water. Buzz offers these tips:

- When washing your car, drive it onto the lawn for an old-fashioned lawn-watering system! Just don't run over any sprinkler heads.

- Place a bucket beneath the shower head in the morning while you're waiting for the water to warm up. That water could be used for flushing toilets in a drought, carried outside to water plants, or poured into a larger container to be used later.

- Even soapy water from a shower, saved in a bucket, is useful for flushing toilets. Just pour it into the top tank and flush.

> *We never know the worth of water till the well is dry.*
> —THOMAS FULLER

Laundry Never Takes a Vacation

I hate laundry with a passion. If I could, I'd buy thirty pairs of underwear, bras, and socks, and worry about laundry only once a month.

Sorting and folding laundry was the first household skill I taught my kids. I called it character training.

Since there is no way to get around laundry, even in a worst-case scenario, a wise Survival Mom has a backup plan for dealing with this never-ending chore if the power should ever go out for an extended period of time.

My recommendation is a child-powered washing system. This can be as simple as two 5-gallon buckets with lids, two new toilet plungers, and round holes cut in the center of both lids for the handles of the plungers. Fill the first bucket with water, a little soap, and a few pieces of dirty clothing and put that kid to work! You can explain that the process is the same as for churning butter. Boys, in particular, might be enticed to work harder if they realize it's a great exercise for building their biceps. Either way, in a few minutes you'll have clothes that are ready to be rinsed in clean water in the second bucket, wrung out, and hung on a clothesline.

An alternative to the Plunge-a-Bucket system is a nifty product called the Wonder Wash. It sells for about $45 and uses a hand crank to agitate clothes in soapy water. Survival Mom Cindy put this to the test on a family camping trip in the Colorado Rockies and had this to say:

> *Each evening we washed three loads: jeans, shirts, sweats, shorts, and underwear for two adults (bigger than size 12) and two (not-so-small) boys. We heated river water, added very little laundry detergent, put in our clothes, and tightened the lid of the Wonder Wash to create pressure inside the tub.*
>
> *After a 2-minute spin, and due to my impatience, I skipped using the drainage tube and simply dumped the water out of the top. We quickly wrung the clothes by hand, returned them to the tub, filled the tub with warm clean water, and gave it a second spin. The entire process took 45 minutes. The clothes came out remarkably clean. The Wonder Wash actually got out the goo from s'mores! We line-dried and wore the clothes the next day.*

The advantage of the Wonder Wash in an emergency or "power down" situation is that it doesn't require any electricity. It uses very little water, making it handy if your crisis includes a water shortage, and only a small amount of soap. Stock up on a clothesline and a dry-

Homemade laundry soap? Yes, you can!

- ½ bar Fels Naptha* soap, finely grated
- 1 cup washing soda (not baking soda)
- 1 cup borax

Mix these ingredients very well and store in an airtight container. For a nicer scent, add 4–5 drops of an essential oil, mix well. Use 2 T. of this mixture per load of laundry. Add a third tablespoon for heavily soiled clothes.

*Any soap without added oils, moisturizers, or perfumes will work.

ing rack or two, and your family will be looking and smelling clean in the midst of chaos or on a camping trip.

If you're the type of mom who longs for the days of Ma Ingalls, washboards and hand-wringers are still available. Lehman's is a company that serves the Amish community, and if it's primitive laundry supplies you're searching for, look no further than www.Lehmans.com!

The next step down on the laundry evolutionary scale is the ancient technique of pounding your laundry on rocks down by the river. To each her own.

Family Preparedness Plan: Water

☑ Water

Water storage rule: at least 1 gallon per person per day and 1 ounce per pound of a pet's weight.

Our family's water goal: _____ gallons.

_____ gallons in portable water bottles

_____ gallons in mid-size containers (e.g., 2-liter soda bottles)

_____ gallons in large containers

Keep track of where your water is stored!

☑ Water purification

The systems we will use are:

☐ Bleach (write expiration date on bottle)

☐ Boiling (have a backup system for heating water, fuel and a metal pot)

☐ Calcium hypochlorite

☐ SteriPEN

☐ Water-purification tablets

☐ Other _____

☐ Other _____

☑ Laundry

In an emergency, we'll use this method for washing and drying laundry:

_____

_____

_____

_____

I need to store _____ bottles/boxes of laundry detergent for 3 months' worth.

CHAPTER 3

Keeping It Clean: The Ins and Outs of Sanitation

For the first 6 years as a mother, I sometimes felt that I was up to my elbows in pee, poop, and vomit. My kids, Lord and Lady Poop-a-lot, earned their nicknames through earnest and sincere effort. My son was known for walking into a room, vomiting on the carpet, and walking out. His pink barf on the day of my daughter's sixth birthday blended nicely with the party decorations. It didn't take long before my carpet cleaner and I were fast friends.

In emergency situations, pee, poop, and vomit don't take vacations, but it's very possible that sanitation workers *will*. Trash disposal could quickly become a nightmare, and a lengthy power outage would affect water treatment plants and sewage systems—not a pretty picture, especially if you're used to hearing, "Mommy, I've gotta go!" a dozen or more times a day.

Like every other area of emergency preparedness and planning ahead, sanitation concerns can be addressed ahead of time. We just have to face the issue boldly, without squeamishness, and then stack that toilet paper to the ceiling.

No Flushing Toilets: It Could Happen to You

No matter how tranquil your life may be at the moment, there are going to be times when convenient and sanitary toilet facilities are

INSTANT SURVIVAL TIP

Restaurant supply stores carry toilet paper in huge quantities. A carton of 100 rolls could last an entire year. Imagine the peace of mind of having more than enough toilet paper for even the worst possible emergency!

Remember, toilet paper is the only thing separating us from animals!

nowhere to be found. You can count on it. I have memories of squatting over earthen holes in the ground in obscure villages in Eastern Europe and balancing over fancy ceramic holes in Japan. In an emergency, it's possible that we may have to creatively cope without modern-day toilet facilities.

One Texas mom experienced something she termed "third-world conditions" when her family evacuated the Houston area to escape Hurricane Rita in June 2005. Her family had left their home about an hour before the recommended evacuation time and thought they would be out of harm's way in no time at all.

In fact, they packed only a few snacks and juice boxes, thinking they would grab a meal at McDonald's on their way north. Fourteen hours later, they were still inside Houston's city limits. She was appalled that her kids had to use the side of the road as a bathroom, with no privacy and in full view of a variety of strangers.

It doesn't take a hurricane to force excessively civilized people to the side of a highway with a couple of Kleenex tissues and embarrassed glances. Our municipal sewage plants operate on electrical systems, which are susceptible to storm damage, power outages, sabotage, or worse. Water pipes can be broken in an earthquake or freezing temperatures. If a terrorist group wanted to bring a city to its knees, forget the suitcase bomb. Just find a way to take out the city's ability to flush toilets.

If you don't believe me, just start making tally marks on a pad of paper every time you hear the toilet flush in your house. That will give you a pretty good idea of how important it is to have at least one backup plan should your toilets ever . . . well, back up.

Actually, this reminds me of one of my worst ever "bad mommy moments" (I've had several). My son rushed out of the hall bathroom with a panicked look on his face.

"Mom! The toilet won't flush!"

"What do you mean it won't flush?"

"I pushed down the handle, but nothing happened. No water came out."

In a moment, I diagnosed our plumbing problem. I had forgotten to pay the water bill. Who knew city water departments could be so cruel? We learned, quickly, how to deal with a situation like this: We went to a hotel.

The Emergency Toilet

When the toilet won't flush, or when flushing toilets aren't within driving distance, having a good, sturdy shovel on hand would be a good idea. However, there are a couple of options a little higher up on the evolutionary scale.

The 5-gallon bucket wasn't invented just for janitorial use. In fact, it can make a mighty fine, albeit temporary, substitute for your toilet. Here's what you'll need:

- A 5-gallon bucket. You can be choosy about the color, but really, in the end, it doesn't matter.

- A snap-on toilet seat will make the experience more comfortable and homey. An old toilet seat works just as well, as long as it doesn't slip off while holding its passenger.

- Heavy-duty trash bags. Plan on using two of these to line the bucket. Commercial liners specifically designed for this purpose can be purchased also.

- A supply of kitty litter, sawdust, peat, or dirt.

- Unscented liquid bleach, diluted with water in a 1:10 solution.

- Air freshener.

Line the bucket with 2 of the trash bags and snap on the toilet lid. Sprinkle a cup or two of kitty litter in the bottom of the bag and after each "Number 2." Additionally, sprinkle a cup or 2 of the bleach solution into the bag to kill bacteria.

We all have big changes in our lives that are more or less a second chance.

—HARRISON FORD

If your own bathroom is available, you can set up a similar system by first emptying the toilet bowl of as much water as possible. Then, line the bowl with trash bags and follow the same steps as listed above. Be sure to keep the seat closed and make good use of your air freshener!

Each day, these emergency toilets will have to be emptied by sealing the bag with a plastic tie and taking it outside. Depending on the type of emergency, you may have to bury these bags on your property. Because so many diseases can originate in human waste, it's vital that waste is buried deeply enough that rodents, insects, and other animals can't dig it up. A 2- to 3-foot-deep hole works just fine, as long as it's at least 50 yards from any water source, including wells and springs.

Unless communication and civilization itself are at a standstill, you can count on government agencies to issue directives for dealing with waste and trash disposal. However, a good rule of thumb is to plan and prepare as if no outside help is forthcoming.

If there's anything you have my permission to be paranoid about, it's dealing with sanitation. Gone are the days when moms would just toss the contents of chamber pots into the streets—and I hope those days never return, since those conditions are what brought about typhoid fever, cholera, and the plague. Workers at sanitation plants are required to have up-to-date vaccines for tetanus and diphtheria, as well as to take extraordinary precautions, since their work is hazardous to their health. Keep that in mind the next time you have to change a diaper, use a porta-potty, or deal with your family's sanitation sans modern plumbing.

‖‖

No Bucket? No Problem!

Here are just a few quick tips in case you and your family are ever stranded without even a bucket on hand. An impromptu toilet can be as simple as a hole dug in the ground. To simplify the process even further, a hole is only necessary if you're going Number Two.

Use a shovel, garden trowel, or flat rock to dig a hole at least 50 yards away from any water source. Just in case you don't have a measuring tape handy, that's about 70–75 paces. The trickling water of a creek may entice your toddler to "go," but with the help of rainfall and

Do not pray for easy lives. Pray to be stronger (wo!)men.

—*JOHN F. KENNEDY (quote modified by The Survival Mom)*

groundwater, human waste has a way of leaching into places it shouldn't.

The hole should be about 6 inches wide, or wide enough for it to have a better than 50/50 chance of collecting the incoming delivery.

If you can, use leaves for wiping, seeing how they are "green"—for real. But if you must use toilet paper, put it in a bag to dispose of elsewhere. Cover the hole with dirt, top with a few rocks, and continue on your way. If you're headed to a location where the waste can be flushed away, scoop it up and take it with you. Who needs a toilet?

For a bit of modesty, try placing an open umbrella on the ground at a strategic angle for maximum privacy. An arrest for indecent exposure could add embarrassment, and possibly a bit of bail money, to an already bad situation.

That Time of the Month

If you're like me, Aunt Flo shows up abruptly at the worst possible moments. I call my three pairs of white pants my "period pants," because wearing them lures Aunt Flo like a moth to a flame. I've stocked up on a couple months' worth of my favorite brand of tampons and a few boxes of panty-liners. This is an area of preparedness that's necessary, though not exactly glamorous.

Shopping store sales with coupons will be the most budget-friendly way of stocking up on what is euphemistically called "feminine protection." If you calculate what you need for 1 month and multiply it by three, you'll have a good idea of how much you need to have stored for 3 months. For planning purposes, be sure to include any other women in your family.

For thousands of years, women around the world did without the handy, individually wrapped tampons or napkins. They used what was available, which in most cases included pieces of fabric. This might be a great way to recycle old T-shirts and the like, but companies such as GladRags.com and Lunapads.com sell cotton pads, liners, and other accessories that can be used, washed, and reused.

One way to deal with Aunt Flo each month in lieu of the traditional tampon and napkin is the menstrual cup. These are soft, reusable silicone cups that, once inserted, can be worn for up to 12 hours. I've found this to be a convenient option, since forgetting about Aunt Flo for an entire day is a relief. The Diva Cup (www.divacup.com) is the most well-known brand of menstrual cup on the market. This device is comfortable, although inserting it correctly takes a little practice. Just think: You could purchase one of these and not worry about stocking up on any other feminine protection for an entire year. The disposable Instead Softcup menstrual cup is a great addition to an emergency kit because Aunt Flo's sudden arrival can, indeed, be considered an emergency, especially if you're miles from home or the nearest drugstore.

The (wo!)man who has done her best has done everything.

—CHARLES M. SCHWAB
(quote modified by
The Survival Mom)

Trash Disposal

Our family regularly fills our city-allotted trash can to the brim and then sneaks our overflow into the trash can of the single grandma living next door. Without our weekly trash pickup, we'd be deep in piles of junk mail, pizza delivery boxes, and orange peels. We wouldn't be alone in our misery, though: Entire cities would be brought to a standstill.

Not only would the piles of garbage smell as bad as any city dump, but insects, rodents, and other animals would soon be attracted to the whole ungodly mess and begin spreading germs and the beginning of

Composting made simple

You could write a book all about composting—and there are dozens of them on the market—but composting is simply combining key ingredients together and letting them rot. It's a lot like what happens in your refrigerator produce drawers, just with a little more forethought and a result that is actually beneficial.

Follow these basic steps:

- Identify a space in your yard away from your house, or use a large container with a lid to begin your compost pile. Some budget-minded moms get used trash containers from their city for this purpose.

- Begin combining organic material from the kitchen and backyard. Neighbors may be only too happy to provide grass clippings and armfuls of dried leaves.

- The addition of any meat or animal products to the mix may attract animals. Use discretion.

- As your pile of compost grows, turn it over every so often with a shovel and add a sprinkling of water to speed the process along. Your mixture should be slightly damp and have an earthy smell. If the mixture is warm to the touch, it's ready to turn over.

- If your compost smells like ammonia, add more brown material (sawdust, wood shavings, straw, dry leaves, shredded newspaper, or dried grass clippings) and mix it in.

- When some or all of your compost is ready for the garden, it will have the consistency of a very rich soil. Use a wire-mesh trash can to shake out the rich humus and leave the larger pieces behind to continue the process.

Black Plague II. The good news is that it's relatively simple to decrease the amount of trash we produce.

Reuse it

Remember how grandma used to smooth out her used silver paper, a.k.a. aluminum foil, and store it in a drawer to reuse? Well, that's not such a bad idea anymore, is it? Aluminum foil—a great item for stocking up, by the way—has multiple uses, and as long as it stays intact, it can be washed and reused over and over again.

Plastic soda bottles can be washed out and used to store dry goods and water. Wash your glass jars and lids in hot, soapy water, and they're ready for food storage as well. They're great for storing dehydrated food and leftovers, and Ziploc storage bags can be cleaned out, dried, and reused. Wash them out with my Survival Mom's All-Purpose Sanitizer and dry them on a baby-bottle drying rack or a dish drying rack.

My kids have discovered fabulous, creative uses for everyday products. Put your kids to work figuring out what to do with empty tuna cans and milk cartons!

Compost it

Virtually all non-meat food scraps can be tossed in a composting pile or bucket, and with the addition of plant cuttings, you can have rich compost for your garden in a matter of a couple of months. Even better, you can add shredded newspaper and cardboard! This single step can reduce the amount of trash your household produces by one-third or more. Just don't store your composting bucket near your back door, or you'll end up with an infestation of gnats like I did. It took weeks to get rid of them.

Feed it

Animals are almost always eager and happy to take the place of your garbage disposal or trash can. If you have any sort of livestock, that's even better. Goats, chickens, pigs, dogs, and cats are handy for dealing with edible leftovers. I mean, am I the only one who gives thanks whenever our dogs clean up the kitchen floor after the kids have knocked over a bowl of ravioli? If you feed your animals food scraps that haven't been cooked yet, you can say they're on a raw food diet.

Recycle it

Depending on future scenarios, local recycling plants may not be in full swing following a disaster or a widespread emergency. If you're reusing, composting, and feeding what you can to your animals, it's likely there's not much trash left for disposal. Pay particular attention to trash that is dangerous to dispose of any other way, such as motor oil, batteries, paint, and household chemicals. Actually, if you mix your own cleaning solutions using natural ingredients like vinegar, baking soda, and lemon juice, you'll have few, if any, leftover chemicals to worry about.

Burn it

If it can't be reused, composted, fed to the animals, or recycled, well, you probably don't have much left to worry about. Congratulations! Most of your paper trash can be burned, but keep this to a minimum. Many townships have outlawed the burning of trash, and during a crisis, air pollution caused by hundreds or thousands of small fires may quickly turn into a major health hazard.

The Survival Mom's all-time favorite, all-natural cleaning solution

- 1 cup white vinegar
- 1 cup water
- 1 drop sweet orange essence oil, or your scent of choice

Combine everything in a spray bottle and use on anything that needs some cleaning. Enjoy the scent. I do.

What About Disposable Diapers?

In the event of an emergency or the end of life as we know it, switching to cloth diapers is a no-brainer. Disposables may be a fact of life for most moms in America, but more than one-third of babies around the world have never worn a disposable diaper. If those moms can manage with cloth diapers, so can you.

Yes, you can stock up on disposables, but babies can tear through a 48-count package of disposables in short order. My recommendation is to purchase a supply of cloth diapers and diaper covers. Diapers have multiple uses, or you can always pass them along to a new mom.

Are your babies grown up, moved out, and with babies of their own? Sometimes emergencies have a way of reuniting family members. If you suspect that an emergency or extended financial difficulties would likely bring your kids with *their* kids back home, it would be smart to stash some cloth diapers and supplies in a back closet, just in case.

Put these on your "no burn" list:

- Particle board
- Coated, painted, or pressure-treated wood
- Plastics of any kind
- Rubber products, such as tires and hoses
- Magazines or junk mail with colored ink
- Wet, rotted, diseased, or moldy wood

The Prepared Family

Take this Survival Mom Trash Challenge with your family to see how little trash you can produce in a week's time.

☑ **Weigh the amount of trash produced by your family over a period of 7 days and record that weight.**

☑ **Have a family brainstorming session and determine how to apply these 5 tasks:**

1. Reuse it
   - What trash might be repurposed for other uses?
2. Compost it
   - If you don't yet have a family garden, start a compost pile now to give yourself a head start!
   - Make sure the kids understand what is safe for composting, and what isn't.
   - This is a great science lesson as kids observe organic materials returning to Mother Earth. Throw in a few earthworms for even more nature lessons.
3. Feed it
   - What scraps could safely be fed to animals? Reptiles make a fine recycling system for scraps of produce. If you're thinking of adding backyard chickens to the family, these animals would be only too happy to take veggies, bread, and crackers off your hands.
4. Recycle it
   - Increase your conscientiousness when it comes to your city's recycling program. If there isn't one, track down plants that recycle aluminum, glass, and paper.
5. Burn it
   - Anything that cannot be sorted into the first four categories may provide fuel for a family bonfire. S'mores are optional.

☑ **Weigh the trash that is produced during the Trash Challenge and compare the results to your baseline data. Chances are, your family has found multiple ways to decrease the amount of trash produced.**

In an emergency, these steps will become even more vital. Mountains of trash create unsanitary conditions, the perfect setting for disease, insects, and other pests. Not only are you doing something friendly for the environment, but you're also establishing important and helpful habits.

Family Preparedness Plan: Sanitation

☑ Emergency toilet

The option we'll use is:

☐ The 5-gallon bucket with the snap-on toilet seat. Stock up on:

    ☐ Heavy-duty plastic bags

    ☐ Kitty litter, sawdust, or ChemiSan

    ☐ The GottaGo portable toilet

    ☐ Adapting our home's toilet for emergency use

☐ Digging a latrine (make sure you have a shovel or two!)

☑ The all-important toilet paper

We use _____ rolls of toilet paper per month. We need to stock up on a total of _____ rolls to last 3 months.

☑ Feminine protection options

Sooner or later, I'm going to need this. I'm stocking up on:

☐ The products I usually use. I'll need _____ packages.

☐ Other females in the family will need _____ packages.

☐ Cloth pads

☐ A menstrual cup

Notes:

CHAPTER 4

The First Steps of Food Storage

From the moment our babies are born, nourishment is the top priority. We nurse them to sleep or pop the nipple of a warmed bottle of formula in their little mouths and marvel at those tiny, perfect lips, eagerly taking in the sustenance we offer. Fast forward a few years, and we can't keep their grubby hands out of the refrigerator and the pantry, and those precious lips are caked with grape jelly and bread crumbs. Let's face it: Growing up takes calories, lots of calories, and enormous amounts of food.

You may never have thought about food storage, but when Survival Moms begin thinking about preparing for emergencies and an uncertain future, food becomes a top concern. A significant loss of income, a natural disaster, or a severe weather event might make it difficult to buy enough food to feed our families, and in some cases, it might be difficult to even *find* the products we're used to. It makes sense to build up our home pantries, but that's easier said than done, and all beginners have plenty of questions:

- How do I plan meals?

- Do I need to learn how to grind wheat?

- What if I buy something my family won't eat?

- How do I keep the food from spoiling?

- Where do I start?

It's tempting to run to the grocery store in a panic and stuff a cart or two with cans of tuna, soup, and beans. I'll admit that's what I did.

The downside to this haphazard approach is that most of the foods stocked at the grocer's aren't meant for long-term storage. Check the expiration dates on your boxes of cereal, and you'll see what I mean. My own first food-storage mishap involved nine boxes of Honey Nut Cheerios. You should have seen the looks on my kids' faces when I told them they had a week to down all those boxes! After all, the cereal had officially expired a month earlier.

Another reason to go about your food storage in a planned and orderly manner is that you need to know *what* you have stored, *how* you will use it, and *how long* the food will last. By following my advice in this chapter for analyzing favorite recipes, stocking up on ingredients that will last long-term, and keeping track of what is on your shelves, you'll have enough food to make satisfying meals for your family. For the purpose of our planning in this chapter, we'll set a food-storage goal of 3 months. It sounds like a long time, a *really* long time, but keep in mind that it's a long-term goal you can work toward a little at a time. Nowadays, unemployment can last for more than a year, and a monumental disaster (think 9–11 or Katrina) can damage the economy of a large region for months. Three months is a reasonable long-term goal.

The Rule of Three applies to food storage, so having three layers is a smart plan: grocery store products, bulk dry foods, and freeze-dried/dehydrated foods. Let's take a closer look at each category.

INSTANT SURVIVAL TIP

Store what you eat and eat what you store. Your pantry isn't meant to be a static hoard that is never touched. If you follow the rule "first in, first out," you'll use the food that has been in your storage the longest and add fresher foods for future use.

Grocery Store Goods

This category is the easiest to acquire. The food is often very inexpensive and easy to prepare—it's all familiar stuff. Open a can, heat up the contents(or not), and dinner is served! During stressful times, almost everyone will appreciate a nice big bowl of Kraft Macaroni & Cheese. Familiar foods are often comfort foods, and parents ignore the importance of these foods at their own peril.

However, with the exception of canned food, this food is usually not packaged with long-term storage in mind. Another downside is that it often contains excessive sodium, high-fructose corn syrup, and other additives you may not wish to feed your family. Still, your local grocery store is a good place to begin with food storage, and this category should account for 25% or so of your total storage.

Bulk Dry Food

INSTANT SURVIVAL TIP

For decades members of the Mormon, or Latter-Day Saints, Church have been actively storing food and preparing for emergencies. They are an excellent resource for new Survival Moms and, if you're lucky, you might even be able to take classes on topics such as food and water storage, gardening, and canning at a nearby LDS cannery or ward (an LDS church).

This category includes rice, beans, cornmeal, wheat, dried milk, and a whole lot more. These foods are designed to last long-term—up to 20 or 30 years in many cases. This food must be stored correctly. Ultimately, it will be the backbone of your food storage.

The foods in this category are *ingredients*, rather than prepared foods. Yes, this means learning how to cook rice and beans from scratch and even grinding wheat for homemade bread, but the payoff is having foods that are the building blocks of hundreds of dishes. Think about it. Your options with a can of ravioli are: eat it cold or warm it up. That's it. On the other hand, individual ingredients can be combined in multiple ways, allowing for a diverse and healthier diet. The majority of your food storage should consist of bulk dry foods.

This layer requires a bit more of an investment, since a bucket of wheat will cost much more than a loaf or two of bread. However, when you calculate that all that wheat will make dozens of loaves and can last for decades, it's obvious that the wheat, not the store-bought bread, is the true bargain.

Most people get these kinds of foods from online sources such as Shelf Reliance. If you live in an area with a high population of Mormons (Latter-Day Saints), there might be food-storage stores nearby, along with a church facility that may allow you to use its equipment to seal your dry goods in large #10 cans.

Cans by the number

In the world of food storage, the ubiquitous #10 can reigns supreme. This large can has a volume of eight-tenths of a gallon. It's the large can you see at Costco and say to yourself, "We could NEVER eat that much nacho cheese sauce!"

Freeze-Dried Foods

Foods in this category make a great addition to your pantry. They are lightweight and have an extended shelf life of up to 30 years. You'll find both entrees and produce that are freeze-dried. However, their main advantage is ease of preparation. With a relatively small amount of hot water—bingo!—you have a meal or close-to-fresh produce.

We decided to stock up on a few cases of entrees after tasting them at a sporting goods store. The macaroni and cheese was almost better than my homemade recipe, and since the meals are so compact, they're a great timesaver on camping trips. I have a few packages in the emergency kit I keep in the Tahoe, in case we're ever stranded by the side of the road. Flat tire? No problem, but wait 'til we've finished eating our turkey tetrazzini!

There is one caveat: Pay attention to serving size. If you have big eaters, you may find yourself zipping through a #10 can of chicken teriyaki in a single meal. Of course, if you serve that teriyaki alongside a big pile of rice, tummies will get fuller faster.

A potential evacuation is one more reason to include this category of food in your storage. In fact, I've stored our cans of freeze-dried entrees near our back door, in case we ever have to skip town . . . er . . . evacuate. If you know you have quick meals ready to grab at a moment's notice, that's one less thing you'll have to worry about if an evacuation becomes necessary.

Survival Moms prepare for the future with the assumption that they will continue to be the backbone of the family, invulnerable to calamity, injury, or illness. Common sense, however, belies this. It's very possible that during a flu epidemic, *you* might be the one in need of care, and your 9-year-old might be in charge of feeding the family. That's the moment you will thank your lucky stars for a stash of freeze-dried entrees and stored water for preparing it.

Freeze-dried food is more expensive up front, but when you price it per serving, it's actually pretty budget-friendly. A can of freeze-dried ground beef runs more than $35 and is about $1.65 per serving. My local grocery store sells the fresh stuff for $1.79 a pound every few weeks, but then, it would hardly last 25 years! As far as food

Recommended freeze-dried produce:

- Mushrooms
- Red & green bell peppers
- Corn
- Pineapple
- Mandarin oranges
- Raspberries

INSTANT SURVIVAL TIP

Try before you buy! It's absolutely vital that you try out dehydrated green onions or freeze-dried chopped beef, for example, before investing in large quantities. Look for small packages of varieties of wheat and grains. Slip them into some familiar dishes to see how your family reacts. Buying a case of #10 cans of freeze-dried peas may not be the smartest move if they cause you to break out in hives.

baby step

Buy just one small can or package of a dehydrated or freeze-dried food you've never tried before. Use it in one or two familiar recipes before you decide whether you want to include it as part of your long-term storage. If you do this two or three times a month, you'll soon know exactly what you want to purchase, when you can afford it.

Recommended dehydrated foods:

- Potatoes
- Sweet potatoes
- Onions
- Green onions
- Hash browns
- Bananas
- Jalapeno peppers
- Carrots

storage goes, most of your protein needs will be met by commercially canned fish, meat, and poultry, as well as beans and possibly canning meat on your own. (Yes, it's easy!) Still, however, the freeze-dried versions are handy. Adding a handful of freeze-dried chicken to a soup or a stew is an easy way to get extra protein and calories in a hurry.

Freeze-dried produce is worth the investment, since the process of freeze-drying maintains up to 95% of the food's original nutrients. Many Survival Moms incorporate these in their daily cooking just for the convenience factor. Freeze-dried blueberries mixed in with your brown-sugared oatmeal in the dead of winter . . . yum! I love the convenience of having freeze-dried mushrooms on hand for my famous Swedish meatballs and gravy.

Dehydrated Foods

The beauty of dehydrated food is that virtually anything you might want to store comes in a dehydrated version: eggs, butter, milk, carrots, potatoes, and even applesauce. Dehydrated food maintains almost as many of the original nutrients as freeze-dried varieties and is just as easy to store. Many dehydrated foods don't come in a freeze-dried version, and dehydrated food is usually less expensive than freeze-dried.

My own favorite dehydrated foods are the ones I dehydrate myself. I bought an inexpensive food dehydrator secondhand and have used it to dry mushrooms, canned fruit, frozen vegetables, and tomato sauce. I've even made beef jerky. Food dehydration is easier than you might think, and I love combining dehydrated foods together and making my own soup and chili mixes. It's also a great way of easily preserving produce before it's on its last leg in your refrigerator.

You probably won't find much dehydrated and freeze-dried food at your local Kroger's. Instead, shop around online and compare prices and shipping charges. One of my favorite brands that I use in my cooking is Shelf Reliance's THRIVE line.

Both freeze-dried and dehydrated foods will need water for rehydration, so it would be wise to store a few extra gallons for this purpose.

Before You Begin Stocking Up . . .

. . . you need an idea of which foods to store for *your* household. No two storage pantries are filled with the exact same foods because each family's tastes and nutritional needs are different. To get a good idea of what should fill *your* long-term storage pantry, first make a list of ten to fifteen of your family's favorite meals and then determine which can most easily be "survivalized."

What types of recipes are the easiest to survivalize? Soups, stews, chili recipes, casseroles, and skillet meals are usually the best choices. Meals that feature a large amount of meat, poultry, fish, or other seafood are more difficult because usually the protein isn't easy to store long-term.

Review the ingredients in your list of favorite recipes and ask the following questions:

- Does the recipe contain ingredients that are canned? Stocking up on canned goods is easy, and most have a shelf life of 2 years and more.
- Are all herbs, spices, and seasonings easily stored? Most can be stored for long periods of time.
- Do all the produce ingredients come in forms that are easily stored, such as canned, dehydrated, or freeze-dried, or can they be home-grown easily?
- If the recipe calls for meat, poultry, fish, or other seafood, is this a minor ingredient and can it be stored long-term?
- Does the recipe contain grains, rice, and/or beans? All of these are excellent choices for food storage.
- Are the dairy ingredients storage-friendly? Dehydrated milk, butter, and sour cream work well in casseroles and other recipes.
- Does the recipe contain eggs? Dehydrated eggs are easily incorporated in recipes. If you've gotta have a steady supply of fresh eggs, get a couple of chickens.
- Does the recipe contain staples such as flour or sugar? These are easy to store and are inexpensive.
- If the recipe contains sauces, such as soy sauce or ketchup, are they easy to stock up on and do they have a long shelf life? Can the sauce be made from scratch?

sur.vi.val.ize (v):
to analyze a recipe and substitute long-term ingredients for those with a short shelf life. Once survivalized, ingredients can then be purchased and stored, so that the recipe could be made at some later date.

baby step

Make a List of Seven

Here's an easy way to get a list of recipes suitable for food storage. Make a list of two soups, one stew, one chili, one casserole, and two skillet dishes your family enjoys. There you go! You now have a list of recipes whose ingredients are very likely compatible with long-term food storage.

Your recipe isn't survival friendly if it contains:

- A large amount of fresh meat, poultry, fish, or other seafood.

- Tortillas, unless you know how to make them and have the ingredients.

- A lot of fresh vegetables. A stir-fry dish, for example, will be difficult to make using only dehydrated veggies.

- A large amount of cheese. Sorry, but unless you can make your own cheese or can afford to stock up on large quantities of freeze-dried cheese (which is excellent, by the way), cheese-heavy recipes just aren't survival-friendly. Maybe you could marry a professional cheese maker or learn how to wax your own cheese (see instructions on page 70).

- Sour cream or cream cheese. Dehydrated sour cream powder is available and works fine when mixed in with other ingredients, but fresh sour cream on its own is impossible to store. Ditto for cream cheese.

- Ingredients that are unusual, hard to find, or very expensive. White truffle oil just isn't on the list of The Top Ten Foods to Store.

Be ready to discover that certain favorite recipes don't transfer well to survivalized versions. One of my favorites, taco lasagna, requires cream cheese, sour cream, cheddar cheese, and corn tortillas. I can keep some of those ingredients in the freezer, but that isn't a long-term solution. I love the recipe too much to toss it out, but I'm not counting on it as a food-storage meal. It's just as well, since I only make it when I'm feeling skinny.

Worries go down better with soup than without.

—*JEWISH PROVERB*

||||||||||||||||||||||||||||||||||||||||||||||||||||||||||||||||||||||||||||||||||||||||||||||||||||||||||

The Survivalized Meal Plan

The next step is to choose the seven most easily survivalized recipes from your original list. These selections should represent hearty and healthy main dishes that will become the backbone of your 3 months of stored food. For planning purposes, we're going to assume you will make each recipe once a week for a total of twelve times per recipe. This is a big job, but once it's completed, you'll have the bulk of your food storage finished!

The next step will be to study every ingredient needed in a recipe and determine how each could be stored so that you could make this recipe 5 years from now. Your goal will be to store as many of the ingredients as possible in forms suitable for long-term storage. Here's an example from my own recipe files.

Italian Meatball Soup

Mix together in a medium-size bowl:

> 1 pound ground beef
> ½ cup bread crumbs
> 1 egg, beaten
> 2 tablespoons milk
> ½ cup chopped onion
> ½ teaspoon Italian seasoning
> ½ teaspoon salt
> ¼ teaspoon pepper

Heat a large skillet over medium heat. Add 4 tablespoons of oil to the heated skillet. Form meat mixture into walnut-size meatballs. Brown in oil, remove from pan, and set aside.

In a large pot, combine these ingredients:

> 14.5-ounce can chopped tomatoes
> 8 ounces tomato sauce
> 2 cups water or beef broth
> 2 teaspoons instant beef bouillon (omit if using beef broth)
> 2–3 teaspoons sugar or ½ teaspoon sugar substitute
> 1 cup each: sliced carrots, celery and zucchini
> ½ to 1 cup chopped onion
> ¼ cup fresh Italian parsley, chopped
> ½ teaspoon dried Italian herbs

Bring mixture to a boil. Reduce heat and simmer for 10 minutes. Add meatballs and cook for an additional 15 minutes. Serve with garlic bread.

There is one thing more exasperating than a wife who can cook and won't, and that's a wife who can't cook and will.

—ROBERT FROST

Here is the survivalized version of the Italian Meatball Soup. Every ingredient in this recipe, except for the ground beef, can be easily stored, in one form or another, long-term. Here is how I organized my list of ingredients:

PACKAGED FOODS	DEHYDRATED / FREEZE DRIED	SPICES/STAPLES
14.5 oz. chopped tomatoes, canned	**1 egg**	**Italian seasoning**
8 oz. tomato sauce	**2 tablespoons milk**	**salt**
	chopped onion*	**pepper**
	carrots*	**beef boullion**
	celery*	**sugar**
	zucchini*	
	Italian parsley*	

I've left out the bread crumbs, since I can quickly make those by toasting or air-drying a few slices of bread. As you can see, this recipe is easily survivalized, with the exception of the meat.

In recipes that include meat, chicken, or fish, you have seven options:

1. Use the canned versions. Commercially produced canned meat and chicken, in various forms, can be purchased through many online companies, as well as your grocery store. Chopped chicken or beef could take the place of the meatballs in this recipe.

2. Can your own meat and chicken. When your grocery's butcher department has a really good sale, stock up, buy plenty of canning jars and lids, and get to work! You'll find dozens of helpful videos on YouTube if you've never done this before, and *Ball Complete Book of Home Preserving* has detailed instructions. One advantage to this DIY canning project is that the meat or chicken you can will contain only the ingredients you add and nothing more. Be sure to follow instructions to the letter, since improperly canned meat and chicken is dangerous to consume. Also, you'll need to use a pressure canner, a metal pot that looks similar to a pressure cooker, in order for your meats to reach the proper temperature and pressure.

3. Another option is to use freeze-dried meat. A can of freeze-dried ground beef retails for around $40, so this isn't an inexpensive option. However, if you have hardcore carnivores to feed, it may be worth the investment.

INSTANT SURVIVAL TIP

When you and I think of calories, we view them as an enemy, standing between us and what we really want to eat! Emergency situations of any type, though, are times of high stress and often increased physical activity, requiring more energy in the form of calories. For this reason, be sure to store more food than you think you will need and don't be shy about stocking up on foods high in both calories and fat, such as olive oil and ultra-high-calorie energy bars.

* Pay attention to the equivalencies of fresh to freeze-dried or dehydrated products when determining how much of these ingredients you will need. For example, 1 cup of fresh chopped onion is a vastly different amount than 1 cup of dehydrated onion! There are directions for equivalencies on each container of dehydrated and freeze-dried food.

4. This won't appeal to carnivores at all, but there's nothing wrong with going vegetarian. Leave out the meat altogether. You can easily boost the protein with a handful of beans. Mix up a lentil burger blend to take the place of meatballs or add rice or pasta to make the soup more filling.

5. Utilize Textured Vegetable Protein (TVP) if you and your family don't mind eating it. It's a soy product that can be purchased in a variety of flavors, including sausage and bacon. Before going crazy buying those big #10 cans because they're so cheap, make sure it doesn't cause tummy troubles for anyone. Of course, it's a no-go if soy is an issue.

6. Try your hand at making wheat meat (seitan), a vegetarian alternative. Wheat meat can be flavored and formed in dozens of different ways, making it a versatile addition to almost any recipe. You'll find a simple recipe in the Extras appendix.

7. Go hunting or fishing, or raise your own meat.

With seven survivalized recipes, you're ready for the next step. Now you'll determine how much of each ingredient you will need in order to make each recipe at least twelve times, or once a week for 3 months.

Using the same categories as in the recipe worksheet, list each ingredient and jot down how much of that ingredient you will need to make that meal twelve times. Adjust your computations if you plan on storing a smaller amount of food. A month's supply is the minimum that I recommend.

Here's my example using my Italian Meatball Soup recipe.

PACKAGED FOODS	DEHYDRATED / FREEZE DRIED	SPICES/STAPLES
(12) 14.5 oz. chopped tomatoes	12 eggs	¼ cup Italian seasoning
(12) 8 oz. tomato sauce	1 cup milk	4 tablespoons salt
	The equivalent of:	2 tablespoons pepper
	6 cups fresh chopped onion	6 tablespoons beef bouillon
	12 cups fresh carrots	12 tablespoons sugar
	12 cups fresh celery	
	12 cups fresh zucchini	
	½ cup fresh Italian parsley	

Your survivalized recipe: _____

_____

Directions: List each ingredient in the appropriate column along with the amount required to make the recipe one time. Use one form for each of your survivalized recipes. When you acquire all ingredients, check the box. This list is your master inventory and a shopping list for this particular recipe. Multiply amounts by twelve for your 3 months' supply.

PACKAGED FOODS	DEHYDRATED / FREEZE DRIED	SPICES/STAPLES
☐ _____	☐ _____	☐ _____
_____	_____	_____
☐ _____	☐ _____	☐ _____
_____	_____	_____
☐ _____	☐ _____	☐ _____
_____	_____	_____
☐ _____	☐ _____	☐ _____
_____	_____	_____
☐ _____	☐ _____	☐ _____
_____	_____	_____
☐ _____	☐ _____	☐ _____
_____	_____	_____
☐ _____	☐ _____	☐ _____
_____	_____	_____
☐ _____	☐ _____	☐ _____
_____	_____	_____
☐ _____	☐ _____	☐ _____
_____	_____	_____

As you work through additional recipes, the quantities of ingredients will expand. Don't be scared by those bigger numbers. Rome wasn't built in a day, and storing enough food to last 3 months is a pretty big deal! You'll be buying groceries for your current needs at the same time. Most people have to pace themselves and even cut back on other expenses in order to make this a reality.

Now your trips to the grocery store have a focus. You can watch for sales, clip coupons, and buy what you can, when you can. With this master list of ingredients as an inventory, you can see at a glance what is needed to stay fully stocked for your set of recipes. When you use ingredients, add those to a shopping list for your next trip to the grocer's.

Is the idea of eating the same meal every week for 12 weeks a huge turnoff? Personally, I need more variety than that, but consider these first seven meals as a starting point. Once you have worked with the first set of recipes, go through the process again to expand your menu. Your only limits are your creativity, space, and budget.

As long as you're adding more recipes, add side dishes and occasional desserts as well. Most good moms serve more than just an entrée at dinnertime. Now, if *I* did that, my family would get very suspicious and wonder what I was trying to cover up. They deeply regret that I didn't major in home cooking in college. Make *your* meals complete with side dishes of additional fruit and vegetables, rice, pasta, and beans. Not only will they provide more nutrients and calories, but also the larger meal will minimize the chances of your kids whining about being hungry 30 minutes after dinner.

As your food storage grows, don't forget to stock up on those meal-stretchers.

Food storage by the numbers

Think about it. You and your family eat breakfasts, lunches, and dinners each day. Get out your calculator, and you'll find that for a family of four it translates to 120 breakfasts, 120 lunches, and 120 dinners *per month*. Plus, your family consumes snacks and drinks. Three months of stored food, then, will be:

360 breakfasts

360 lunches

360 dinners

Plus snacks and beverages

Watching for bargains and taking advantage of coupons has never been more important!

|||||||||||||||||||||||||||||||||||||||||||||||||||||||||||||||||||||||||||||||||||||||||||||||||||||||||||||||||||||||||||

Keeping Track of All This Food

Last week my kids were craving ravioli for breakfast and stole two cans of the stuff from my food storage! Yesterday it was grape jelly, and I know they have their eyes on those boxes of Capri Sun for the swim meet tomorrow afternoon!

You'll be using the food you have in your food storage, either out of necessity for meal preparation or to rotate food that is close to its expiration date. Keeping track of this in-and-out process can make you crazy. If you think of your food storage as a library, though, it's easier to track what needs to be replaced. Keep a pad of paper *with a pen* near your pantry. As you, or anyone else in the family, remove an item, jot it down. This creates a handy shopping list for the next time you head to the grocery store.

As you're replacing those items, try to add a few more, as your budget allows. It's amazing how quickly those "extras" add up.

Who wants to cook three meals from scratch every day?

From a food-storage standpoint, it's best to plan for one hearty meal a day. If you think about it, anytime you might be 100% dependent on your stored food will almost certainly be a time of high stress, worry, and, possibly, even displacement. Planning and preparing three meals a day may not be possible or desirable. Come to think of it, that's pretty much my attitude toward cooking on any given day of the week.

||||||||||||||||||||||||||||||||||||||||||||||||||||||||||||||||||||||||||||||||||||||||||||||||||||||||||||||

Breakfast: The Most Important Meal

Most people prefer simple breakfasts. I'm not sure why, but for some reason eating the same breakfast every day doesn't seem to bother most of us. It's kind of like the way dogs get all excited over yet another serving of the same food they've been eating every day for 10 years. This monotony makes storing breakfast meals easy. As long as attention is paid to the nutritional and caloric makeup of this "most important" meal, repetition and simplicity are called for. Follow the same steps to survivalize your breakfasts as you did for the set of seven main dishes. Here are a few breakfast dishes I commonly make, along with a list of ingredients.

Breakfast main dishes:

- Oatmeal
- French toast
- Pancakes
- Eggs, toast, and meat
- Quick bread/muffins
- Cold cereal
- Breakfast casseroles
- Waffles
- Granola
- Breakfast burritos
- Smoothies

Side dishes:

- Applesauce
- Fruit
- Potatoes
- Rice
- Tang orange drink

PACKAGED FOODS*	DEHYDRATED / FREEZE DRIED	SPICES/STAPLES
syrup	milk	honey
pancake mix	butter	sugar
Tang drink mix	eggs	flour/wheat
chopped green chilies	hash browns	yeast
salsa	bacon- and sausage-flavored TVP	salt
cereal	chopped onion	
protein powder	freeze-dried cheese	
	peaches	
	pears	

A solid breakfast that provides protein and plenty of calories will satisfy most appetites all morning long. A hearty late lunch and then a light dinner of leftovers or a quick sandwich is not only suitable for emergencies and survival situations but isn't a bad way to dine under any circumstances.

If your family isn't all that crazy about traditional breakfast foods, just increase your repertoire of main dishes, including plenty of soups. If store-bought bread isn't easily available for any reason, plan on baking a loaf of bread a few times a week, depending on the size of your family and their appetites. Not only is it a great meal-stretcher, but it also gives you the option of making sandwiches, one of the quickest meal options ever invented.

Oats: The queen of breakfasts

My kids aren't too picky about what they eat for breakfast. Just this morning my 9-year-old son was eating a package of ramen soup, dry. Yeah, it's not my cup of tea, either. My daughter ate a bowl of Cheerios, with plenty of sugar added. Usually, breakfast is the easiest meal for stocking up, but for food storage, I'd like to suggest that you consider meals that are hearty, filling, and nutritious. Cheerios and dry ramen won't cut it.

My favorite breakfast for storage is either oatmeal or granola. Both can be "adjusted to taste" by adding nuts, dried fruit, honey, and many other possibilities. Even if your kids aren't big fans of oatmeal and granola, surely there's a customized version that will make them happy.

Figuring out how much to store is easy. Calculate how much each family member eats in a typical breakfast, keep track of the various

*These can be homemade or purchased from a grocery store.

baby step

Store enough food for just 2 weeks. You'll be ready for most short-term emergencies, and this step won't tax your budget.

Many emergencies last a week or less, so this will help get you ready. Don't stop once you get those first two weeks stored, though! Keep going in order to be ready for a long-term catastrophe.

Oatmeal Inspirations

Add a few frozen blueberries. Mix in some cool yogurt just before serving. A pat of butter adds a savory flavor. Garnish with frozen peaches, chopped walnuts, and maple syrup! Stir in a tablespoon of peanut butter and a bit of honey.

add-ins and come up with a total per breakfast. When you multiply those amounts by thirty, you'll know just how much to stock up on for a full month's worth of breakfasts.

Here's the tally for the four of us in our family—enough for one oatmeal breakfast per person every day for a month:

- Oatmeal: 60 cups (½ cup per person per day)
- Brown sugar: 8 cups (1 tablespoon per person per day)
- Raisins: 7 ½ cups (1 tablespoon per person per day)
- Walnuts: 2 cups (1 tablespoon for 30 days—I'm the only one who likes walnuts)

Sometimes I pour a bit of milk over our oatmeal, and for variety, replace raisins with the same amount of chopped, dried apricots or apples.

Here are a few more tips for utilizing oats in your breakfast meals and storage:

1. Fortunately, when oatmeal becomes tiresome—and it will—you can use many of the same ingredients to make homemade granola and granola bars.

2. Another break from oatmeal is a different hot cereal, such as cream of wheat, with similar toppings.

3. Be sure to have a breakfast option that doesn't require cooking for those power-outage mornings. Granola bars, for example.

4. Use oats and a few baking ingredients to make a loaf of nutritious breakfast bread or muffins for another change.

5. Experiment with different versions of oatmeal—steel-cut grain, oat groats, or a multigrain mix.

6. Quick oats have their place in food storage, although rolled oats are preferred for their additional fiber and nutrition. Quick oats are handy for days when heating up some water is the only way a hot breakfast is going to happen.

7. To store oats long-term, use cleaned-out 2-liter soda bottles, Mylar bags, or buckets—with one or two oxygen absorbers in each. Keep the oats in a cool, dry, and dark location (more on storage later).

My Survivalized Seven

Here are seven recipes my family and friends enjoy whose ingredients are easily stored for years. If you're feeling too lazy to survivalize your own recipes or just need examples for getting started, here you go.

Rice & Beans with a Bam!

1 tablespoon olive oil

½ cup chopped onion

¼ cup chopped red bell pepper, either freeze-dried
  or dehydrated

3 minced garlic cloves or ½ teaspoon garlic powder

1 cup water

2 teaspoons chili powder

1 teaspoon salt or to taste

1 teaspoon ground cumin

1 teaspoon dried oregano

½ teaspoon dried coriander

¼ teaspoon ground red pepper, optional

3 15-ounce cans black beans, rinsed and drained

5–6 cups cooked, hot rice

1 ounce or more cheddar cheese, optional

Heat oil in a nonstick skillet over medium heat. Add onion and bell pepper and cook for 5 minutes or until tender, stirring occasionally. Add garlic and cook for 1 more minute. Add water and remaining ingredients, except for the rice and cheese. Bring to a boil. Cover, reduce heat, and simmer for 10 minutes or until thoroughly heated. Put rice on plates and top with bean mixture and grated cheese.

Serves 4–6.

Macho Mexican Rice

2 cups uncooked white rice or 2 cups Super Rice mixture

½ chopped onion or the dried equivalent

3 tablespoons olive oil

3 cups water or chicken broth

2 cloves of garlic, pressed

½ teaspoon salt or to taste

Super Rice

3 cups long-grain white rice

½ cup quinoa

½ cup millet

6–8 cups water

Use a rice cooker or a covered skillet on the stovetop set on medium-low to cook the rice. Use this mixture just as you would use plain white rice; it has the added nutrition, protein, and fiber that quinoa and millet provide.

Serves 6

2 tablespoons tomato paste or 1–2 tablespoons tomato
   powder, depending on how tomato-ey you like your
   Mexican rice
   Customize to your own preferences by adding any or
   all of the following during the simmering time:
½–1 teaspoon cumin
1 teaspoon chili powder
½ cup corn, canned or freeze-dried
½ cup of salsa or chopped canned tomatoes
diced green chilies
sliced black olives
chopped cilantro, fresh or dried

In a 10-inch skillet, heat the olive oil over medium heat. Add rice and onion and stir until the rice is slightly browned. Be careful to not burn the rice. Add the water or chicken broth, tomato paste, salt, and garlic. Stir until the tomato paste is dissolved and then add any or all of the additional ingredients. Bring mixture to a simmer, lower heat, and cover with a well-fitting lid. Continue cooking for 20 minutes or until the rice is cooked but not mushy. Serve piping hot. Optional: Top your finished rice with sour cream or grated cheddar cheese, and for a hearty main dish, stir in 2 cups of any cooked, diced meat.

Serves 6.

Not-from-a-Jar Magnificent Marinara

2 28–ounce cans whole Italian tomatoes, chopped
¼ cup tomato paste or 4 tablespoons tomato powder
   and ¼ cup water
½ cup olive oil
1 crushed garlic clove or more, depending on how many
   vampires you plan on warding off later
1 tablespoon minced onion or 2 teaspoons dehydrated
   onion
2 tablespoons minced parsley or 1 teaspoon dried parsley
½ teaspoon crushed dry oregano
1–2 tablespoons fresh basil, thinly sliced, or
   1 tablespoon dehydrated basil
1 teaspoon salt
black pepper

There is no sight on earth more appealing than the sight of a woman making dinner for someone she loves.

—THOMAS WOLFE

Place all ingredients in a large saucepan. Bring to a boil. Reduce heat and cover with a lid. Simmer for 40 minutes or until the sauce is reduced to about 1 quart, stirring occasionally. This fresh-tasting sauce is marvelous served over hot pasta or in any dish that calls for marinara sauce. It can also be made in larger batches and canned.

Dehydrated-to-Death Chili

- 4 15-ounce cans kidney and/or black beans, drained and rinsed
- 4 6-ounce cans tomato sauce
- 2 tablespoons dried, chopped onion
- 2 tablespoons chili powder
- 2 teaspoons cumin
- 1 teaspoon salt
- ½ teaspoon garlic powder
- ⅛ teaspoon black pepper
- 1–2 cups cooked ground beef, optional

TheSurvivalMom.com

For more great recipes using food storage ingredients, visit my blog, www.thesurvivalmom.com.

To make this recipe as a one-pot meal, combine all ingredients in a large pot and cook uncovered for 30 minutes. If a thinner consistency is desired, add up to 1 cup of water.

If you'd like to make the dehydrated version, follow these instructions:

Combine the tomato sauce with dehydrated onions and all seasonings in a medium-size bowl. Stir well. Divide the tomato sauce mixture into four parts and spread each portion onto four nonstick drying sheets. Next, spread a can of the drained and rinsed beans onto a dehydrating tray. Repeat with the remaining beans. You will have eight trays ready for the dehydrator.

Dehydrate at 120 degrees or according to the instruction manual for your particular dehydrator. The beans will be ready in about 4 hours. Some of the beans will split open. This can be avoided by dehydrating for 2 hours and then removing the trays from the dehydrator and air-drying until the beans become crispy. The tomato sauce mixture will be completely dried when it can be easily peeled away from the nonstick sheets. This will take about 6 hours.

To store your dehydrated chili, combine the sheets of tomato sauce and dried beans in a canning jar with a tight-fitting lid, a FoodSaver bag, or even a Ziploc bag, depending on how long you wish to store it. Add one oxygen absorber if you plan on keeping it stored for more than 6 months.

Cooking the dehydrated chili is a dream. Pour the dry ingredients in a large pot, along with 8 cups of water. Cook over medium heat for at least 20 minutes or until the beans are completely rehydrated. You can add cooked ground beef or canned tomatoes at this point. The chili will thicken as it cooks. You may want to add more water for a thinner consistency.

Serve alone, over rice, or with my Crispy Cornbread! ▼

Serves 6.

Crispy Cornbread

3 tablespoons oil, shortening, or butter for skillet

1 cup cornmeal

1 cup self-rising flour or 1 cup flour and 4 teaspoons baking powder

1 teaspoon salt

¼ teaspoon garlic powder

⅓ cup dried milk

1 tablespoon butter powder

¼ cup freeze-dried bell peppers or 3 tablespoons dehydrated peppers, rehydrated

1 tablespoon egg powder

1 cup and 2 tablespoons water

¼ cup oil, melted shortening, or melted butter

Pour 3 tablespoons of oil, shortening, or butter in a cast-iron skillet and place the skillet in a 425-degree oven to preheat. Combine all dry ingredients in a medium-size bowl and mix thoroughly. Add rehydrated peppers, water, and oil and stir until just combined. Pour into the hot skillet and bake for 20–25 minutes. The cornbread will be done when the edges are slightly browned and an inserted toothpick comes out clean.

Remove from heat. Place a cooling rack over the hot cornbread and carefully flip the cornbread onto the rack using oven mitts or pot holders. Serve hot with the Dehydrated-to-Death Chili.

Roasted Corn and Confetti Chowder

2 cups fresh, canned, or freeze-dried, rehydrated corn

2 tablespoons olive oil, divided

¼ cup chopped onion or 2 tablespoons dehydrated onion, rehydrated

1 clove garlic, pressed

6 cups chicken broth or 6 cups water and 3 teaspoons chicken bouillon

3 cups diced potatoes or 1½ cups dehydrated potato dices

¼ cup dehydrated carrots, diced

¼ cup freeze-dried bell peppers

1 tablespoon freeze-dried or dehydrated green onion

½ teaspoon dried thyme or 1½ teaspoons fresh thyme
⅔ cup dried milk
1 cup water
salt and black pepper to taste

Preheat the oven to 400 degrees. Spread corn over a medium-size sheet pan and drizzle 1 tablespoon of olive oil over the corn. Roast in oven for 10–12 minutes or until the corn begins to slightly brown.

In the meantime, heat the remaining oil in a 4-quart pot over medium-high heat. When the oil is hot, add chopped onion. If using rehydrated onion, be aware that the moistened onion will spatter a bit when added to the hot oil. Stir until the onion is tender and then add pressed garlic. Cook for 1 minute.

Pour broth or water/bouillon mixture into pot and add potato dices, carrots, bell peppers, and green onion. Bring to a simmer and cook until potatoes are tender, for about 10 minutes.

Whisk together the dried milk and water and set aside. When potatoes are tender, add the thyme, milk mixture, roasted corn, salt, and pepper. Cook for an additional 5 minutes.

Serves 6.

Open Sesame Stir-Fried Rice

4 cups cooked rice
¼ cup oil, separated
1 tablespoon sesame seeds
1 teaspoon sesame oil
2 cloves garlic, pressed
2 tablespoons dehydrated onion, rehydrated
¼ cup soy sauce
black pepper to taste
2 tablespoons dehydrated or freeze-dried green onion,
    rehydrated
½ cup freeze-dried, chopped, and rehydrated mushrooms
    or 1 4.5-ounce can mushroom pieces
¼ cup freeze-dried, rehydrated celery or 2 tablespoons
    dehydrated celery, rehydrated
2 tablespoons dehydrated carrots, rehydrated

INSTANT
SURVIVAL TIP

Rice, potatoes, pasta, and beans have long been staples in food storage. Yes, you can eat them as a main dish, but they're even handier when used as a meal-stretcher. A cup of beef stew over a cup of pasta is a very satisfying meal. A cup of teriyaki chicken over a cup or two of rice—yum! Meal-stretchers are an economical way to extend a meal a whole lot further while still providing nutrients and calories, and there will be more variety than the dreaded "rice and beans" meal!

2 tablespoons freeze-dried peas, rehydrated
pinch red chili flakes, optional
To increase protein, add your choice of:
1–2 cups chopped chicken, beef, pork, or other meat
4 eggs, whisked, cooked, and broken into small pieces

Note: Replace any or all freeze-dried or dehydrated vegetables with fresh ones, if you have them.

Rehydrate the freeze-dried and/or dehydrated ingredients in separate bowls according to package directions. Drain and pat dry with paper towels.

In a large nonstick skillet, heat 2 tablespoons of oil plus the sesame oil over medium-high heat. Add the sesame seeds and cook until they are slightly golden-brown and toasted. Add the pressed garlic and onion and continue cooking for 1 minute or until the garlic is cooked and fragrant. Add the rehydrated vegetables, black pepper, and red chili flakes and cook for an additional 3–4 minutes, or until they are heated. Remove sesame seeds and vegetables from the pan.

Add the remaining oil to the pan, heat, and add the cooked rice. As the rice cooks, drizzle soy sauce over the rice, stirring continually until the sauce is evenly distributed. Cook for 5 minutes and then add the vegetable mixture. Continue stirring until all ingredients are thoroughly combined.

Serves 4–5.

Any Day Chicken & Rice Soup

Who says that a nice, hot bowl of chicken soup is for wintertime only?

¼ cup dehydrated onion, chopped
⅓ cup freeze-dried celery
⅓ cup freeze-dried carrots, diced
⅓ cup freeze-dried mushrooms
1 or 2 12.5-ounce cans chicken
2 garlic cloves, pressed, or ½ teaspoon garlic powder
4 teaspoons chicken bouillon
½ teaspoon black pepper or to taste
12 cups water
1 tablespoon dried parsley
2 cups uncooked rice
1 teaspoon salt or to taste

Combine all ingredients in a large pot over medium heat. Bring to a simmer and cook for 30 minutes or until the vegetables are tender. Serve with hot Crispy Cornbread and butter.

||||||||||||||||||||||||||||||||||||||||||||||||||||||||||||||||||||||||||||||||||||||||||||||||||||||||

Your Food Storage Will Be Incomplete Without These Six Fresh Foods!

Think fast: What food items always seem to be on the short list when you head to the grocery store? Chances are, foods with the shortest shelf life will be included on that list; e.g., milk, bread, eggs, and produce. Foods that spoil or rot within a couple of weeks are also the ones that we depend on for variety and a well-rounded diet. It's a good idea to have these foods in multiple forms, such as canned, dried, and frozen.

What the heck is an oxy absorber?

Oxygen is one of the five enemies of food storage (see page 100). One way to protect food from its effects is to pack an oxygen absorber inside the container of food. It removes oxygen, and your food will stay fresh longer.

Make a note: canned foods don't last forever.

Many of the shelves in my pantry are filled with canned foods: chili, soup, broth, fruits, and vegetables. I even have a couple of cases of Dinty Moore stew. It's tempting to consider those cans as having the same 20- to 30-year shelf life as wheat and rice, but I'm afraid that's not quite the case.

It's true that the U.S. Army has found canned meats, veggies, and jam in "excellent states of preservation" after 46 years, but that's pushing it just a bit!

Foods are classified as either high-acid or low-acid, and those categories determine their shelf life when canned. High-acid foods include fruits, tomatoes, and pickled products. Officially, they have a shelf life of only 18–24 months. Low-acid foods, such as meat and vegetables, have the official USDA sanction of remaining good for 2 to 5 years.

When stocking up on high-acid foods, plan on rotating through the cans a little more frequently while also stocking up on dehydrated and freeze-dried versions. If you're in love with pickles or other pickled foods, mark the expiration date on the container and just plan on having a grand-old pickle party prior to that date!

Your food storage will be incomplete without these six fresh foods:

Milk—Milk can be stored long-term canned or in the form of dried milk. If you live near a dairy plant, you may be able to purchase dried milk in large quantities from it at a reasonable price. You can repackage it in food-safe plastic containers, jars with airtight lids, and Mylar bags, along with an oxygen absorber; for the best long-term results, however, buy it commercially packaged. If you live in a humid climate, the shelf life of dried milk will be shorter, and nonfat dried milk will have a much longer shelf life than dried whole milk. Canned milk or boxed milk comes in handy when you need a small amount of milk for a recipe. I keep several gallons of milk in the freezer in addition to these two other forms.

Bread—For short-term storage, say a month or so, commercially baked bread can stay in the freezer and taste just fine when your kids are clamoring for PB&J. For long-term, however, there really is no substitute for baking your own. Store-bought white flour can be stored for a year or so in airtight containers. To avoid any insect problems, put newly purchased bags of flour in the freezer for 2 weeks to ensure that anything remotely resembling an insect egg is dead.

To make sure your family has bread in the long run, though, there's just no way to get around storing wheat and grinding your own flour. You might as well start learning how to bake your own bread, crackers, and tortillas now and avoid the learning curve if you're ever under pressure to produce a loaf of bread for sandwiches *now*! By the way, watch for wheat grinders on Craigslist, eBay, and even in thrift stores. One sharp-eyed friend of mine has found not one but two wheat grinders at Goodwill.

Eggs—How do you feel about adding a few chickens to the family? A coop in your backyard is probably the best way to ensure a supply of fresh eggs. Eggs can be frozen quite easily by cracking one or two in Ziploc bags, sealing, and freezing. Keep in mind, however, that many emergencies cause power outages, and anything frozen will be ruined within a couple of days. Add powdered eggs to your pantry for an excellent long-term option. They are easy to use in recipes, and a single #10 can has the equivalency of more than 200 eggs!

Produce—Fruits and vegetables can be canned, frozen, freeze-dried, dehydrated, or grown right at home. Home-canning ensures that fresh produce contains none of the undesirable additives found in commercial counterparts, although commercially canned varieties are often too inexpensive to pass up. DIY dehydrating is so simple, it's silly. The first veggies I dehydrated were the ones I usually include in soups and stews: carrots, celery, onions, and potatoes. Look for more information on stocking up on produce and more dehydration how-to's on page 93.

If you don't yet have a garden somewhere on your property, get one started now! The learning curve can be quite daunting. Even if you *have* grown your own produce, a different home or even a different location in the same backyard can present new challenges, and you can pretty well count on at least a few dead plants before you reap that fabulous harvest. The first casualties in my garden this year were four heads of leaf lettuce; a couple of pepper plants look mortally wounded.

Cheese—Is life without cheese even worth living? I'm not so sure, but I'm also not thrilled with my options when it comes to long-term storage. I think I'd be lost if I couldn't whip up a quick quesadilla for my kids' lunches, and powdered cheese just doesn't cut it—no pun intended. Freezing softer cheese, such as cheddar and mozzarella, effectively stores it for a few months, if properly wrapped, but it can affect the texture. Powdered Parmesan in the famous green can will probably last right through Armageddon, but it's not my favorite form of cheese, although it would do in a pinch. (Have you ever had Alfredo sauce made with the powdered stuff? Ewwwww!)

I suppose the next level of preparation for cheese lovers would be to make their own cheese, but eventually moms will start asking themselves, "Just how committed am I to having cheese in my long-term storage?" Some moms will reply, "Whatever it takes!" Others, however, will say, "If I don't have the time *now* to make my own cheese, do you really think I'll have time in the middle of a natural disaster or collapse of civilization?" Survival Moms will be called upon to make tough decisions, and I hope your decision about how to handle cheese in your food storage is the most difficult one you'll ever face!

Plant a cook's garden

If seed catalogs leave you dazed and confused, narrow your focus to only the specific produce you use in a given recipe. I love having a salsa garden out back: tomatoes, onions, cilantro, garlic, and jalapenos. A soup garden is just dandy: carrots, celery, parsley, potatoes, tomatoes, and onions. Another way to decide what to plant is to keep track of the fruits and veggies your family eats and enjoys most often. It doesn't make sense to plant kale if your family never eats it. Plant plenty of your favorites instead!

If you can wax your legs, you can wax cheese!

The truly adventurous Survival Mom—or really, any cheese-head—should try waxing cheese. It's a whole lot easier than waxing your moustache or brows, and it doesn't take much practice to become a pro at it. Here's what you'll need:

- Official cheese wax—no substitutions allowed. Cheese wax is pliable when it's cooled down and is designed to adhere to the cheese. Darker colors are better, since they will protect the cheese from light, one of the enemies of food. Cheese wax is available at www.thecheesemaker.com or www.blendedwaxes.com.
- Cheese. Hard, dry cheeses, such as Colby, Swiss, and Parmesan, work best. If you like cheddar, begin with mild cheddar, since it will sharpen as it ages. Use paper towels to thoroughly dry the exterior of the cheese before applying the wax and allow the cheese to dry for a few hours prior to waxing. Cut the blocks of cheese into a size that will be used within a couple of days once the wax is removed.
- Food-handling gloves. You don't want to transmit skin oil from your hands to the cheese. I buy these gloves in packs of 500, and they last forever!
- Wax paper to provide a nonstick surface for your wax-covered cheese as it cools.
- A double boiler. Be sure to use a pan for melting the wax that will become your official Cheese-Wax Melting Pan because you'll never get all the wax out of the pan. An inexpensive pan from a garage sale should work well for this purpose.
- A food thermometer.
- A natural boar-bristle brush.

Melt the wax in the double boiler to 160°F or until melted; do not overheat it. Dip the block of cheese halfway into the wax. Allow the wax to cool down a bit before dipping the remaining half of the cheese into the wax. Repeat this dipping process at least two more times. Make sure every little groove and dimple is filled in with wax by using the natural bristle brush to add yet another final coat of wax. If you wish to label the cheese, and you should, slap the label on the waxed cheese before the final coat. Store the cheese in a cool, dark place—but not inside a closed container, as cheese needs circulating air. Be sure to check the cheese periodically; look for cracks or signs of mold. If you see mold, cut it away and rewax the affected area of the cheese.

> *Learn as much as you can while you are young, since life becomes too busy later.*
>
> —DANA STEWART SCOTT

Be ready for power outages

Has it ever occurred to you just how many emergencies involve a power outage? Earthquakes, severe winter weather, flooding, tornadoes, heat waves, hurricanes, and more are all likely to cause a disruption in your electrical service. When you consider how vulnerable our power connections are and how reliant we've become on the ready and steady supply of energy, suddenly having to do without is a scary and foreign prospect.

This is one reason I don't recommend including frozen food as part of your food-storage goals. A freezer is a valuable appliance, but if you've ever had to clean one out that was filled with melted and rotten food, I'm sure you said, "Never again!"

As you're clipping coupons and watching for grocery bargains, take a look at my Handy No-Cook Foods checklist and stock up on a variety of foods that require no refrigeration and can be eaten at room temperature. These foods will become part of your food storage, *and* you'll be ready for the next big storm. Anything and everything on this list is a perfect fit for any emergency bag.

Handy No-Cook Foods

- MREs (packaged military meals)
- Energy bars (high-calorie)
- Almonds and other nuts
- V8 juice
- Canned pasta
- Gatorade mix
- Cocoa mix
- Peanut butter
- Jerky
- Dried fruit
- Canned fruit
- Applesauce/fruit cups
- Fruit leather
- Rice cakes
- Pilot bread/Triscuits
- Hard candies
- Tuna packs
- Cookies
- Crackers
- Cheese spread in jars
- Pudding cups
- Instant coffee (if ya just gotta have it!)
- Packets of dry milk
- Breakfast bars
- Sunflower seeds

Butter—It's been years and years since I've used margarine. I have about 30 pounds of real butter in my freezer at any given time, and that's the way I like it. Frozen butter stores very well for months, and when I find it at $2.49 a pound or less, I stock up. When the power goes out, butter can be stored safely at room temperature for a couple of weeks—until it's used up.

If you love butter, you're going to love commercially canned butter. The best-known brand is Red Feather. This stuff will really fool you into thinking you're eating butter straight from the fridge. It's expensive but worth adding to your pantry, a can or two at a time. It melts beautifully.

Powdered butter can be reconstituted with a bit of water, giving it the consistency of whipped butter but with a milkier flavor. Unfortunately, powdered butter doesn't melt, so using it to pour over hot popcorn isn't an option. However, it makes a flavorful spread for bread and muffins and is very useful in recipes that call for butter when the fresh stuff isn't available.

Why not just buy one of those ready-made "Food for a Year" packages?

Ahhh . . . I love to sit back and let someone else do all my work for me. What mom doesn't? However, relying on an anonymous committee at some food-storage company to decide what you and your family will eat every day for 365 days doesn't sound too smart, and it could end up being a huge waste of money.

There's no guarantee that the foods this company chooses will be acceptable to you, tasty, or nutritious enough, especially for active, growing kids. When you take a close look at these "food for a year" packages, some only provide 1,200 calories per day. The average active adult requires 2,500 calories, and growing teenagers need even more.

The cans of foods from these packages may also include unwanted additives and cause allergic reactions. What could possibly be worse than being stuck in a bomb shelter, serving dehydrated peas for the first time, and discovering that they induce diarrhea in your youngest kid? Save your money and devote your time to carefully planning a personalized stock of food.

Can a Whole Foods Mom Make Peace with Food Storage?

You may have noticed that many of the foods on storage lists are not exactly compatible with moms who want to serve their families organic foods with few additives and no extra sugar. I call these moms Whole Foods Moms, whether or not they actually shop at the Whole Foods Market, because in their dreams, their storage pantry would be filled with just the type of food Whole Foods sells. Is there any hope for these moms when it comes to survival food storage? I think there is.

A Whole Foods Mom may not end up with the variety she's used to, but ideally our food storage isn't meant to provide 100% of our diets, either. We can grow at least some of our own produce, raise chickens (free range, of course!) for eggs and poultry, and even buy the fresh ingredients we enjoy from local farmers, co-ops, and other gardeners.

Begin keeping track of what your family currently eats. If you enjoy gourmet granola, learn how to make your own and begin stocking up on those ingredients, making sure they are packaged for long-term storage. The ingredients in a favorite salad or a main dish from Whole Foods just might be very easy to add to your pantry for your replication in the future. Recipes containing grains and different legumes are usually very storage-friendly.

Take a look at the THRIVE line of foods from Shelf Reliance. You'll find that much of their produce is GMO-free (non-genetically modified) and freeze-dried. Freeze-dried produce retains about 95% or more of the food's original nutrients, giving you and your family a very healthy and nutrient-dense option to fresh. Mountain House sells a few organic, freeze-dried foods but at a premium price.

If God had intended us to follow recipes, He wouldn't have given us grandmothers.

—LINDA HENLEY

One compromise that might come easy is to stock up on non-organic basics. Wheat, rice, other grains, and beans can be purchased inexpensively in bulk, freeing up a good deal of money if the purchase of more organic or "natural" products seems too expensive. These basic foods will give you hundreds of meal options that you can transform into delicious meals with healthy additions, such as spices, herbs, and wholesome produce. A meal of couscous with organically grown veggies and free-range chicken (home-canned) could rival any Whole Foods' entree, and it's entirely possible within the realm of food storage.

Each Survival Mom has to determine what is most important when she buys food intended for storage. If price is the main consideration, then she'll have more cans of Campbell's Tomato Soup on her shelves than organic, free-range chicken broth. If there are special dietary considerations, those may have to come first regardless of cost, and if a Whole Foods Mom absolutely must have the freshest foods with few additives—and organic if possible—then she'll have to decide how to best make that happen.

There is no one-size-fits-all plan when it comes to food storage. Each of us has to do what's best for our family, within the constraints of budget, time, food sensitivities and allergies, location, and space. It's all about "doing your best, wherever you are and with what you have."

A roundup of some of the more bizarre storage foods

A Whole Foods Mom might turn her nose up at some of these, but they can really come in handy.

- **Shortening powder**—As if shortening weren't bad enough, here comes the powder! Actually, this food could save your bacon someday, when you need shortening for a recipe but don't have any on hand. It can be used in recipes interchangeably with butter powder. If biscuits are a staple in your family, this product is a must—and it won't go rancid, unlike shortening and oil. It's hardly an "all natural" product, but again, it's nice to have on hand for baking.

- **Freeze-dried cheese**—The day this was invented should really be a holiday. This is real cheese. It looks exactly like the grated cheese you buy at the store, except that it's bone-dry. To use it, just soak it in warm water, wait a few minutes, drain, and pat dry. It melts beautifully, and you'll never know the difference in your quesadillas or cheese enchiladas.

- **Freeze-dried cottage cheese**—Calcium is a major mineral that is vital for strong bones and teeth and overall good health. Families with young children and nursing mothers should, especially, have multiple sources of calcium in their food storage. With a bit of water, freeze-dried cottage cheese can be reconstituted and eaten as is (better if chilled). It can also be served as a yummy layer in lasagna while providing a healthy dose of calcium.

- **Sour cream powder**—I wish I could say this stuff is identical to its cool and creamy counterpart found in the dairy section, but it's not. However, it does provide the flavor of sour cream in recipes, including creamy casseroles and potato dishes.

- **Freeze-dried grapes**—These are definitely one of the more unusual freeze-dried fruits. They are still purple and still oval-shaped, but now they're crunchy! This is one freeze-dried fruit that is especially sensitive to humidity, so before you open that #10 can, have a plan for keeping the contents nice and dry.

- **Powdered eggs**—I'd like to say that these come from powdered chickens, but that would be too easy. Rather, they are dehydrated eggs that have been powdered. Because each #10 can contains the equivalent of a couple of hundred eggs, this is a cost-effective way to always have eggs for your baking and cooking needs.

A Sassy Survival Mom Survives with Sauces

Say *that* three times fast! Around our house I've learned that our refrigerator better contain ketchup and ranch dressing—or else! I wish my son had never discovered the joys of dipping slices of pizza in ranch dressing because that stuff can be pretty darn expensive, and of course, he completely rejects the cheap stuff.

While you're stocking up, keep track of the sauces you frequently use. We use a lot of soy sauce, in addition to ketchup and ranch dressing, and if I'm eating French fries, I've gotta have my HP sauce! Here's a quick checklist to jog your memory of sauces that are must-haves for keeping your family happy and you sane.

If you don't like something change it; if you can't change it, change the way you think about it.

—MARY ENGELBREIT

- Soy sauce
- Teriyaki sauce
- Tabasco or other hot sauce
- Worcestershire
- A-1
- HP sauce (a British favorite)
- Ketchup
- Heinz 57
- Oyster sauce
- Fish sauce
- Mustard
- Barbecue sauce
- Ranch dressing

Keeping your favorite sauces around is all well and good, but the really smart idea is to experiment with recipes to make your own, if possible. Some of these sauces can spoil, so once again, it's important to keep an eye on expiration dates and rotate.

Spices, Herbs, and Seasonings

Can you imagine eating a diet of bland white rice and tasteless pinto beans? I can't, but a lot of families who are stocking up on those two staples seem to be setting themselves up for multiple meals of monotone flavor. Personally, I like to use a lot of spice when I cook and have been stocking up accordingly.

My Macho Mexican Rice is a good example of taking a staple ingredient, adding a few ingredients from your food storage, and ending up with a dish that's anything but boring. The combination of spices is what makes the difference.

Basic spices that should be in your storage pantry, as well as in your kitchen for daily use, are basil, garlic powder, minced onion, chili powder, ground cinnamon, ground ginger, oregano, paprika, rosemary, parsley, and thyme. I don't know about you, but these, along with cumin, are the spices I reach for time and again. If Mexican food is your thing, you'll want to include cumin and cilantro; Italian food lovers will find that they also need Italian seasoning and, perhaps, fennel and crushed red pepper. If there are certain canning recipes you use regularly, be sure to include those spices in your stash. Use this list as a guide for stocking up on herbs, seasonings, and spices you use most often.

Herbs

- Basil
- Bay leaves
- Chives
- Cilantro
- Coriander
- Dill
- Fennel
- Herbes de Provence
- Marjoram
- Mint
- Oregano
- Parsley
- Rosemary
- Sage
- Tarragon
- Thyme
- Turmeric

Seasonings

- Celery salt
- Dried minced garlic
- Dried onion flakes
- Garlic powder
- Onion powder
- Onion salt
- Sea salt
- Table salt

- Italian seasoning
- Kosher salt
- Montreal steak seasoning
- Taco seasoning
- Seasoned salt

Spices

- Allspice
- Caraway seeds
- Cayenne powder
- Celery seed
- Chili powder
- Chinese 5-spice powder
- Cinnamon
- Cloves
- Crushed red pepper
- Cumin
- Curry powder
- Ginger
- Mustard powder
- Paprika
- Pepper
- Peppercorns

IIIIIIIIIIIIIIIIIIIIIIIIIIIIIIIIIIIIIIIIIIIIIIIIIIIIIIIIIIIIIIIIIIIIIIIIIIIIIIIIIIIIIIIIIII

Staying Healthy and Strong, for Your Family's Sake

Nutrition is part of staying healthy, and I recommend stocking up on 6–12 months' worth of vitamins and nutritional supplements. Even products like Ensure deliver a hefty dose of nutrients, although they are more expensive per dose. Supplementing your diet with extra nutrients could become very important in a time of food shortages or escalating prices. It may be tempting to buy the biggest bottles possible, but remember that each time you open any container, air and moisture enter and affect the shelf life of whatever is inside—vitamins and supplements included. Buy smaller amounts, keep track of expiration dates, and rotate to be sure that the vitamins retain their highest levels of potency. Remember that kids need different dosages than adults, so plan and stock up accordingly.

Picture this: You're with your kids or grandkids in a Costco or a Walmart when you hear gunshots and screams coming from across the store. From the terrifying sounds you know you only have a few seconds to get to safety, and an EXIT door is about 30 yards away. Do

> It is surprising what a woman can do when she has to, and how little most women will do when they don't have to.
>
> —WALTER LINN
> (gender adaptation by The Survival Mom!)

A Survival Mom's Story

Teddi Johnson, West Virginia

A true Survival Mom doesn't sit and wait for things to happen. She *makes* them happen. A few years ago Teddi decided she wanted to learn how to make her own cheese, so with the help of a few library books, she mastered the art and makes her own feta, cream cheese, and other varieties. She credits her mother with her array of solid skills, including sewing, cooking from scratch, primitive camping skills, gardening, and preserving food. She said, "To me, it's unusual to *not* know how to do these things."

She has vivid memories of being a young child and traveling with her family to visit Grandma in Bakersfield, California, just before Christmas. A freak blizzard roared in, stranding the family on the road for two days. Most of us would be freaking out right along with the blizzard, but Teddi's family took it in stride. They had wisely packed winter clothing and extra food. Her dad melted snow, so they had a ready supply of water. When the Highway Patrol came by, on foot, to check on their welfare, the family was doing just fine. In the meantime, hundreds of other stranded passengers, some wearing shorts and sandals, had to be evacuated on foot. "After that," she says, "I never go anywhere without a sleeping bag in the back of the car. Even though I was only 5 years old, that experience prepared me for a lot of things later on."

One of those was the 1992 Big Bear earthquake in California. Her home was without water and electricity for 3 days. Panicked, desperate people were stealing groceries at gunpoint, but again, she had everything her family needed right there at home, from a bucket toilet to stored water and food. She had a one-year-old child at the time and was determined that she, as a new mom, would take care of her family.

She showed her mother grizzly side once when her husband, Wulf, was working graveyard shifts and she heard someone enter her house through a window. Without a thought, she grabbed her husband's .22 rifle, confronted the intruder, and terrified him so much that he didn't move a muscle until the sheriff arrived. When Teddi said, "If you even breathe hard, I'll shoot you," apparently, the young man believed her, and so did the sheriff when he had to pry the rifle from her hand.

Interestingly, she admits that if she had been in the house alone, she wouldn't have acted so boldly. "I probably would have just locked myself in the bathroom and called 911, but my baby was in the same room as the intruder."

Teddi is committed to survival and made a difficult decision last year when she realized that her weight had reduced her mobility to the point that she was vulnerable in a catastrophe. She began one of the most difficult journeys of her life, losing weight. To date, she has lost 150 pounds. Her commitment has improved her family's health as well. The Johnson family is in good hands with this Survival Mom.

you have the physical conditioning and stamina to grab the kids—pick them up, if necessary—and run fast enough to escape with your lives? Or, would those extra pounds and flabby muscles slow you down and make a quick escape impossible?

I'm the first to admit that a quick sprint across the store would be pretty difficult for me. I could do it, but it sure wouldn't be impressive in terms of speed or style. I've missed way too many workouts at the gym. I'm typical of millions of Americans, yet as someone who has preparedness as a top goal, I know that someday my survival may depend on being physically fit.

How about you? Could you depend on your fitness level to run fast and far if your life, and the lives of your children, depended on it? Building up our bodies to be as strong as possible and losing some of the pounds that slow us down are a survival and preparedness must. No, it's not an easy step, and there are hundreds of excuses to procrastinate—with most of them printed on restaurant menus!

The necessity of getting in shape and building up my physical strength has been a big pill for me to swallow. I'm not a runner—far from it—but I've been making a point of walking or bicycling as many days of the week as I can, as well as doing a series of strength-building calisthenics (floor exercises). When I feel like turning on the TV or plopping down with the latest Daniel Silva book, here's what I tell myself:

- Upper-body strength will help improve my target shooting.

- I'm setting a good example for the kids. They love physical activity, and I want them to keep that attitude.

- Stronger leg muscles are more attractive and much better for running from a dangerous situation—and also for kicking bad guys in the groin.

- As I build up my cardiovascular system, my overall health improves, hopefully keeping me healthy for many, many years to come. Who knows what our health care system will look like in a few years? I'd just as soon stay healthy and limit my dependence on the medical system.

- I am so vain, it's embarrassing. Heck, I just want to look cuter in my jeans!

- If gasoline prices climb to levels beyond my budget, we'll be walking a whole lot more.

- The future could very well bring more expensive energy overall. If I have to use my household appliances less often, I'll be doing a lot more manual labor and will need a stronger body and more energy.

Moms are known for putting everything and everyone ahead of their own needs, but right now it's vital that you take care of your own physical, medical, and dental issues as soon as they arise. An uncertain future could mean longer waits for doctors' appointments and higher medical costs. Please don't put off getting routine exams and taking care of little things that might not be so little. Above all, your kids need a healthy and strong Survival Mom, so do everything in your power to make sure you survive!

The Prepared Family

How do you introduce your children to the idea of food storage without causing them to worry? We started by reading the story of Joseph from Genesis 41 in the Bible. The story has been retold in a beautifully made animated film by DreamWorks Animation, *Joseph: King of Dreams*. Here are some of the lessons my kids learned from Joseph's life.

- Joseph understood the signs that difficult times were coming. Although we don't know *exactly* what lies ahead, our eyes and ears tell us that it's smart to prepare.

- Joseph kept adding a little each day and each week, and over time it added up to enough food for an entire country. Our jars of peanut butter and cans of tuna may not look like much, but when we add a little each week, it will soon be enough to last for a long time.

- Joseph's food wasn't for *now*, it was for *later*. No, we can't dig into those boxes of granola bars right now! They're for *later*!

- Joseph shared. Because of his foresight, planning, and *doing*, there was enough food stored for everyone, including hungry neighbors. Our food storage isn't something selfish, meant only for our family. We hope to have plenty to share.

Another option is to read "The Ant & the Grasshopper." Children love stories about animals, and the lessons from this ancient fable won't be lost on them.

Preparedness is a theme in other children's literature as well, including the Little House on the Prairie series.

Make food storage an adventure! Have the kids taste-test new freeze-dried foods. Help them make their own snack mixes using freeze-dried or dehydrated fruit, nuts, and dry cereal.

Family Preparedness Plan: Food-Storage Planning

Guiding Principles: Keep it simple! Serving size counts!

☐ Master Meal List—Breakfasts:

☐ 1. _____

☐ 2. _____

☐ 3. _____

☐ 4. _____

☐ 5. _____

☐ 6. _____

☐ 7. _____

☐ Master Meal List—Main Dishes:

☐ 1. _____

☐ 2. _____

☐ 3. _____

☐ 4. _____

☐ 5. _____

☐ 6. _____

☐ 7. _____

Putting the pieces together

☐ Survivalize each recipe.

☐ Develop a Master Grocery List that can be used for both shopping and an inventory of the ingredients necessary for a survivalized menu.

☐ Survivalize additional recipes for added variety.

☐ Stock up on Handy No-Cook Foods (see page 71) to prepare for a power outage or other emergency.

☐ Review the lists of sauces, herbs, and seasonings and inventory my stash. Add needed items to my To Buy list.

☐ Assess level of physical fitness and make a "No Excuses" plan for improvement.

☐ List physical, medical, and dental issues. Prioritize them in order of urgency, and begin making appointments.

CHAPTER 5

Increase Your Food Storage Savvy

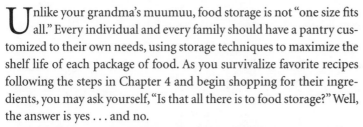

U nlike your grandma's muumuu, food storage is not "one size fits all." Every individual and every family should have a pantry customized to their own needs, using storage techniques to maximize the shelf life of each package of food. As you survivalize favorite recipes following the steps in Chapter 4 and begin shopping for their ingredients, you may ask yourself, "Is that all there is to food storage?" Well, the answer is yes . . . and no.

By following my Survivalized Meal Plan in Chapter 4, you will be ready to prepare complete meals using your favorite recipes. However, there are certain foods that are so versatile and so shelf-stable that they need to be included in your pantry regardless of whether they show up in your recipes.

I call these my "Top Ten Foods to Store."

In addition to buying your recipe ingredients as detailed in the previous chapter, buying these Top Ten Foods will expand your repertoire. What if none of your survivalized recipes include rice? Rice has an immensely long shelf life, is versatile, and makes a great meal-stretcher to boot. Take a look at my Top Ten and then keep an eye out for them whenever you shop. Most are among the lowest-priced groceries you'll find.

1. Wheat

It's not called the "staff of life" for nothing. Just about every baked good you can think of, from crackers to bagels and tortillas, uses wheat as its most important ingredient. There are three main categories of wheat you should know about.

baby step

Purchase 1 pound of hard white wheat. If you don't have a grain mill or know anyone who does, cook up a batch of wheat berries to get an idea of the flavor and texture of real, live wheat.

Hard white wheat—I call this my "go to" wheat and use it for almost everything. Whenever you make a recipe that calls for yeast, you'll be using either hard white or hard red wheat. Hard white yields a flavorful loaf of bread that resembles store-bought "wheat" bread, except that yours will be the real thing! Plan on this wheat to be 40–50% of your total wheat storage.

The "hard" wheats contain more gluten, which produces the sticky, elastic dough necessary for baking bread.

Hard red wheat—This wheat yields a loaf of bread that is darker in color, with a heartier flavor. Some families love hard red wheat and use it for all of their bread-baking, but it can be harder on the digestive system for some. Others prefer to combine hard red with hard white for a customized flavor. Try making a loaf of bread using hard red and see how your family likes it. If they turn up their noses, and you end up feeding the rest of the loaf to the birds, next time try a 50/50 combination with hard white. Continue experimenting until you come up with a loaf everybody loves.

Soft white wheat—A woman does not live by bread alone. We need our brownies, our cookies, and our cupcakes, too! Soft white wheat is the wheat you'll use for baking these recipes and any others that do not call for yeast. It doesn't contain as much protein as the hard wheat, but who eats brownies for their protein?

Please don't be afraid of wheat! When it's ground using a grain mill, you end up with flour. There's no mystery or sorcery involved.

The reason wheat is recommended for storage is because it has a shelf life of up to 30 years. You could easily bequeath it to a loved one in your will. Flour, on the other hand, is only good for about a year or so before it can take on a nasty flavor and lose its nutritional value. Baked goods made with old flour just don't turn out right. However, you might still get some use out of it as a breading ingredient for meat, chicken, and veggies before frying, but only if the flavor of the flour isn't distasteful.

By the way, once wheat is ground into flour, it begins losing nutrients, so always grind only the amount of wheat you'll be using within a couple of days or freeze whatever is left over to prevent the oils in the ground wheat from becoming rancid with time.

Cooked Wheat Berries: It's what's for breakfast!

This hot cereal is versatile, and you'll surely be able to create a version everyone in your family will love. Here's the basic recipe:

> 1 cup hard white wheat, sometimes called "wheat berries"
> 2½ cups water
> dash of salt

The easiest way to prepare this hot cereal is to combine the wheat and water in a slow cooker, set on low, and cook overnight or throughout the day. For the stovetop, combine ingredients in a medium-size pan over medium-high heat. Bring to a boil, lower the heat, cover, and simmer until the berries are plump and chewy. This will take about an hour.

Add brown sugar, honey, cinnamon, or dried fruit for a heavenly breakfast.

The Ultimate Wheat Berry Salad

First, prepare cooked wheat berries using either the slow cooker or stovetop method. You can make this recipe while the berries are still warm or after they've cooled.

Place 3 cups of the berries in a medium-size bowl and add:

> 4 tablespoons olive oil
> 3 tablespoons balsamic vinegar
> salt and pepper to taste (optional)
> ⅓ cup finely sliced basil
> ¼ cup chopped rehydrated or fresh tomatoes
> ¼ cup fresh or rehydrated celery
> 3 tablespoons finely chopped red onion

Food Calculator Suggestion

150 pounds of wheat per person per year, ages 7+ years

75 pounds of wheat per child per year, ages 0–6 years

A note about food calculator quantities: Since much of your stored food will have a long shelf life, your now-young kids may be ravenous teenagers by the time you need to rely on your stored food. Therefore, you may want to stock up on the larger recommended amounts per person.

This is delicious as is, but you can add olives, feta, and any fresh herbs you may have growing in your garden. This salad is absolutely delicious! You can thank me later. Cooked wheat berries can be added to other salads as well.

The nitty-gritty on grain mills

Soon after you buy that first bag or bucket of wheat, begin shopping around for grain mills. Not many people use a stone metate anymore to grind their wheat and corn, so a mill will have to do! Your first dilemma will be: electric or manual?

Making bread can be time-consuming on its own, without the added time involved with grinding wheat in a manual grinder. For that reason, I recommend an electric mill. Two of the highest-rated brands are the Nutrimill and the WonderMill. I give them both a thumbs-up for their relative quietness, grinding speeds, and larger capacities for the wheat and the ground flour. You really can't go wrong with either brand.

A manual mill is important as a backup. You definitely don't want to be caught in a power outage with 500 pounds of wheat and a useless electric mill. Two mills in this category that I recommend are the WonderMill Junior and the more expensive but top-notch Country Living mill. There are smaller and less expensive mills on the market, but some of them produce flour at such a slow rate that you could, literally, be grinding for 20 minutes or more to produce just one cup of flour! When it's *your* arm doing the work, that's no fun at all!

Whatever mill you purchase, look for one that is capable of grinding other foods, such as rice, corn, coffee, and herbs. Not all mills are designed to do this. If possible, test the mill with a bit of wheat and check for loudness. One of my friends has a mill that is so loud that she has to wear ear protection!

Finally, if you're just getting started, I recommend looking for a mill on Craigslist, eBay, or even Freecycle. Once you're a pro at making bread and are grinding wheat frequently, then invest in something more expensive, durable, and of a higher quality.

Did you know?

All-purpose flour is made up of a mixture of both hard and soft wheats. The combination is usually around 60% hard and 40% soft, making it suitable for a wide variety of recipes.

2. Rice

Along with wheat, rice is extraordinarily versatile. It's no wonder that 50% of the world's population relies on rice for 80% of its diet! Depending on which recipe you choose, you could mix up a spicy batch of Macho Mexican Rice one night and serve your family jambalaya the next night! They'll never realize they ate rice two nights in a row!

Brown rice is considered to be a whole grain because its bran covering is intact. It provides extra fiber and nutrients, so it's worth having in the pantry. If you're interested in stocking up on brown rice, you should know that it will have a shorter shelf life than white rice because of the oils in its hulls. You can lengthen that shelf life by storing brown rice in the freezer or refrigerator in airtight containers. Another option is to store it in vacuum-packed bags or jars. Oxygen is the cause of rancidity, and if you can eliminate oxygen from a package, you can lengthen the life of the food.

White rice may not have all of the extra nutritional goodies of brown rice, but you can work a bit of magic to change that. Check out my recipe for Super Rice in the previous chapter.

If someone in your family has celiac disease or must be on a gluten-free diet, you can make your own rice flour by grinding it in a mill that specifically allows the grinding of rice.

Food Calculator Suggestion

50 pounds of rice per person per year, ages 7+ years

25 pounds of rice per child per year, ages 0–6 years

3. Dried milk

You may have bad memories of being forced to drink a watery, white beverage your mom called "instant milk," but dried milk is still an ingredient that is useful in your food storage. For the longest shelf life, buy it from commercial vendors that have packaged it in airtight #10 cans. If you're ever forced to drink it again, mix it up the night before, add a tablespoon or so of coffee creamer or a little vanilla extract, and chill it overnight. I suppose if you're really dreading taking that first sip, you could add a shot of Kahlua! Otherwise, it's smart to have this as an option when making recipes that call for fresh milk.

Nonfat dried milk has the longest shelf life and is definitely the best form for storage. Shop around online for the best prices. Overwhelmingly, the favored brands for dried milk are Augason Farms and Rainy Day.

You'll probably encounter "milk alternatives" in your shopping. These are milk-based products that have additives to make them taste better. Be sure to read the label before buying if you're avoiding things like partially hydrogenated vegetable oil and high-fructose corn syrup.

Food Calculator Suggestion

60 pounds of dry milk per person per year, ages 7+ years

30 pounds of dry milk per child per year, ages 0–6 years

If your brain refuses to accept dried milk or if you just want to have a backup, consider shelf-stable milk. This is milk in liquid form. It is packaged in the same type of cardboard containers as juice boxes are. It's been said that shelf-stable milk will never do two things: go bad or taste good! Another backup is the old standby—evaporated milk. When you only need a small amount of milk for cooking or baking and there's no fresh milk available, it's very convenient to just pop one of these cans open. It has a shelf life of 12–15 months, so you'll want to rotate it in with your cooking as you add additional cans for future use.

If you have young children or if there's a nursing mom in the home, milk, in whatever form, is going to be necessary for proper growth. Toddlers, in particular, need the fats found in whole milk. Dried whole milk is available from a variety of online sources, including King Arthur Flour (believe it or not) and The Great American Spice Company, and you'll find Nestle's Nido Instant Dry Whole Milk at local grocery stores. Rice milk and soy milk are two other options for special dietary needs. Both come in shelf-stable versions, as well as powdered.

My biggest problem with dried milk has been our cat, Daisy. She somehow manages to ferret out our packaged dried milk no matter where in the pantry it's hidden and has so far chewed through a cardboard box and a Mylar bag. She hasn't been quite as successful with our powdered milk packed into jars!

4. Salt

Did you know that salt was once so valuable it was used as a currency? In fact, we get our word "salary" from the days when Roman legionnaires received salt as payment for their service. Nowadays, salt is so inexpensive and comes in so many varieties that it makes sense to have at least 5 pounds stored per person in your family.

Salt is an important nutrient that our bodies need. In the kitchen, it's necessary for adding flavor to foods. You'll also need salt if pickling or canning foods is on your To Do list. In years gone by, long before every home had a freezer, Survival Moms preserved meat and fish by salting them. Mineral-dense sea salt is also useful for its healing properties; entire industries have been built selling beauty and health products containing high levels of salt from the Dead Sea.

There are four salts you should keep in your pantry:

Iodized salt will help protect the body from diseases related to iodine deficiency. This is the table salt you probably use every day in your cooking and baking. It's cheap, and you could probably buy a year's worth in one shopping trip.

Canning salt will be necessary if you plan on pickling produce from your garden. Pickled zucchini, okra, and green beans are delicious! Canning salt doesn't contain iodine or any other additives. This ensures that your homemade pickles will be swimming in perfectly clear brine. One word of caution: Canning salt will clump and cake in humid weather, so be sure to store it in a dry location and in a container with a tight lid.

Kosher salt is my family's favorite when it comes to flavoring food. It has a coarser grain but a milder flavor than table salt.

Sea salt is beloved by chefs and home cooks alike for its exceptional flavor and usefulness in preserving foods. Some experts swear by Celtic sea salt, in particular.

Food Calculator Suggestion

5 pounds of salt per person per year, ages 7+ years

3 pounds of salt per child per year, ages 0–6 years

For long-term storage, especially if you live in a humid climate, repackage your salt in plastic or glass containers with a tight lid. In case of a leaky roof or flooding (you never know!), your salt will be kept nice and dry. Unless exposed to humidity, salt stores indefinitely.

5. Beans

A terrific addition in the meal-stretcher category, beans offer healthy doses of fiber, nutrients, and calories. Get to know all of your bean options because some beans are higher in folic acid and iron than others. White beans and Mung beans, in particular, pack a pretty hefty nutritional punch. Check out my Nutritional Value of Beans chart below to learn more about which beans you may want the most in your pantry.

This may come as a surprise, but dry beans can actually dry out. Really! That bag of dried pinto beans can, over time, become so hard

Is your stomach tough enough?

Food Calculator Suggestion

60 pounds of beans per person per year, ages 7+ years

24 pounds of beans per child per year, ages 0–6 years

If you have not been including beans, bread from freshly ground wheat, and lots of fiber in your diet, you and your family may experience what is politely called "tummy troubles" until your systems become accustomed to higher fiber content. You can avoid these issues by serving one or two bean-based meals per week and using less store-bought bread and more homemade bread made from whole wheat.

I've thought about what life would be like trapped in a bunker with my 9-year-old son while eating beans three times a day. Not coincidentally, I've stocked up on a dozen or so cans of my favorite air freshener from Bath & Body Works!

Basic guide to sprouting

Great seeds to sprout

- Chia
- Wheat
- Alfalfa
- Radish
- Red clover
- Mung beans
- Arugula
- Garlic
- Amaranth
- Broccoli

There is a wide variety of beans and seeds suitable for sprouting, and experimenting to find your favorites is half the fun. If you have a canning jar and some beans around the house, you're ready to go!

You'll need a canning jar with the screw band and a 5-inch square of porous fabric (pantyhose are good for this purpose) or a piece of mesh or netting cut to fit the jar opening. You'll also need seeds or beans and water. Measure out about 1 teaspoon of seeds if they are tiny or 2 tablespoons if they are larger.

Pour the seeds into the jar and fill halfway with water. Place the porous fabric over the top of the jar and screw on the band. Swish seeds and water and then pour out the water into your sink. Repeat this process twice a day until the beans have sprouted.

I use the Victorio Kitchen Seed Sprouter, which allows me to sprout three different types of beans or seeds at the same time in separate trays. Experiment with different types of seeds/beans to see which flavors are your favorites. I was surprised to find out how much I liked wheat sprouts.

Use your sprouts in salads, sandwiches, and even atop soups and stews for extra crunch and nutrition.

You'll find more information at www.sproutpeople.com.

Nutrional Values of Beans

Type	Calories	Protein	Carbs	Fiber	Sugars	Calcium	Iron	Potassium	Niacin	Folate
Anasazi	600	40g	108g	36g		8g	10.8mg			
Black	662	42g	121g	29g	4g	239mg	9.7mg	2877mg	3.8mg	861mcg
Fava	512	39g	87g	37.5g	8.55g	154mg	10mg	1593mg	4.2mg	634mcg
Gr. Northern	620	40g	114g	37g	4g	320mg	10mg	2538mg	3.6mg	882mcg
Kidney	613	43g	110g	46g	4g	263mg	15mg	2587mg	3.8mg	725mcg
Mung	718	49g	129g	33.7g	13.66g	273mg	13.95mg	2579mg	4.7mg	1294mcg
Navy	701	46g	126g	51g	8g	306mg	11mg	2465mg	4.5mg	757mcg
Pink	720	44g	135g	27g	4.5g	273mg	14mg	3074mg	4.5mg	757mcg
Pinto	670	41g	120g	30g	4g	218mg	10mg	2688mg	2.3mg	1013mcg
White	673	47g	122g	30g	4.26g	485mg	21mg	3626mg	1mg	784mcg

Values per cup. Data from USDA National Nutrient Database.

and dry that no amount of cooking will make the beans edible. It will be tempting to toss them out, but try grinding them using your wheat grinder and adding bean flour to various dishes for extra nutrients and fiber. A word of caution: Check the manufacturer's directions for your mill to ensure that it's designed to grind beans.

You may have enjoyed bean sprouts in your salads and in many Asian dishes, but did you ever think of growing bean sprouts yourself? That's one more reason to stock up on beans. Every variety can be sprouted, adding massive amounts of important micronutrients to your family's diet.

Don't forget the lowly canned bean! There may be times when water is precious, and soaking beans overnight and then boiling them the next day might not be the wisest use of water. Canned beans are already cooked and ready to eat or be added to a recipe.

Include your assortment of canned beans in your family's storage goal. If you're a fan of refried beans, include those, both canned and dehydrated, as well as bean soup mixes.

6. Tomatoes

I've singled out tomatoes from other veggies because they are particularly versatile. If you think about it, in the past week you may have eaten a tomato-based food product every day! Think salsa, ketchup, and marinara sauce. Mexican and Italian restaurants would shut down if tomatoes ever ceased to exist! Tomatoes are loaded with a terrific array of micronutrients and are the basis of many soup, stew, and sauce recipes. Go ahead and buy them canned and in different forms, such as sauce, paste, diced, and whole.

Canned tomatoes need to be monitored once you've had them on the shelf for more than a year. They are one of the high-acid foods and have a shorter shelf life than some other canned foods.

The Paranoid Dad's Salsa for Champions

In a saucepan over low heat, combine these ingredients until thoroughly dissolved:

> **3 tablespoons oil**
> **3 tablespoons vinegar**
> **3 teaspoons salt**
> **3 teaspoons sugar**
> **3 cloves garlic, pressed**
> **chopped cilantro (optional)**
> **thinly sliced green onion (optional)**

Pour warmed liquid into a bowl and add a 28-ounce can of tomatoes (chopped or pureed), one chopped white onion, and one or more chopped jalapeno peppers, to taste. Add a nice big bag of tortilla chips, and dinner is served!

If you have the slightest green thumb, plan on starting your own tomato garden. It's not unusual for a single tomato plant to produce more than 20 pounds of tomatoes. As you watch those red globes get bigger and bigger, you'd better have a plan for preserving some of them! It's easy to either can or dehydrate your extra tomatoes. Mix up large batches of your favorite salsa or marinara sauce and can those, following the proper procedures to the letter.

If growing your own is not possible, search for produce co-ops, farmers markets, and produce stands in your area. Tomatoes are an extremely prolific crop. I've even seen kids standing on a neighborhood corner with a sign that read, "Free Tomatoes!" No kidding!

Once you have a batch of tomatoes, they're quite easy to preserve for a long shelf life. If you want to avoid canned products or additives, here are my own favorite ways to preserve fresh tomatoes.

Let our advance worrying become advance thinking and planning!

—WINSTON CHURCHILL

Dehydrated tomatoes

- Wash fresh tomatoes and remove core.

- Slice each tomato into ¼-inch-thick slices.

- Lay tomato slices on the dehydrating trays. It's okay if the slices touch each other.

- Dehydrate at 135–140 degrees for 8–10 hours.

- The slices should be brittle when they are completely dry.

- For more specific instructions, check the manufacturer's manual for your dehydrator.

Food dehydrating basics

A food dehydrator can cost a few dollars at a garage sale or more than $200 if you buy the Excalibur, which is considered to be the best dehydrator on the market. Here are some tips for getting the most out of a dehydrator:

- A dehydrator with a fan at the back of the unit will give better results than one with the fan on top.

- Plastic mesh tray inserts will help keep tiny pieces of food from falling through to the trays below.

- A temperature of 120 degrees is good for drying most foods.

- Spray trays with a light coating of vegetable oil to prevent food from sticking.

- When just getting started, record what you dehydrate, how long it takes, and what the volume of the finished food turns out to be.

- Fruit leather trays are a good investment. They enable you to dehydrate applesauce, tomato sauce, and other thick, liquid foods.

- Even if all you have is an herb garden, a dehydrator will become your best friend for preserving those herbs and any other edible products that come from your garden. Dehydrating food is light years easier than canning.

- Buy bags of frozen veggies and fruit when they're on sale, empty the bag onto dehydrating trays, and turn on the dehydrator. Frozen foods are already cut and clean and ready to be dried.

- Dehydrated foods can be stored in Food-Saver bags, jars, or other airtight containers. Add one oxygen absorber (more on oxygen absorbers on page 104) and store in a dark, cool location.

- The two books I recommend for learning more are *Mary Bell's Complete Dehydrator Cookbook* by Mary T. Bell and *How to Dry Foods* by Deanna DeLong.

- Visit www.dehydrate2store.com for inspiring instructional videos.

Tomato powder

- Tomato powder is intensely flavored and can be reconstituted with water to create your own "fresh" tomato sauce and tomato paste.
- Begin by filling a blender or food processor about half-full with dehydrated tomato slices.
- I blend everything—peel, seeds, and all.
- Blend on "high" or "puree" setting until all slices have been powdered.
- Store your freshly made tomato powder in a jar with an airtight lid.

Dehydrated tomato sauce

It may surprise you, but marinara sauce and even salsa can be dehydrated. This is especially helpful for moms who want to pack their own homemade dehydrated meals for camping trips. Check out my recipe for Dehydrated-to-Death Chili in Chapter 4 for an example of putting dehydrated tomato sauce to work in a recipe.

- Start with either canned or homemade tomato sauce.
- If you know what recipes you'll be using the sauce for, mix in the salt, herbs, and spices accordingly.
- Marinara sauce can also be dehydrated using this technique.
- Spread the sauce evenly on your dehydrator's fruit leather trays or nonstick sheets.
- Dehydrate at 130 degrees.
- The sauce is fully dehydrated when there are no wet or tacky spots. Peel it off the trays, roll or fold it up, and store it in a small glass jar.
- It's easily rehydrated with a cup or two of water, depending on the desired thickness of the sauce, and provides you with portable sauce for camping trips or inclusion in a dehydrated mix.

Canned tomatoes

When it comes to canning, nothing beats learning at the feet of a master. That would be your grandma or some other canning pro who would love to share his or her expertise. My friend Barbara would, I'm sure, spend an entire weekend instructing me on the intricacies of

A canner's shopping list

- Canning jars in various sizes
- Jar lids and screw bands
- Reusable lids from TATTLER (the hottest things in the canning world)
- Jar lifter
- Wide-neck canning funnel
- Magnetic lid lifter
- A boiling-water canner with rack
- Tongs
- Pressure canner— necessary for canning chicken and meats

Can chocolate chips, coffee beans, and M&Ms!

Glass canning jars are ideal for food storage in more ways that you might think. With a FoodSaver Wide-Mouth Jar Sealer, you can vacuum-pack just about anything in an oxygen-free environment. Chocolate won't turn white, and coffee beans will stay fresh. Go ahead and buy those bags of Christmas M&Ms on December 26. They'll taste just as good next year!

canning everything from applesauce and strawberry jam to bread-and-butter pickles. If there's no canning expert in your world, the *Ball Complete Book of Home Preserving* might become your new best friend.

- The most basic canning recipe simply requires fresh tomatoes, lemon juice, and an optional dose of salt. Tomatoes are one of the easiest veggies to home can.

- I recommend packing the fresh tomatoes in water or tomato juice, since so many recipes call for both tomatoes and their juice.

- Flavor your canned tomatoes with herbs, spices, and seasonings according to the type of cooking you do the most. For example, if you cook a lot of Italian recipes, include oregano, garlic, basil, and thyme with your tomatoes. Just make sure you label your jars.

- Buy canning supplies whenever and wherever you can. Even if you don't use all the jars and lids you've collected, you can use them to store just about anything else that needs an airtight home.

7. Produce

When you see produce on sale, whether fresh, frozen, or canned, stock up according to your family's preferences. It's hard to overstock vegetables and fruit, since they are so versatile. It would be far better to have too much produce, in any form, than too little.

Vegetables and fruit provide micronutrients, fiber, and variety to our diets. This is a perfect example of the Rule of Three: How can you provide produce to your family from three different sources?

Food Calculator Suggestion

Figuring out how many tomato products to store is a little tricky because there are so many varieties of them. If you plan to grow your own tomatoes, that will also affect your storage goals. These tips may help:

Keep track of how much ketchup and salsa your family eats per month. Set a goal to stock up on those items, multiplied by three, for a 3-month supply.

Because canned tomato products have a shorter shelf life, don't stock up on more than you could use in an 18-month period. Again, begin keeping track of what you typically use in a month and use those numbers as a storage goal for a 3-month period.

Tomato sauce _____
Tomato paste _____
Canned tomatoes (chopped? pureed? whole? Italian? Southwest? can size?) _____

- Fresh is always best, especially if you've grown it yourself.

- Produce co-ops have sprouted all over the country, as more and more people seek out the healthiest options for their families.

- Local farmers often sell direct to customers.

- Meet-up groups sometimes connect home gardeners with each other, allowing for the exchange of seeds and produce.

- Check Craigslist. I found a great source of wheat and pinto beans this way.

- Don't overlook canned and frozen produce. Both can be easily dehydrated for a longer shelf life.

- Check with a local LDS church for leads to local growers. These growers may even sell produce and other foods directly to you.

Buying dehydrated and freeze-dried produce is another good option and is often more cost-effective than preparing the foods yourself. Consider this: I can purchase a #10 can of sliced, freeze-dried green onions for under $7. This can holds about 10 cups of green onions. I would have to grow or buy an enormous amount of fresh onions to produce an equivalent 10 cups, not to mention the investment of time to dehydrate them! There are times when the most budget-friendly option is buying commercially dehydrated or freeze-dried produce.

When it comes to food storage, it's sometimes easy to overlook snacks. If snacks are a part of your family's diet, however, don't overlook them now! In fact, they may become even more important as a source of nutrients and calories. Here's where veggies and fruit can play an especially important role. They're nutritious and healthy, and I've yet to meet a kid who doesn't like freeze-dried apples!

If fresh produce ever becomes a scarce commodity, we could see the return of nutritional-deficiency diseases, such as scurvy. This is one more reason to boost your family's supply of fruit and vegetables—the more the merrier!

Finally, with the huge variety of vegetables and fruit out there, how do you decide which to stock up on first? Here are six suggestions:

1. Keep track of the produce you already buy and use. As always, it's best to begin with the familiar and branch out from there.

2. Begin setting aside favorite recipes and make a list of the produce needed for each. This will help you narrow your focus.

3. Consider stocking up on the most common veggies used in soups and stews, such as potatoes, onions, corn, carrots, and celery.

4. Take note of which veggies and fruits are difficult, impractical, or impossible to grow in your zone. I have stocked up on freeze-dried pineapple, mango, and bananas applying this principle.

5. Don't forget hot and cold cereal mix-ins. Oatmeal isn't the same without raisins or dried cranberries.

6. What fruits and veggies do your kids enjoy as snacks? Sometimes we get so busy stocking up on the basics that we forget how comforting and fun a snack can be.

8. Peanut butter

I include peanut butter on this list because it is such a nutrient-dense food, packed with healthy oils and calories. It's an excellent source of protein and is a particularly good food to include in emergency kits because of its long shelf life. I love it when my kids ask for peanut butter sandwiches because I know it's a real "stick to your ribs" meal, and they won't be begging for food 30 minutes later!

Better yet, though, peanut butter has an extremely long shelf life even after it's been opened. It has a very low moisture content that doesn't support mold and/or bacterial growth. Unopened peanut butter will last just about forever because the oil content has to be exposed to air in order to go rancid.

Powdered peanut butter is a product I recommend as a backup, as well as a handy ingredient for recipes. You get all the same nutrients but none of the fat. I use the powder in my morning smoothies, but it can be mixed with a bit of water to create a peanut butter spread.

Peanut allergies don't have to mean the end to handy, nutty spreads. Almond and cashew butters have a shelf life of about 1 year, and the love of my life, Nutella, has a similar shelf life to peanut butter when it's unopened.

If you're a mom who shies away from anything containing hydrogenated oil—and, therefore, from most commercial peanut butter—making your own nutty spread is very easy, as long as you have a mill that has the capability of grinding legumes.

Food Calculator Suggestion

4 pounds of peanut butter per person per year, ages 7+ years

2 pounds per child per year, ages 0–6 years

I recommend more, particularly for families with young children.

9. Oil

Unless you stock up on oil, you'll be stuck with having to boil and bake all your food. However, oil is very tricky to store long-term. Bottled oils generally have a shelf life of just a year, so it's important to keep track of dates and use the older oil first. Oil has a bad habit of going rancid even before it *smells* that way. Even *I* have been known to shun brownies made with rancid oil.

In general, oil is the one food that is better stored in smaller containers and rotated very frequently. Sure, you can use rancid oil to make your own soap, but if it was intended for cooking, then it's gone to waste.

When you purchase oil, keep in mind the five enemies of food (see page 100). Always store oil in a cool, dark place, such as a cabinet or a cupboard. Some moms store theirs in a covered plastic bin. If you have a choice between buying oil in clear or opaque containers, opaque is better.

Oil can also be refrigerated or even kept in the freezer. I recommend taking this step, especially if you live in a warm climate. If one part of your house is cooler during the summer, then that should be where your oil is stored.

Consider how often you use oil and which types you use. I rarely use vegetable or canola oil, except in baking. We use olive oil for everything else. Analyzing your oil usage will be helpful in determining which types to store.

When it comes to olive oil, quality counts. If possible, purchase the freshest 100% extra-virgin olive oil you can afford. Sometimes this can be purchased in metal cans, which will help protect the oil from the harmful effects of oxygen and light. Otherwise, buy it in smaller amounts, rotate frequently, and store in a cool, dark place.

Coconut oil is a good alternative that you may not have considered. It has a longer shelf life than other oils and some amazing health benefits, although your fried chicken may smell like it was outside sunbathing, with a nice coating of Coppertone! I've put coconut oil to good use by adding a tablespoon to my morning smoothies. It's an excellent source of healthy fats and additional calories, if necessary. Virgin coconut oil can be purchased online from Tropical Traditions, in health food stores, or at Whole Foods.

Food Storage Mini Worksheet

Vegetable/canola oil used per month: _____

Olive oil used per month: _____

Other oil usage: _____

Calculate each total and multiply by three to figure how much extra oil to store for a 3-month supply.

What about my sweet tooth?

Sugar is an absolute must, as well as honey. Both have extremely long shelf lives—just be sure to keep sugar in an airtight package, especially if you live in a humid climate. Honey can double as an amazing healing agent for your first-aid kit and is the only food that never spoils.

Food Calculator Suggestion

40 pounds of sugar and 3 pounds of honey per person per year ages 7+ years.

20 pounds of sugar and 1 pound of honey per person per year ages 0-6 years.

If you have a whole set of sweet teeth or plan on doing more than a little canning, you may want to increase these amounts.

Food Calculator Suggestion

4 pounds of shortening per person per year, ages 7+ years

2 pounds of shortening per child per year, ages 0–6 years

2 gallons of oil per person per year, ages 7+ years

1 gallon of oil per child per year, ages 0–6 years

One other option to storing oil is to stock up on shortening. I know, I know. Health experts have decried the use of shortening for most of our lives, but when shortening is packaged in either its original metal container or repackaged in vacuum-packed jars using a FoodSaver Wide-Mouth Jar Sealer and canning jars, it has an indefinite shelf life. Melt whatever you need for a recipe, and you've got oil. It's an option worth considering. However, note that much of the Crisco-brand shortening is packaged in a mutant cardboard/metal container, which is *not* meant for long-term storage. It will have to be packed into a canning jar and sealed with a jar sealer.

If you've ever suffered a few weeks on an ultra-low-fat diet, you may have noticed dry skin and hair and other effects. The fact is, our bodies require healthy oils. One of the drawbacks of freeze-dried and dehydrated foods is that they contain no oils. When you start adding those foods to your family's diet, be sure to supplement them with doses of healthy oils during your meal preparation.

Keep in mind that a moderately active adult requires around 2,500 calories each day. In an emergency situation, the use of healthy oils will boost calories, which, in turn, will give you and your family members increased energy.

10. Dried pasta

Pasta is one more versatile meal-stretcher and a family pleaser, all in one. It doesn't have the long shelf life of most other foods on this list, but that can be helped by repackaging it in vacuum-packed jars or bags or in Mylar bags with an oxygen absorber. Buy a nice variety of pasta, including whole wheat. Many grocery stores now carry gluten-free pasta for families with special dietary needs.

For pasta purists

If you can't imagine life without pasta, the best long-term option for you is storing durum wheat. Durum has the highest amount of protein of the wheat varieties, and when ground, it's the main ingredient used in pasta. You can buy durum wheat online from Walton Feed. Learn how to make pasta by hand or buy a manual pasta machine. The Norpro Pasta Machine is a particularly good brand. Homemade is always best, and when it comes to pasta, that's the golden rule!

Adding the Top Ten Foods to your Survivalized Meal Plan from Chapter 4 will help round out your food-storage pantry. If the Top Ten are all you have, you'll still have the ingredients for preparing dozens of different meals and have extra food for snacking.

Homemade brown sugar

There's no need to stock up on brown sugar. Just mix 1 cup of granulated sugar with 1 tablespoon of molasses. Mix well, and you have fresh brown sugar!

These ingredients may not show up on your survivalized recipe list or in my Top Ten, but no pantry is complete without them:

- Vinegar, both white and apple cider
- Balsamic vinegar
- Baking soda
- Baking powder
- Cooking spray
- Cornstarch
- Flavored extracts
- Vanilla
- Nuts, stored in vacuum-packed containers and bags
- Powdered sugar
- Granulated sugar
- Bouillon powder or cubes: beef, chicken, or vegetable
- Molasses

The Five Enemies of Food

As your pantry begins to fill up, there are five enemies that will shorten the life of your food or, in some cases, completely ruin it. You're investing time, money, and effort in establishing a well-stocked pantry for future emergencies, so it's important to know how to properly store that food in order to ensure the longest possible shelf life.

When I first began stocking up, I paid no attention to details such as shelf life and food-storage methods. At first, it was just reassuring to *have* all those extra cans of chili and tuna, and I took a lot of pride in watching my stash grow. However, it only took one instance of opening a box of potato flakes and finding little black bugs inside to realize that I had just wasted an otherwise perfectly good box of instant potatoes by not paying attention to its date stamp and packaging.

These five enemies will affect food whether it's in your pantry, your emergency kit, or your bunker.

1. Heat

The optimal temperature for stored food is 70°F. For every 10 degrees warmer, the shelf life of your food will be shortened by years. Conversely, every 10 degrees colder will double the shelf life of food. Just remember that cooler is better and consistent cool is best of all. Fluctuating temperatures affect the life span of food.

If you're watching your heating or cooling bills, it may be difficult to maintain a steady temperature in your pantry or food-storage area. Do the best that you can in your circumstances. Try storing food underneath beds and clearing out clutter in closets and cupboards for food-storage areas. If your 20-year-old announces that he's going to

Storage Life Differences Depending on Temperature

Constant Storage Temperature (°F)	Storage Life
39.76°	40 yrs.
49.84°	30 yrs.
59.92°	20 yrs.
70.00°	10 yrs.
80.08°	5 yrs.
90.16°	2.5 yrs.
100.24°	1.25 yrs.

Note: The above chart is not for a specific food but shows the relationship between temperature and storage life. Source: Waltonfeed.com

spend the next 6 months traveling through Asia, wish him the best, sell his bedroom furniture, and you've got an entire new space to fill!

Lucky Survival Moms with cellars or basements will find it easier to maintain a steady, cool temperature. Above all, don't be tempted to store food out in the garage or in an outbuilding with no insulation or temperature control. If you have a food that would last for 10 years at 70 degrees, it might be good for 20 years if stored just below 60 degrees but would be preserved only for 2.5 years if stored at 90 degrees. That's the difference temperature has on stored food!

Living in Phoenix, I know a thing or two about hot weather. If you live in a part of the country where hot summers are a fact of life, too, consider these survival tips for your food:

- Buy food in smaller containers, so you'll rotate through them more quickly.

- De-clutter living spaces, such as bedrooms, and find ways to store food in those rooms.

- If all your stored food is in one room, purchase a small air conditioning unit to help maintain a consistent temperature in that area during the summer months.

- Store non-food items, such as toilet paper, in the garage or an attic in order to expand indoor storage space.

2. Humidity

The second enemy of food is humidity, both ambient humidity and moisture within food containers. Dry goods such as beans and wheat will, naturally, contain far less moisture than home-dehydrated peaches or tomatoes. If you are packaging your own food in jars, buckets, or Mylar bags, you can add a desiccant if humidity is a factor where you live. You've seen desiccants before: They're those little packets of silica beads found in packages of new shoes or electronics. Their job is to absorb moisture, and they can do this for your food.

I suggest purchasing ready-made packets from Sorbent Systems, although you can make your own by purchasing indicating silica gel. "Indicating" means that the silica beads change color as they absorb moisture. This is especially helpful if you live in a tropical climate with enough humidity to keep your skin looking beautiful but also to pro-

Housework, if it is done right, can kill you.

—JOHN SKOW

Desiccant Amounts for Common Food-Storage Capacities	
½ teaspoon	24-ounce canning jar
1 ¼ teaspoons	32-ounce jar
1 tablespoon	1-gallon container
¼ cup	5-gallon bucket

vide a happy home for dozens of varieties of mold! (An important tip for minimizing the effects of humidity is to store food away from outside walls.)

To make your own desiccant packet, pour the amount of silica gel listed in the chart above into a square of porous cloth and tie with a string. Make sure your cloth is woven tightly enough to prevent the beads from sneaking past the threads, yet loosely enough to allow the air to easily pass through. Examples would be gauze or heavyweight cheesecloth.

The really good news about the indicating silica gel is that once it becomes fully saturated with moisture, it can be reactivated simply by being heated in a 300°F oven for 10 minutes. It will then return to its original color and will be ready for use again.

If you want to forget all your other troubles, wear too tight shoes.

—THE HOUGHTON LINE, NOVEMBER 1965

When you're packaging your food for storage, it's perfectly fine to use both oxygen absorbers and desiccants, if the latter is necessary.

Is all your food stored in one room? If so, a dehumidifier can help remove excess moisture in the air, helping to extend the shelf life of your food.

Home-dehydrated foods will need to be either vacuum-packed or stored with a desiccant packet to achieve a shelf life of more than a year. A home dehydrator isn't as efficient as the big units used in food plants. Ideally, stored foods should have no more than 10% moisture, but it's impossible to detect that accurately at home. So, plan on rotating through your home-dehydrated food on a regular basis and keep it stored in a dark and dry environment.

3. Oxygen

Have you ever found some old Easter candy and opened it excitedly, only to find that the chocolate bunny was now a funny color of white?

Oxidation caused that change. Oxygen is most definitely not friendly to stored food.

Most of the air we breathe is made up of nitrogen—78%, in fact—which is a food-friendly gas. Unfortunately for our food, although fortunately for *us*, there's plenty of oxygen in the air as well. Luckily, it really doesn't take much effort to eliminate oxygen from your stored food.

There are two methods most often used by Survival Moms for eliminating oxygen in stored food:

Oxygen absorbers are the little packets you sometimes find in dried soup mixes and other foods. They aren't the same as desiccants because they absorb oxygen, not moisture. Don't get the two confused!

Oxygen absorbers are inexpensive, effective, and seem to be the current preference of many food-storage experts, since they are so easy for beginners to use. The procedure couldn't be simpler: add one or more absorbers to a container of food and seal the container. That's it.

Oxygen absorbers can be purchased in varying sizes measured in cubic centimeters (cc). A 100-cc absorber will absorb 100 cc of oxygen. Refer to the chart below to determine the correct type and number of absorbers for your food container. When in doubt, add an extra absorber, but don't go crazy: Containers have been known to implode when too many absorbers were added.

It's pretty amazing to watch these absorbers do their job. Once your container is sealed and if it has soft sides, you can watch the package become more and more compact as oxygen is absorbed.

Here's a key point about oxygen absorbers: These absorbers begin absorbing oxygen as soon as they encounter the air, and this means that the process begins as soon as their packaging is opened. They usually come in packs of 50 or 100. If you won't be using all of your absorbers at once, the extras will need to be repackaged in a vacuum-

A woman begins cutting her wisdom teeth the first time she bites off more than she can chew.

—HERB CAEN

Oxygen Absorbers for Common Food-Storage Containers

100 cc	32-ounce large canning jar
300 cc	#10 can
300 cc	1-gallon container
1500 cc	5-gallon container

sealed bag using a FoodSaver system, a Seal-a-Meal system, or something similar. Another option is to store them in a canning jar with a tight-fitting lid. The absorbers will absorb whatever oxygen is present in the jar, but no more.

Let me tell you about the first time I used these babies. I had 25 containers of oats and rice ready to be sealed and a package of 50 oxygen absorbers. It took more than an hour to get all of the containers filled. Then I had to find the matching lid for each container and have all of them at the ready, because I knew that once I open the package of absorbers, I would be on borrowed time. By the time I got to the end of the line and had capped every container, I was a hot and sweaty mess. I believe some yelling was involved as well, since two of the screw-on lids had disappeared when my son had come on the scene.

Lessons learned:

- Buy the smallest number of absorbers possible, unless you are tackling a particularly huge packaging job.
- Assemble a large amount of food, so that you can use most or all of your absorbers at once and have a major task behind you.
- Have more containers on hand than you think you'll need.
- Fill the food containers first and make sure the matching lid is nearby.
- Open the package of absorbers and count out the number needed for your packaging project.
- Quickly insert absorbers into each container, sealing each container as you go.
- Use a food vacuum system to repackage the unused oxygen absorbers as soon as possible or put them in an empty canning jar. Once the jar is capped with a gasket and a screw lid, there will be very little air left inside to be absorbed. The canning jar will have a tighter seal than a regular jar.
- It's handy to have another person help with this process.

As effective as oxygen absorbers are, many food containers will begin to either absorb a bit of air or allow air in through the seal over time—and with that air comes more oxygen.

Once an absorber has absorbed all the oxygen it can hold, it will have to be replaced. Otherwise, oxidation will begin affecting your food, causing it to become discolored or rancid.

To make sure your food remains safe from the effects of oxygen, keep track of the date it was sealed and check for signs of leaks. With a Sharpie or China marker, mark the date it was sealed on the outside of the container. As you add more packages of food to your pantry, remember to place the newest packages behind the older ones. This will help with rotating your food *and* keeping an eye for any storage issues, such as loose lids or cracked containers.

baby step

Begin saving large jars and lids as future storage containers. Classico pasta-sauce jars are especially good because their top openings are the same size as standard canning lids.

Dry ice is a second way to remove oxygen from grains stored in buckets. It's a little more complicated than tossing in a few oxygen absorbers, but it's also less expensive. Additionally, for most people, dry ice is easier to acquire than oxygen absorbers.

Wheat, barley, oats, corn, rice, and other grains need to be packaged just as carefully as any other food, and this method is inexpensive if you have a lot to pack. Plus, it has the added advantage of killing off insect eggs.

Dry ice is solidified carbon dioxide. As it melts, the carbon dioxide is released, forcing oxygen out of a container but allowing nitrogen to remain.

You can buy dry ice at most grocery stores. It comes wrapped in paper and must be handled carefully. Always use gloves when handling the ice directly. You'll need approximately 1 ounce of dry ice per gallon capacity of the container you're using, or ¼ pound per 5-gallon storage bucket. A small food scale is handy for measuring out the correct amount of ice.

DO use dry ice to package dry goods, such as oats, beans, wheat, and white rice.

DON'T use dry ice with any type of powdered food.

DO use dry ice in Mylar bags and food-safe buckets.

DON'T use dry ice in metal containers of any kind.

To package your dry goods using dry ice, follow these instructions:

1. Measure out the correct amount of dry ice. Wipe away any frost crystals from the ice using a clean, dry cloth.

2. Place the dry ice on the bottom of the container. Make sure it's centered, allowing for even distribution of carbon dioxide.

3. Pour the grain, beans, or other dry, granular food on top of the ice. Leave 1 inch of head space at the top.

4. Place the lid on top of the bucket. Press the lid down to partially seal the bucket, leaving it about halfway open. The oxygen will need to escape as the ice dissipates.

5. Before completely sealing the bucket, check to see if the bottom of the bucket is cold. If so, the ice has not yet melted completely. It may take 5–6 hours for the dry ice to completely evaporate.

6. If you are using a Mylar bag, either as a liner within a bucket or on its own, follow steps 1-3. Use a hot iron to seal the Mylar bag as instructed on page 111, leaving 3 to 4 inches open for the escaping carbon dioxide. Check the bottom of the bag to see if the ice is still present. Once it is completely gone, finish sealing the bag. Make sure the top seam is tightly sealed before storing.

Before you haul those buckets away for storage, check to see if any of them have a bulging lid. If so, lift the lid slightly to relieve the pressure. If the lid or the Mylar bag appears to have been "vacuum-packed," that's perfectly normal.

It's not easy taking my problems one at a time when they refuse to get in line.

—ASHLEIGH BRILLIANT

4. Light

How many times have you read directions that said to store spices or some other food in a "cool, dark place"? Well, there's a good reason for that. Light, as well as heat, can destroy the food's nutrients and shorten its shelf life. I even store my water in dark closets and under beds. Certain nutrients, such as vitamins A, D, E, and K, are particularly susceptible to light. When the time comes to actually prepare and eat the food you've stored, it should be as nutrient-dense as possible.

If you don't have a dark pantry or have run out of cupboard and shelf space, store glass jars and clear plastic containers in labeled boxes or bins and then close them tightly.

My family had the mother of all garage sales one spring to get rid of unnecessary and unwanted stuff. My ulterior motive was to clear out space for more food and water storage. It worked, and we pocketed a little over $400, which was then used for . . . more food!

5. Pests

In my house, children top the list of pests in this final category! I don't even bother buying granola bars anymore, since I find discarded wrappers all over the house and empty boxes in the pantry. What I *really* need is a high-tech security system for my pantry door and some sort of a drop-down net to trap small, two-legged creatures as they attempt to breach my pantry's perimeter!

Usually, though, the pest category refers to the ugly little vermin and rodents who manage to turn even the yummiest-looking food into something disgusting. I'm talking about creatures like weevils, beetles, and even moths. How do these insects get in our food anyway? Can they really chew their way through cardboard, plastic, and other packaging material?

Well, the answer is yes, they can—although usually they are already in our food in the form of eggs. These eggs are microscopic, and try as they may, food-processing plants find it virtually impossible to detect and remove them. Foods most susceptible to these infestations are dry goods, such as cereal, flour, pasta, and grains.

Fortunately, it's easy to ensure that these eggs never hatch. Place airtight packages of food in your freezer for 2 weeks, and those little buggers will be *dead*. Forever. That's a comforting thought, isn't it?

When you use either oxygen absorbers or dry ice to package food, these eggs get deprived of oxygen, which effectively kills them.

Why should you care about nutrient loss in stored foods?

- Nutrients susceptible to deterioration by light are fat-soluble. This means they are stored in your fat for days and, sometimes, weeks. Your body uses these vitamins as needed.

- In a crisis, you want to remain as healthy as possible. Medical care may not be easily accessible.

- A healthy family has a better chance of surviving.

Mason Jars, Buckets, and Mylar Bags—Oh My!

How well you can protect your food from these five enemies determines the actual shelf life of any given food in your pantry. Where heat is a concern, shelf life will be different in Phoenix than, say, Waukesha. Humidity is a factor if you live in Hawaii but not so much if Santa Fe is your home.

The best anyone can do is to keep these food enemies in mind and develop strategies to protect against them. Proper packaging is one way to do this.

Jars

I first realized the need to start saving and cleaning jars when I began dehydrating food in earnest. I would end up with a cup of dried basil or 3 cups of dehydrated corn and look around in vain for storage containers. Ziploc bags are *not* the way to go, believe me, unless your plan is to use the food within a few weeks. So, I started saving pickle jars, pasta-sauce jars, and jelly jars. They certainly aren't fancy, but sometimes all you need is a small container. If you plan on storing these foods for more than a month, add one oxygen absorber to the jar along with the food before tightening the lid.

Mason and Ball jars are worth buying, either new or at yard sales. Their standardized sizes and shapes make them easier to stack on shelves and purchase lid replacements for. The jars themselves last forever, or until your toddler drops one, but the lids will need to be replaced if you've used them in the canning process.

TATTLER created quite a stir around the country with its introduction of Reusable Canning Lids. If you enjoy canning, preserving, and/ or pickling, or those skills are on your To Learn list, these lids will be worth the initial expense.

Don't kick the buckets. Save them!

White plastic buckets of varying sizes will be found in every home where food storage is taken even a bit seriously. Food-grade buckets can be purchased from Walmart, online sources such as Ready Made Resources, container stores, and food-storage stores.

Personally, I get most of my buckets for free. Grocery-store bakeries, restaurants, delis, and pizza places all receive bulk foods in just the type of food-safe buckets we're looking for. It's worth asking around to see if any of these businesses will give their used buckets away for free or for a nominal fee. They may also hand you matching lids, but I don't recommend using these secondhand lids, unless you're planning to use the buckets in combination with Mylar bags, because they probably do not have an airtight seal anymore.

Instead, take a look at a great product called Gamma Seal lids. These reusable lids come in two parts: an outer ring that snaps down on the top of the bucket and an inner screw-on lid that is very easy to open and close. I buy one for each bucket that contains food actually in use. Food stored in newly purchased buckets and meant for long-term storage can be capped with the snap-on-type lid they came with.

Gamma Seal lids come in a variety of sizes and colors, which can be helpful for identifying buckets of different foods. For example, you can put a red lid on a bucket of hard red wheat, a yellow lid on a bucket of hard white wheat, and a blue lid on a bucket of rice.

A filled 5-gallon bucket is going to weigh as much as a good-size second-grader—hardly lightweight enough to casually tote around the house. Smaller buckets may be a better choice for a lot of families and individuals. When I consult with singles and senior citizens, I suggest purchasing two or three smaller buckets, 1 or 2 gallons in size, in place of the larger ones. They are easier to handle, stack, and carry. Plus, once these smaller buckets are opened, those with smaller appetites or fewer mouths to feed will consume the contents more quickly. Smaller buckets are a great option.

Another big plus for buckets of all sizes is their versatility. Who said you could only use them to store wheat? I have buckets labeled "Dental Supplies," "Kitchen Soap," and "Batteries." Square buckets, in particular, are easy to store and stack due to their shape, but all of them have so many uses other than storing wheat.

Important: Store filled buckets off the ground to allow for air flow beneath them and don't store more than three buckets on top of each other—the buckets themselves or their lids could crack under too much weight.

What about buckets from home improvement stores?

On their own, these buckets are not safe for food storage. However, if you use a Mylar bag liner inside the bucket, they're perfectly fine. They're also great for holding non-food items, such as camping gear, or as an emergency kit.

Mylar bags

I fell in love with Mylar bags the moment I realized they can help protect food from four of the five enemies of food: oxygen, light, humidity, and pests.

Very, very determined insects can chew their way through Mylar bags, but these bags are still a lot more heavy-duty than many other food containers.

If you know what a Mylar balloon is, just think stronger and thicker, and you have Mylar for food storage. Storing wheat in large Mylar bags inside plastic buckets is common, and many companies, such as Walton Feed, sell their buckets of wheat with a Mylar liner.

Once a bag is filled, you can add oxygen absorbers (see chart on page 104 for correct quantities), fold the top of the bag over a tabletop or other hard surface, and seal the opening by using an iron, a flat iron (the kind used to straighten hair), or a sealer specifically designed for Mylar bags. When you apply heat, the Mylar melts together and creates an airtight seal. It's very, very important that the bag is completely sealed, so once it has cooled, carefully check it for any gaps. If it isn't fully sealed, repeat the sealing process.

By snipping off all or part of the sealed end, you can access the food inside later and then reseal. One reason Mylar is so popular is because it can be resealed over and over. Just remember to add a new oxygen absorber, or absorbers, each time.

Unless I don't plan on opening a bucket of wheat or other food for years, I really like the options that smaller Mylar bags provide. Think

A match made in heaven!

When you use a Mylar bag as a liner inside a bucket, you get the best of both worlds. The bag provides an extra layer of protection against oxygen, light, pests, and moisture, and the bucket provides a structured container for the bag, as well as handles to make transportation easier. The combination of these two receives my highest recommendation when it comes to storing food for the long haul.

about it. Smaller quantities allow for more frequent rotation and are smaller and lighter than heavy buckets. In an evacuation, these smaller packages would be easier to grab and pack. If you make your own dehydrated food mixes, they can be sealed in small Mylar bags, and then the bags can be reused. For organization, store the bags in labeled bins or boxes. You can still stock up on large amounts; the only difference is in the quantities stored in each container.

Once the Mylar bag has been sealed, the food is safe for years, depending on storage conditions and the food itself. It's even possible to store water in these bags.

Here are some simple tasks that kids can help with when it comes to food storage:

- Help pour food into storage containers. Give them the job of pounding the container against the countertop in order to force out as much air as possible before sealing.

- Help keep an inventory of what is in your storage pantry. A three-ring binder with a section for each letter of the alphabet will allow them to track everything from adzuki beans to zucchini.

- For kids who love to cook, give them the task of finding new recipes using mostly food in the pantry.

- Learn how to sprout wheat and other seeds as a family. It's a great science lesson, and they'll be introduced to new foods at the same time.

☑ The Prepared Family Challenge!

When your pantry is comfortably full, set a date to challenge yourself and your family to use *only* foods in your storage for one full week. Use your own Survivalized Meal Plan recipes and the recipes in this book to get going. Here are a few tips for a successful challenge.

1. Let the family know ahead of time. Get them excited about completing the challenge successfully.

2. Every meal counts! Pack survivalized lunches for your kids and hubby and plan ahead for snacks.

3. Write out the week's menu and make sure you have all of the ingredients before you launch. Running to the grocery store during the challenge is a no-no!

4. Keep a daily diary of what recipes worked well and which didn't. If you need to tweak a survivalized recipe for future use, this is the time to do it.

5. At the end of the 7 days, evaluate your success. Did you run out of ingredients? Did the family get bored with their meals? What could you do better next time, considering that "next time" could be a genuine emergency?

6. Take the family out to their favorite restaurant or ice cream shop, no matter the results of the challenge!

The Prepared Family

Family Preparedness Plan: Food Storage, Phase 2

I need to stock up on these Top Ten Foods:

Total needed for my family for 3 months:

☐ Wheat (hard white/hard red/soft white) _____

☐ Rice (white/brown) _____

☐ Dried milk _____

☐ Salt _____

☐ Beans _____

☐ Tomatoes _____

   ☐ *tomato paste* _____

   ☐ *tomato sauce* _____

   ☐ *tomatoes (whole, diced, etc.)* _____

☐ Produce _____

☐ Peanut butter or other nut butters _____

☐ Oil _____

☐ Dried pasta _____

Putting the pieces together

☐ Buy an electric grain mill.

☐ Buy a manual grain mill.

☐ Learn how to sprout seeds.

☐ Start a garden and grow my own fresh produce.

☐ Learn how to dehydrate food.

☐ Learn how to can produce or try canning a food I've never tried preserving before.

☐ Master two or three bread recipes.

☐ Check my pantry for the five enemies of food: heat, humidity, oxygen, light, and pests.

☐ Track down free food-grade buckets.

☐ Other _____

☐ Other _____

CHAPTER 6

Your Home Base

I'm a homebody—always have been and always will be. I may not be a gourmet cook, and my house is nearly never pristine, but when my family walks through the door, I want them to breathe a sigh of relief. I even have a plaque by the back door that reads: "You can relax now. You're home."

A Survival Mom's home is more than just a place to sleep and eat. It's the eye of the storm. It's the one place you have control over when everything else has gone to hell. My husband lived on Guam for many years and experienced dozens of typhoons (hurricanes). He only experienced being in the eye of the storm four times but tells me that it was peaceful. The eye is calm, often without a cloud in the sky. It's not affected by the turmoil and pressure around it, and, in fact, is protected by the eyewall—a ring of towering, powerful thunderstorms.

Your home can become an amazing refuge for your family! It sets the stage for preparedness and survival when it's free of chaos, prepared for the unexpected, and secure from outside dangers.

If chaos reigns within your home's four walls, how can you be ready to face an everyday crisis or a worst-case scenario? How can you be sure that you have important survival tools and supplies if you have to push clutter aside just to answer the phone? Could your family survive days or weeks without electricity? And just how safe is your home from intruders and other ne'er-do-wells?

There are three key steps to transforming your home into an eye of the storm:

- Create calm and bring order with decluttering, organization, and routines.
- Survivalize your home by preparing for unexpected emergencies.
- Assess your home's security.

Calm, order, preparedness, and security will provide your family with the safest possible environment, no matter what comes.

||||||||||||||||||||||||||||||||||||||||||||||||||||||||||||||||||||||||||||||||||||||||||||||||||||||||||||||||||

Bringing Order

When my kids were in the toddler and preschool stages, every day was filled with pandemonium and, often, anarchy. I can't tell you how many times we missed out on field trips because we couldn't find a pair of matching shoes for each of us. If we had been pressed to flee our burning home or an oncoming tornado, it would have been every man for himself.

In a crisis, moms are expected to assess emergencies, respond calmly—calling out orders in clear, firm voices—and get any situation under control quickly. In a chaotic setting, that sort of response is impossible, but with some adjustments here and there—and maybe even a major overhaul in some cases—your own eye of the storm will become the refuge your family needs.

There are three demons that turn our homes from havens to hellholes. These demons are merciless and attack hovels and mansions alike. They can only be conquered with super-human focus and effort, which, of course, every Survival Mom possesses.

Do these demons look familiar to you?

- Clutter
- Disorganization
- Lack of routine

They slither and cavort around my home, daring me to oppose them. The only way to survivalize your home and create that eye of the storm is to conquer these demons once and for all.

> I have always drawn strength from being close to home.
>
> —ARTHUR ASHE

Lose the Clutter

Let's start here, because there are very few drawers, cupboards, and rooms that aren't infected by this particular nasty critter. Survival Moms tend to be energetic people who want a problem solved all at once, but clutter isn't that type of problem. Clutter is best tackled one small area at a time. No mom ever woke up as a candidate for an episode of *Hoarders* after going to bed in an immaculate home the night before! This particular demon starts small and becomes mighty over many weeks and months. Eventually, we feel helpless against its powers because we don't know where to begin.

Erin Gentry, an organizing expert with Rubbermaid, calls clutter "postponed decisions." It begins with a single piece of paper or a magazine that you're not quite sure what to do with. Maybe you want to hold on to a coupon flyer, just in case. That magazine article looks interesting, but you don't have the time to sit down and read it right now. That is where clutter gets a foothold and doesn't let go. Once you postpone the decision of how you will handle that piece of paper and set the paper down, you have a designated place for . . . more clutter! I swear, it breeds like rabbits!

Erin describes the best process for eliminating clutter as **EASY**!

- **E**—*Empty* out that drawer, refrigerator, trunk, or anything else you want to declutter. Start with a cleaned-out space.

- **A**—*Assess* each item and make a decision right then and there. Should you *toss* the item? If it's stained, broken, outdated, and won't ever be used, heartlessly throw it in the trash. Is the item still useful but nothing you will ever put to use? Then *donate* it. Have an area set aside for the things you decide to *keep* and another area for things you want to hold on to but won't be using right away. Those you will *store*.

- **S**—*Separate* what remains into like groups. For example, if you're cleaning out the garage, sort gardening tools from sports equipment and hand tools from car maintenance items.

- **Y**—Keep *you* in mind. Everything about your home is unique to *you*. Trust your own judgment when you're making those decluttering decisions, and remember that just about anything you decide to toss can be replaced if need be.

This project may take months, but when you're finished, you will never again buy something just for the sake of buying it. You'll question every item that comes into your home because you'll remember how hard it was to exorcise that clutter demon from your house. Plus, you'll be enjoying a home that is much easier to maintain.

Getting rid of clutter is an absolute necessity for Survival Moms. We need to know what we have and where to find it. Clutter can be tricky because it can fool you into thinking you have something that you don't! As you clear away clutter from cupboards, drawers, garage, and entire rooms, you'll discover space—space for stored food, water bottles, and so much more!

The Grab-n-Go Binder

If your home is anything like mine, a good portion of your clutter is paper, Public Enemy #1. I have receipts, coupons, old mail, and more receipts on just about every flat surface in the house. Sometimes, mingled with all that other paper are more important documents, such as insurance policies and medical records. One of the most important steps you can take as you declutter is to locate all your vital records and store them in one place. Some Survival Moms like the idea of storing them in a lockbox, but another option is to use a Grab-n-Go Binder.

This binder begins with an ordinary three-ring binder, dividers, and a box of top-loading plastic page protectors. You'll be gathering copies of important financial documents, medical records, education and employment documentation, and other vital records. The originals should be placed in a safe deposit box or a safe, but having these copies in a single location will be invaluable.

Label the dividers with the names of each family member, as well as with "Household Records," "Legal Documents," "Medical Documents," and "Financial Records." Use the Grab-n-Go checklist opposite to pull all of these documents together in one location. Your records will be organized and ready to grab at a moment's notice. Be sure that other members of your family know where the binder is located.

A way to keep your documents even more secure is to scan them and save the images on a CD or a flash drive. Give the CD or the flash drive to a trusted relative and keep another copy in a safe deposit box or other secure location. Use an encryption program, such as TrueCrypt, to protect your information even further.

Keep the binder stored in a secure place—preferably a heavy, fireproof safe that can be bolted to a wall or the floor. If you can pick up and tote the safe or the strongbox yourself, so can a thief. Large safes, however, can cost hundreds and even thousands of dollars. If that is out of your budget, a smaller fireproof file box is still a good option. Imagine a scenario in which you have mere minutes to evacuate your home. You grab the kids, your cell phone, the file box, and your purse, and you're good to go—or at least as good as it gets in that frantic scenario! If you end up at an evacuation center, you have birth certificates, insurance policies, passports, and even an inventory of your home's contents. Smart girl!

Ready to get started?

Financial documents

- Copies of the fronts and backs of debit/credit cards
- Copies of property deeds and car titles
- Names, addresses, and phone numbers of all banks
- Other important documents related to employment and/or family business
- Copies of your insurance policies (life, health, auto, homeowners, etc.)
- Copies of car registrations and maintenance records
- Name, address, and contact information for anyone who sends you a bill
- Copies of savings bonds, stocks, and bonds
- Copies of statements from investment firms

Personal documents

Organize items in sections for each family member.

- Names, addresses, phone numbers, and e-mail addresses of relatives and close friends
- Recent photos of each family member and each pet
- Pet vaccine records

When it's time to GO!

The floodwaters or wildfires are on their way, and you have moments to get out of the house. Your binder is ready, but one addition you may want to add is a sealed envelope filled with a bit of cash. During the initial hours of an evacuation, you may have no idea how long it will be before you can return home, and local businesses and banks may also be closed. That cash may be your ticket to a cozy hotel room, a few hot meals, and gas for the car.

- Copies of:
  - Marriage license
  - Birth certificates
  - Driver's licenses
  - Concealed Carry Weapon (CCW) permits
  - Passports
  - Social Security cards
  - Military documents
  - Diplomas and transcripts
- Resumes
- Immunization records

Household documents

- Color photos of your house and each room in the house
- Photos of anything of particular value
- Appraisals of valuable objects, such as art, jewelry, and collectibles
- A list of firearm serial numbers
- Receipts for furniture, appliances, electronics, fitness equipment, and other high-ticket items
- A copy of the rent or lease agreement

Legal documents

- Legal documents pertaining to child custody or adoption
- Legal documents related to a divorce
- A copy of your will, living trust, or family trust
- Copies of both past and current, binding contracts
- Names, addresses, and phone numbers of your attorneys

Medical documents

- Copies of health insurance cards
- A list of blood types for each family member
- Names, addresses, and phone numbers of all doctors
- Medical histories of each family member
- A list of current prescriptions, dosage, and pharmacy contact information
- Copies of medical records and test results for anyone in the family with a significant health issue

On average a person wastes ninety minutes a day looking for lost or misplaced things.

—THE GET ORGANIZED ANSWER BOOK

One way to determine any other records to include in your Grab-n-Go Binder is to imagine that your home has been destroyed, you have nothing left, and you're trying to put your life back together. What documentation might you need? Would you need documents necessary for applying for a job or school enrollment; insurance policy information to file a claim; photos of your pets or children, in case you become separated; or immunization records, in case you temporarily have to enroll your children in a different school?

Finally, you don't want these documents to fall into the wrong hands, so label the spine of your binder with something boring and innocuous, such as "Great-Grandma's Recipes" or "Report Cards"—and for heaven's sake, don't forget where you put your binder!

Homes in harm's way

Do you live in Tornado Alley or at the base of an active volcano? If your home is in an area prone to natural disasters or extreme weather, store a copy of your Grab-n-Go Binder's contents at a location 50–100 miles away.

||||||||||||||||||||||||||||||||||||||||||||||||||||||||||||||||||||||||||||||||||||||||||||||||||

A Life Free of Clutter!

When a home is thoroughly decluttered, you can react quickly to everyday emergencies and significant crises. You know exactly where to find emergency kits, the Grab-n-Go Binder, and an ice pack. Everything is right where it should be, and no one is tripping over house debris while

The joy of having less

The more you have, the more you are occupied. The less you have, the more free you are.
—*Mother Teresa*

Have you ever analyzed why you're so relaxed when you stay at a hotel or a resort? Yes, the ambiance has a lot to do with it, and being away from household chores is another big plus, but one of the reasons it's so peaceful is because we're away from all of our *stuff*.

The clutter on the kitchen table, the pile of books by your bed, and all of the receipts and mail to be filed—are nowhere to be seen. Your hotel room contains only the most important things for survival and comfort and nothing else.

One of the most peaceful and joyous summers of my life was spent on a kibbutz in Israel. I had taken with me only a few changes of clothes, a notebook, some toiletries, and not much else. I slept on a foam mattress in a dorm room cooled only by an oscillating fan, and life was so simple. I could pack up a few things and go on a day trip with friends. Laundry was simple; housekeeping was simple; and it was mostly so because I wasn't bogged down with belongings.

Have you ever thought about what *stuff* really costs beyond the price tag? Stuff has to be dusted, mended, insured, stored, guarded, arranged, repaired, polished, washed, and hauled. Then, we end up getting rid of it in one way or another!

trying to race to safety or locate a life-saving tool. Even smaller crises, such as a typical first-aid emergency, are easier to handle. The first-aid kit is stocked and easily located. Emergency phone numbers have been posted where everyone can find them. You're prepared!

A pleasant side effect of decluttering is that it will likely save you money. During the sorting process, you'll probably find some of the very same tools or supplies you've been meaning to buy!

Do you know what's it like to lose a good amount of weight? You breathe easier, move around easier, and just feel better about life. That's what decluttering feels like, except your jeans' size doesn't change! Keep in mind that just like maintaining that girlish figure, a decluttered environment is an ongoing effort—it never really ends. Sorry!

INSTANT SURVIVAL TIP

Storage space is at a premium in many homes. Have you ever thought of renting a storage unit for the spillover—and maybe even as a location to store your preparedness goods? If the unit is air-conditioned, it's even a good option for storing your extra food. Just make sure it's close enough to access in an emergency.

Get Organized

An ever-present companion of clutter is disorganization. This particular demon loves to infiltrate homes and fill them with confusion because irritability is sure to follow.

"Where are the scissors and tape?" I have yelled those words possibly a hundred times since my daughter discovered the joys of both items. A lesson I am still teaching is, "Scissors and tape always go back in the same drawer!" She'll have the same issue with her daughter someday, and she'll deserve it!

A Survival Mom has a thousand things to do on any given day. She's shopping for food-storage bargains, learning how to use a solar oven for cooking, reviewing her front doors and windows for security issues, and training her kids how to hide from black helicopters. All that takes a lot of time, and she doesn't have time for disorganization. However, *time* is exactly what disorganization steals from us.

On Monday, for example, you might spend 8 minutes looking for matching shoes and socks for each person and then 5 more minutes searching for the car keys. You then sit in the car and wait for Little Suzie to find her notebook and permission slip, and 6 minutes later she's successful. At dinnertime, you realize that you're out of a key ingredient for a favorite recipe, so you have to stop everything and run to the store. You're back 25 minutes later, and now everyone is grouchy because dinner is going to be an hour late. Do you see how that little demon works? The whole evening is ruined because of disorganization.

Disorganization is a killer, especially in a Survival Mom's home. Not only are we focused on what needs to be done on a daily basis, but we also have an eye on the future, not to mention on all of that extra food in the pantry! If our families are going to be ready to face an uncertain future or a worst-case scenario, well, survival *is* a mom's job, and there's no time to waste.

An organized food pantry

As your pantry fills, one of the immediate benefits is having all of the ingredients you need for whatever recipe you're in the mood for. When Greek penne with sun-dried tomatoes and walnuts sounds good, lo and behold, every ingredient is in the pantry! There's no need to run to the store because your food-storage pantry now serves as a customized mini-mart!

Of course, a disorganized pantry is a whole other story. Several months ago I was featured on the local Fox network affiliate as a food-storage expert. The cameraman displayed my pantry for all to see. They filmed as I ground wheat and showed off my collection of water bottles, and I think I looked pretty darn impressive. Not a week later, I sent my kids to the neighbor's house to borrow brown sugar. Naturally, these neighbors had seen me on TV, and I'll never live down not having something as basic as brown sugar. Here's the rub, though: I *did* have that darn sugar! It was sitting behind two large boxes of baking soda and underneath a large bag of macaroni on the top shelf of the pantry.

I learned my lesson that day: It's far better to run to the grocery store than to ask a neighbor for anything, if you know what's good for you.

Since that sorry episode, my pantry is the neatest room of the house. Here are some of my favorite tips for getting it organized, so that you're always able to find what you need, when you need it, *and* keep track of what's in stock.

Group similar foods and supplies together—About 25% of my total stored food is canned goods. All vegetables are grouped in one area and then sorted by type; e.g., carrots or green beans. Canned fruit is on another shelf, again grouped by type, and I've done the same thing with soups, canned pasta, chili, and tuna.

INSTANT SURVIVAL TIP

Food must be stored in a cool, dark, and dry area. Food isn't picky about which room of the house best fits that description. If you need to empty out cupboards in a playroom or the entertainment center, it's okay. The important thing is that your food is happy.

You probably have your local grocery store's layout memorized, so organizing your own food in a similar manner should be second nature. Who knows better how to organize food? Here are some helpful categories found in typical grocery stores:

- Dairy products: butter, milk, cheese, sour cream, and cottage cheese. It doesn't matter how they're packaged. Store them all together in one area.

- Condiments: relish, ketchup, salsa, mustard, and anything else found on my Condiments/Sauces list. When it's time for Burger Night, you'll be glad these are all stored together. Vinegar, oil, and salad dressings are aisle buddies in the store, so keep them together in your pantry.

- Snack foods: packaged cookies, pretzels, chips, crackers, and more. Actually, I prefer to hide these in different locations—safe from grubby little hands—but if we're being 100% consistent, they should be in the same area. *Note:* These foods have short shelf lives, so keep track of their expiration dates.

- Seasonings: spices, herbs, and seasoning mixes. It makes recipe preparation so much easier when these are all together. If you have a lot of spices, consider placing them in several small bins, grouped alphabetically: e.g., A–G for allspice, basil, cinnamon, ginger. To free up space in your kitchen cupboards, store only your more frequently used spices and herbs there and everything else with the rest of your food storage.

- Beverages and beverage mixes: Gatorade, Kool-Aid, Crystal Lite, coffee, tea, and the like will be much easier to find when they are all together. I place the smaller packages of drink mixes together in a small bin. Every little bit of organization helps.

- Canned meat, poultry, and fish. When you run out of canned chicken, you can grab the beef. When you run out of beef, you can start using the tuna, until you're finally down to that case of oil-packed sardines.

- Baking ingredients: Flour, sugar, brown sugar, salt, baking powder and soda, and cocoa powder, for example, all belong together.

- Packaged mixes: brownie (I'd be lying if I said I didn't have at least a dozen of these), cookie, cake, pancake, and biscuit mixes.

- Starchy processed dishes: Stuffing, potato, and rice mixes are handy as side dishes and should be stored near each other.

Don't own so much clutter that you will be relieved to see your house catch fire.

—WENDELL BERRY

If you've dehydrated or canned your own food, include those jars and containers right alongside commercially packaged foods for the sake of organization. Since they may be packaged in glass jars, it's important to take steps to avoid breakage, in case of an earthquake or a 2-year-old. Some Survival Moms put all glass jars in covered, plastic bins or even cardboard boxes to protect them from breakage *and* the damaging effects of light. Label these containers, and you're golden.

Store by use—Even with orderly shelves, my pantry was a bit topsy-turvy until I began paying attention to ingredients I reached for over and over again. Making bread was frustrating because the ingredients were scattered all over and dried milk had to be scooped out of a gallon bucket every time I needed it. Who wants to make bread under those conditions? When I made soup, it took several minutes just to track down the usual suspects: canned tomatoes, herbs, garlic, green beans, corn, potatoes, and carrots. It gets ridiculous when assembling the ingredients takes more time than making the actual recipe!

If there are certain recipes you make often, group those ingredients close together, even if it means storing a specific item in two different places. For example, my 48 jars of pasta sauce are placed right next to

The pantry inventory on paper

When you make a shopping list, you probably organize it by category. Use those same categories to create an inventory of your food storage. This is especially helpful in determining if you have too much or not enough of any given item. Typical grocery list categories are:

- Baby supplies
- Baking items
- Canned foods
- Cleaning and laundry supplies
- Condiments
- Cooking items
- Dairy and eggs
- Fruits and vegetables
- Herbs and spices
- Meat, poultry, and fish
- Miscellaneous
- Paper products
- Pasta and grains
- Personal supplies
- Shortening and oils
- Snack items

Create a page for each category and then begin keeping track of what you have in each category and the amounts of each. Kids from about the age of 10 should be able to do this and free up important nap time for you!

my pasta collection. I can grab one of each, and dinner is (almost) served! I sometimes add mushrooms to my sauce, so I have a few cans stored by the pasta and the remaining cans on the shelf where I store my vegetables. It's okay to "file" one food in more than one location.

Organize The Big Three: wheat, rice, and beans—These survival staples are often the backbone of most preparedness pantries. I dig into my stashes for my everyday cooking, and yet I have enough stored that I won't use it up any time soon. In fact, I've written my buckets of wheat into my Last Will & Testament. They may very well outlive me.

Keeping The Big Three organized is simple because they are usually stored in large buckets. You can stack buckets and place them in rows, but it's not any more complicated than that. As long as they're labeled and dated, storage couldn't be easier. If you've followed my instructions in Chapter 4 for filling buckets, your dry goods will be edible for years to come.

In my pantry, buckets are labeled "Hard White Wheat," "White Rice," "Pinto Beans," and so on, but I also need smaller containers of the same foods because I use them in my cooking throughout the week. Smaller containers are lightweight, small enough to store in kitchen cupboards, and you can rotate through them more quickly than through larger buckets. Big families won't have a problem rotating through 5 gallons of rice or pinto beans, but singles and smaller families will appreciate keeping these staples on hand in 1-gallon Mylar bags, 1-gallon buckets, or other small containers. Clean 2-liter soda bottles make an ideal container for storing many dry ingredients long-term.

Pay attention to dates—The most frequent dates a Survival Mom is likely to encounter are the ones stamped on jars, cans, and boxes of food. Don't worry. Food doesn't suddenly dissolve the day after an expiration date, but as you're stocking up, circle or write the food's expiration date where you can clearly see it and then place the newly purchased food in the back. This will ensure that the older food will be used up sooner rather than later.

Speaking of dates, please don't toss out food just because of an expiration date. If the food has been kept in a cool, dry, and, preferably, dark place, it may very well be perfectly fine. Give it the sniff test, and

TheSurvivalMom.com

Need more tips on organization and decluttering? Visit my blog, www.thesurvivalmom.com.

if it doesn't smell rancid, it is fine to eat. If no mold or mildew is present, again, it's fine.

I'll bet you thought that there was some government agency setting these dates and that awful things happen to people who ignore them. Nope. Baby formula and some baby foods are the only foods required by federal law to be labeled with expiration dates. Think about it. Is it possible that food producers stick a date on the package so you'll need to buy more sooner? Hmmm . . .

Of course, use your common sense when it comes to these dates, but if properly stored food smells and looks fine, go ahead and use it.

Storing your stash of nonedibles

How can I say this nicely? Normal people don't store 40 tubes of toothpaste, 30 bottles of hand sanitizer, and bushels of toilet paper. They just don't. But who needs normal if there's a shortage of basic supplies? One never knows when all that hand sanitizer may come in handy. You can always use it for barter, right?

Not everything you store will be edible. My 180 rolls of toilet paper line a back wall, batteries are stored in a labeled box, as are dental supplies (floss, toothpaste, and toothbrushes), and there's even an entire labeled box of antiperspirant. I want to smell fresh even if the world does come to a crashing end.

To determine what you and your family should store, carry a small notepad around with you for 2 or 3 days and jot down every consumable supply you use, such as razors, contact lens solution, laundry softener, and baby wipes. Add to the list the items you use less frequently, both indoors and outdoors, such as plant fertilizer or WD-40.

You may not be a coupon queen at the moment, but when it comes to these necessary supplies, the coupons in Sunday's newspaper could be your best friend. Without question, they will help you stock up on almost everything on your list. The first time you get eight toothbrushes for *free* because you used a manufacturer's coupon combined with a store sale, you'll be hooked. In one trip to the store, with enough coupons you could easily stock up on a year's worth of items like liquid soap and deodorant.

You may be working hard to protect your food storage from heat, humidity, light, oxygen, and pests, but when it comes to shampoo, Windex, and paper plates, you can relax. Many of these supplies can

Ten nonedibles for your stash

- Feminine products
- Bar soap
- Ziploc bags of all sizes
- Rope for clothesline and clothespins
- Tylenol PM, lots of it
- Birth control
- Hair coloring
- Multivitamins
- Duct tape
- Hydrogen peroxide

be stored in areas that would terrify your food. Go ahead and store all that toilet paper out in the garage. I haven't yet heard of an insect that yearned to feast on shampoo and conditioner, so feel free to store those anywhere you like.

One step you will need to take, however, is grouping similar supplies together. Because so many of them are small, such as boxes of Band-Aids and tubes of Vaseline, store them as a group in a labeled box. Shoe boxes work just fine, and small plastic bins and other containers are found at nearly every thrift store and garage sale.

Don't forget, those buckets normally used for storing wheat are a terrific choice for storing nonedibles. In fact, you won't even need food-grade buckets for mouthwash and baby wipes. Make sure these storage buckets have lids, however. It's all too easy to knock one over, and what Survival Mom needs one more hassle to deal with?

There's no need to color-coordinate your labeled containers; nor must they match in type or size. Why do I need to say this? Because I know some of you! You're already planning a massive shopping trip to IKEA for those attractive black-and-white storage boxes in various sizes. Trust me: As long as your supplies are grouped together and labeled, when necessary, nothing more needs to be done. Turn your energy elsewhere, Survival Mom—like to alphabetizing your cans of beans!

Where to find inexpensive containers:

- Craigslist
- Freecycle
- Restaurants/delis
- Garage sales
- Friends/family
- Dollar stores

||||||||||||||||||||||||||||||||||||||||||||||||||||||||||||||||||||||||||||||||||||||||||||||||||||||||||||

Life in a Small Space

In my lifetime, I've lived in a rented-out single room, a spacious 3,000-square-foot home, and just about everything in between, and I've gotta tell ya: When it comes to storage, bigger is better.

I remember the days of living in a one-bedroom apartment and feeling cramped, even without 6 months' worth of food and toilet paper! For sure, a Survival Mom living in a small space will have to be doubly creative. Once you've done a thorough job of decluttering, Erin Gentry of Rubbermaid suggests classifying your remaining belongings into three categories:

A—items you use daily or weekly
B—items you use once a month or less
C—seasonal items, including clothing

Items in Category A, which are used frequently, should be easily accessible and in locations that are the easiest to reach. You'll drive yourself crazy if you have to find a stepstool to reach a rice cooker that you use three or four times a week. Save those high cupboards and shelves for Category B. If it's a pain in the neck to reach, it's the perfect spot for everything in this category! I keep my food processor out in the garage and a tortilla press above the refrigerator. There's no need to waste precious kitchen storage space on those particular tools that I use only occasionally.

Everything in Category C should be boxed up, labeled, and stored far away from your living space. Those Fourth of July tablecloths and ceramic Easter bunnies should only show their faces at the appointed time. And what should be done with anything Christmas-y? Lock it away somewhere safe until the day after Thanksgiving! Once these seasonal items are cleared out, you'll have more space for those cans of soup and bags of sugar. Besides, don't you just hate seeing holiday stuff long after the holiday has passed?

Prepositions to the rescue!

Remember learning parts of speech in grade school? Prepositions specify time, location, and direction. This may sound crazy, but prepositions can help you find even more storage space!

Above—What can you store above the refrigerator and above the washer and dryer? What about all that unused space above the clothes in your closet? And wouldn't that plant shelf be more useful for storing something other than silk plants?

Behind—What's behind your couch, behind the piano, and behind those boxes in the garage? Store canned food behind books on a bookshelf.

Inside—Put small things inside bigger things. For example, 14 tubes of toothpaste and 80 bars of soap would fit quite nicely inside a carry-on suitcase.

Outside—Using your garage for storage is a given, but what about utilizing the space in a covered trailer, a camper, or a garden shed?

Under—Look under the beds and other pieces of furniture for space. You might find extra space under a staircase or even under floorboards or a crawlspace.

A good plan that is implemented today is better than a perfect plan that is implemented tomorrow.

—GEORGE PATTON

Utilizing these miscellaneous spaces doesn't mean you have to end up with an unsightly mess. My friend Chrystalyn actually uses her food storage as home decor! She fills clear, matching containers with grains and beans, sticks a cute label on them, and then arranges them on her plant shelves, along with silk sunflowers and ivy! I don't think a casual observer would ever realize that her family actually eats that food!

Here are a few more tips I've used to maximize storage space in my own home:

- Install high shelves in closets, a laundry room, and even bedrooms. Utilize all that space above your head! If you rent, be sure to check with your landlord first.

- Purchase or build pieces of furniture that can pull double duty. Any time you're shopping for furniture, make sure it can also be used for storage. For example, a chest makes a perfectly good end table. A bench is a handy piece to have, but be sure it can provide stash space. A trundle bed can be used as a storage box once the mattress is removed.

- Look for dead space as a result of poor architectural planning. My son's closet stretches more than 2 full feet beyond the closet door opening. Several small shelves would fit perfectly in that area, or we could build a false wall and store valuables, firearms, and, yes, extra food in that space.

- Clean out file cabinets of everything but your most pertinent records and use that extra drawer space for storage. Keep tax records for 7 years, but receipts from Christmas 2005, as well as those appliance manuals from your old house, can be safely tossed!

- Consolidate. Can you combine the contents of two medicine cabinets into just one? Can you combine kitchen towels and washcloths into one drawer instead of two? Every time you can do this, an extra drawer, cupboard, or closet is freed up.

Keeping track of it all

It won't take long to realize that you have a little something stored in every room of the house, not to mention in all of those cubbyholes outside! It would be nothing short of a disaster to be in dire need of that propane heater, only to find the heater but not the extra bottles of propane! It's important to be methodical as you store essential supplies and know where everything is.

You can do this by labeling containers with a list of their contents. Group like things together and then label. It doesn't have to be fancy. A hand-written phrase or list works just fine. When you store it away, record the location on a Home Inventory Record. Record the room or the area of storage, items stored, and the date. Keep these inventories in your Survival Mom Binder.

It's a good idea to *not* store everything in one place. If thieves are looking for food in a true end-of-the-world scenario, it's far better to have smaller amounts of food stored in numerous locations than all of it in one place, waiting to be hauled out in a wheelbarrow.

The video inventory

The simplest inventory of all is a video recording of the contents of each room. Once you've made this video, keep a copy in a safe or a lockbox and another copy at a location away from your home. If you have receipts for expensive furniture and electronics, your insurance agent will love you if you ever need to make a claim following a house fire or a natural disaster.

||||||||||||||||||||||||||||||||||||||||||||||||||||||||||||||||||||||||||||||||||||||||||||||||||

Establish Proactive Routines for Crises Large and Small

When it comes to preparedness and survival, there's a lot to be said for family routines, plans, and clear-cut directives. When everyone knows what to do and what to expect in both everyday and scary situations, there's more confidence and security. Routines teach kids responsibility and organization and help quell fears. Rehearsing routines empowers kids even further.

Kids worry about the unknown and don't always end up with an accurate assessment. What if *our* house catches fire? What if my mom gets hurt? What if an earthquake happens and I'm away from home? When my own two kids heard about a family losing their home, they asked if their friends would have to live under a bridge. Who knows where they got that idea, except perhaps I read "Billy Goats Gruff" to them one time too many. Sometimes I've wished they were a little less observant and didn't think so darn much.

Put a few routines into place to address scary situations, and you'll be better prepared when a disaster of some sort looms or a sudden emergency arises. Small routines, already in place, can minimize panic and maximize your family's security. Three survival scenarios to plan

Every Survival Mom should know . . .

- CPR
- How to clean and bandage a wound
- How to wrap a sprain with an ACE bandage
- How to apply a splint
- How to stop severe bleeding until help arrives
- How to move an injured person
- How to perform the Heimlich maneuver
- Who to help first if there are multiple injuries

for are a sudden medical crisis, an evacuation, and a scenario in which parents aren't around to take care of everything.

A sudden medical crisis

A broken bone, a bad fall, or an unresponsive loved one causes immediate emotional reactions that are made far worse when family members are unsure about what to do, who to contact, and where to find important information. All of this can be alleviated with just a couple of hours of planning, training, and rehearsing with your family.

It took all of 10 minutes to instruct my kids on how to handle a situation if a family member or a friend is injured or is unresponsive. My oldest child will call 911 from a house phone (not a cell phone) and the youngest one will follow whatever directions are given by the 911 operator and call either my husband or me. Calling from a house phone provides the 911 operator with an address. When you call from a cell phone, he or she has no way of knowing where you are or where the emergency is.

The first step in putting together a family plan for a medical emergency is to decide what each child is capable of handling. Is your 7-year-old mature enough to dial 911? Is a tween or teen old enough to take a first-aid class and handle basic triage?

Second, delegate a task to each child or person in the home. Once you've given an assignment, make sure everyone knows exactly what to do. Rehearse together a 911 phone call, running to get the first-aid kit, securing pets for the arrival of the first responders, and even performing basic first aid.

Third, write out the entire routine, along with each delegated task. Remember to print and not use cursive if you have young children!

Review the written plan together and make sure it's posted where everyone can find it.

Here is an example of a routine based on a crisis in which children must handle a medical emergency on their own, without any adults present.

1. Decide if a medical emergency requires a 911 call. If you answer yes to any of these, make that call!
   a. Is the person unable to get up or move?
   b. Are you not able to wake the person up?
   c. Is the person bleeding rapidly?

2. Kid #1 calls 911 on a home phone.

3. Kid #2 follows any instructions given by the 911 operator and calls Mom, Dad, or another adult family member.

4. Get the house ready for the first responders. Even young children can help with these important steps:
   a. Secure all pets in a bedroom.
   b. Unlock the front door, so emergency responders can enter the house quickly.
   c. Make sure all lights are on in the house.
   d. The oldest child goes outside to signal emergency vehicles.

5. Remain calm.

Once your plan is in writing, post one or more copies around the house. Keep a copy in your Survival Mom Binder. Even the best routine will be useless if it's forgotten. Set aside time to review these steps. We all forget important information, and kids are no exception.

Note: At least one adult in your home should go through basic first aid and CPR training, at the minimum. The American Red Cross conducts classes for children as young as 11 years of age. Training alleviates a great deal of fear and panic.

If you're really serious about this type of training, seek out courses in wilderness first aid. These courses teach skills based on the assumption that no help is coming—just the type of training you need in a survival situation. Regardless of which class you attend, knowing what to do during the first few minutes of a medical crisis could make the difference between life and death, *and* you'll be able to share what you've learned with your kids.

A recipe for rehydration

Mix up two or three dozen batches of this formula, pack in snack-size Ziploc bags, and you'll be ready to deal with sicknesses that involve vomiting and diarrhea:

- 3 tablespoons sugar
- 1 teaspoon salt

When this sugar/salt combo is mixed with a liter of clean water, you have an effective rehydration fluid that will go a long way toward helping someone recover from a bout with diarrhea and/or vomiting.

Plan for an evacuation from home

Fewer than half of all Americans have any type of evacuation plan in the event it is no longer safe to stay at home. The most common calamities that force families from their homes are anything but exotic. Floods, hurricanes, and earthquakes are relatively commonplace but force thousands of families to seek refuge elsewhere every year. Usually our homes are the safest place to be, but when they're not, a Survival Mom should have an evacuation plan in place, along with family routines that will ensure a safe and speedy exit.

You'll find more detailed directions for a complete evacuation plan in Chapter 11, but consider putting small routines in place *now* to avoid mass chaos and critical delays later. Some of these simple routines may already be a part of your family's lifestyle.

Keep your fears to yourself, but share your courage with others.

—ROBERT LOUIS STEVENSON

- Have a set place for keys, wallet, and purse. (A master key ring that holds a spare key for *everything* is a good idea—allowing you to have keys for cars, house, storage unit, vacation home, bicycle locks, and Grandma's house all in one place. Be sure to label each key.)
- Store emergency kits near an exit (more about these kits in Chapter 11).
- Establish a laundry routine that ensures clean clothes are always available in their designated closets and drawers.
- Set up a system for notifying close friends and family members when you leave home.
- Always keep the gas tank at least half full.
- Renew prescriptions promptly and, if possible, have at least a month's supply as a backup. Mark your calendar with your pharmacy's phone number so you'll be reminded to call in the renewal each month.

If your home is decluttered and organized, and these routines are in place, getting out of Dodge shouldn't be a problem at all.

The kids home alone

Every Survival Mom plans and prepares as though she will be the one leading the charge in a crisis, organizing the troops and managing every detail. But what if Mom *isn't* around? What if Mom or Dad is sidelined by a serious injury or illness or simply can't make it back home? The kids will have to cope, but if they have no idea where to find the can opener or how to prepare a freeze-dried meal, things could get ugly fast.

At first glance, it may seem that preparing kids to be on their own will scare them silly and be counter-productive. The opposite is true, however. Kids gain confidence and learn self-reliance when they know how to do "grown-up" things around the house. My daughter nearly bursts with pride whenever she serves a dessert made from scratch. She can follow a recipe to a "T," knows where all of the ingredients are, and can safely put a baking dish in the oven and take it out again. I have every confidence that my little 12-year-old could manage to keep my son and husband fed with three meals a day if she had to. Yeah, she'd complain, but at least no one would starve!

Lead your children gently to a higher and higher level of independence and just watch them blossom! Here are some of the basic routines and bits of information to teach at *age-appropriate* levels:

■ Preparing meals

Teach this from an early age, beginning with cereal and milk and PB&J sandwiches. Young kids can whisk, stir, pour, measure, and then graduate to follow simple recipes. If they've been helping unload and put away groceries and are familiar with the pantry, they'll be serving you breakfast in bed before you know it! Here are some routines and skills to teach them:

- Location of ingredients, including those in your food storage
- Location of and how to use basic kitchen tools, including a can opener
- Basic kitchen safety
  — How to use a knife safely
  — How to use a stove, oven, and microwave safely
    • How to handle and prepare food in a sanitary manner
    • What to do if there's a kitchen fire
    • How to handle hot pots and pans safely
- Using small kitchen appliances correctly
- Following simple recipes

■ Handling family finances

If your kids are ever home alone for a lengthy period of time, they'll need to begin taking care of financial matters. They should know:

The simplest foods for kids to make

1. PB&J, tuna, and other types of sandwiches
2. Can of soup, heated in the microwave
3. Can of anything, heated or not!
4. Quesadillas
5. Hot dogs
6. Salad
7. Cereal
8. Oatmeal
9. Beans and franks

- Value of standard currencies and how to read prices
- Location of extra cash
- What bills need to be paid and how to pay them
- Where your bank is located and how to get there
- How to use an ATM
- How to make a bank deposit

Taking care of laundry

- How to follow a set laundry routine
- How to follow a schedule of family laundry
- How to sort laundry: whites, colors, jeans, towels, etc.
- How to start a load of laundry and measure out detergent
- How to start the dryer and clean out the lint catcher
- How to sort and fold dry clothes and put them away
- How to do simple mending with a needle and thread and sew on a button by hand

Dealing with trash

- Location of every trash can in the house
- Location of large trash bags
- Which items go in the recycle bin
- How to empty the smaller trash containers into a larger bag
- How to take out the trash
- Schedule of trash pickup days

Caring for pets

Having multiple animals in the household will add to the workload when the kids are on their own, but most kids will gladly put in that extra effort in order to keep their animal friends healthy and safe. Here are some basic routines to teach your kids now so that the animals will be well cared for.

- Location of food for each animal
- How much food each animal gets and location of the feeding containers

- Providing fresh water daily
- Cleaning up poop or cleaning out fish tank or birdcage
- The safest routes for walking the dog
- How to change the litter box and what to do if there is no more litter
- What to do if the animal's food runs out
- Phone numbers for the veterinarian and his/her address

Cleaning each room of the house

Establish a written routine, or a list of tasks, for cleaning each room. Teach those individual tasks, one at a time. Here are some general principles that should be part of those routines:

- Location of household cleaners and cleaning tools
- Which cleaner does what (use homemade cleaning mixtures to avoid dangerous chemicals)
- Which tasks should be done daily, weekly, or only occasionally
- How to use the vacuum
- How to sweep and mop the floor
- How to dust

Taking care of outside responsibilities

- How to mow the lawn, rake leaves, pull weeds
- Watering the garden
  — Location of the watering hose and containers
  — When and how to water which plants
- Knowing when to harvest produce
- If there's a water shortage, what to water and what not to water

Caring for younger children

A Red Cross babysitting class will teach much of this information, and many cities provide babysitting classes as well.

- Follow established morning and nighttime routines
- Know how to bathe babies and toddlers safely
- Know how to change a diaper and the location of supplies
- Ways to comfort younger siblings when parents aren't around

Do we not realize that self-respect comes with self-reliance?

—*ABDUL KALAM*

Home security issues

- Know how to arm and disarm a home security system
- Know what to do if the smoke or carbon monoxide alarms go off
- Actions to take in case of a power outage
- Know how to secure all doors and windows

Dealing with routine health issues, such as allergies and asthma

- Know where all vital medications are located
- Have a list of phone numbers for the pharmacy, the doctors, and the ambulance
- Know when a medical crisis requires professional help

Safely use a variety of hand tools such as a hammer, screwdriver, multi-tool, saw, and drill

I've found the easiest way to develop independent kids is to involve them in nearly everything that goes on in our household. They learn where to find things when *they* have to put them away. They should routinely put away the groceries, unload the dishwasher, locate the ingredients in the refrigerator or the pantry, and put away the laundry for every member of the family. My son always knows where everything is, and this has made him quite an independent little fourth-grader. Of course, this includes my secret stash of birthday and Christmas gifts, but I guess a mom's gotta take the good with the bad!

By the time a child is 14 or 15 years of age, depending on his or her individual level of maturity, he or she should be able to follow most of the listed routines and be well on the way to being self-reliant. Children will always need their mom, but knowing what they are capable of will bring you some peace of mind.

Oh, and—please!—don't ever tell your kids, "I'm teaching you this in case I ever die!" Just naturally involve your kids in daily household routines.

Family Preparedness Plan: Home Base

Rank these demons according to which are our home's biggest bugaboos. The worst culprit is a "1."

_____ Clutter _____ Disorganization _____ Lack of routine

Addressing all three is important to establish a calm and orderly home, but we may want to tackle our worst enemy first.

Declutter room by room:

Empty (empty out)—Assess (toss, donate, keep, store)—Separate (classify)—You (customize)

Living Room

☐ Cupboards

☐ Shelves

☐ Drawers

☐ Tabletops

☐ Other storage containers and furnishings

☐ Windowsills

☐ Other _____

Family Room/Den/Bonus Room

☐ Cupboards

☐ Shelves

☐ Drawers

☐ Tabletops

☐ Other storage containers and furnishings

☐ Windowsills

☐ Other _____

Kitchen

☐ Cupboards

☐ Shelves

☐ Drawers

☐ Countertops

☐ Refrigerator

☐ Other storage containers

☐ Pantry

☐ Windowsills

☐ Other _____

Bathroom #1

☐ Cupboards

☐ Shelves

☐ Drawers

☐ Countertop

☐ Other storage containers and furnishings

☐ Windowsills

☐ Other _____

Bathroom #2

- ☐ Cupboards
- ☐ Shelves
- ☐ Drawers
- ☐ Countertop
- ☐ Other storage containers and furnishings
- ☐ Windowsills
- ☐ Other _____

Bedroom #1

- ☐ Closets
- ☐ Shelves
- ☐ Drawers
- ☐ Tabletops
- ☐ Other storage containers and furnishings
- ☐ Windowsills
- ☐ Other _____

Bedroom #2

- ☐ Closets
- ☐ Shelves
- ☐ Drawers
- ☐ Tabletops
- ☐ Other storage containers and furnishings
- ☐ Windowsills
- ☐ Other _____

Bedroom #3

- ☐ Closets
- ☐ Shelves
- ☐ Drawers
- ☐ Tabletops
- ☐ Other storage containers and furnishings
- ☐ Windowsills
- ☐ Other _____

Garage

- ☐ Cupboards
- ☐ Shelves
- ☐ Drawers
- ☐ Workbench
- ☐ Storage containers
- ☐ Other _____

Other

- ☐ Closets
- ☐ Cupboards
- ☐ Shelves
- ☐ Drawers
- ☐ Tabletops
- ☐ Countertops
- ☐ Other storage containers and furnishings
- ☐ Windowsills
- ☐ Other _____

Putting the pieces together

- ☐ Make a Grab-n-Go Binder:
  - Assemble vital documents as listed on page 118.
  - Scan the information and store it on CDs and/or flash drives.
  - Put either a CD or a flash drive in your Bug Out Bag.
  - Store the binder in a safe place.
- ☐ Organize pantry:
  - Group similar foods and supplies together.
  - Store by use.
  - Organize The Big Three: wheat, rice, and beans.
  - Begin a pantry inventory on paper or an Excel spreadsheet.
- ☐ Organize nonedibles.
- ☐ Store all seasonal items in labeled containers. Keep them in a remote location, such as an attic or a storage shed.
- ☐ Make a video of our home's contents and store it in a safe place.

Establish family routines

- ☐ Our family's medical emergency plan:
  - What constitutes a medical emergency:

    _____

    _____

    _____

  - Person to call 911:

    _____

  - Person to follow instructions from 911 operator:

    _____

  - Other delegated tasks:

    _____

    _____

    _____

    _____

- ☐ Household routines for children to learn:
  - Preparing meals
  - Handling family finances
  - Laundry routine
  - Family trash routine
  - Caring for pets
  - Housecleaning, room by room
  - Outdoor responsibilities
  - Caring for younger children
  - Handling routine health issues

CHAPTER 7

The Unplugged Home: Learning to Live Without Electricity

Sooner or later your home will be surrounded by tempests you cannot control. They may be severe weather events that threaten to rip your home apart, natural disasters that jeopardize your safety, or societal chaos brought on by a collapsing economy. If your household is running like a well-oiled machine, you only need to add a few supplies and plans for weathering future storms.

Perhaps the most important way to prepare your home is to prepare for a Stone Age lifestyle. In other words, how would your family survive without electricity? Have you ever realized just how many emergencies involve a power outage? Earthquakes, severe winter weather, flooding, tornadoes, heat waves, hurricanes, and more are all likely to cause a disruption to your electrical service. Worst-case scenarios involving terrorist attacks, war, or an EMP (electromagnetic pulse) can easily take down the power grid for weeks, months, or even much longer. When you consider how vulnerable our power connections are and how reliant we've become on the ready and steady supply of energy, suddenly having to do without electricity is a scary prospect.

Make contingency plans for the next power outage in your area by listing everything you routinely do that relies on electricity or gas and then consider how you would cope in a power-down scenario. For example:

Hot water for showers and washing dishes—How will you heat water? Will you be able to sanitize dishes to ward off sicknesses related to food contamination? The best off-grid solution is a solar hot water heater, if you can afford one and if your backyard provides full, or nearly full, sunlight year-round. Otherwise, you'll be heating water the way great-great-grandma did—over a campfire or a cook stove.

Pure drinking water may be another concern. All municipal water systems run on electricity with generators as a backup, but what happens when the fuel tanks on the generators run dry? Chapter 2 details several strategies for making sure your family's water is always safe to drink and use.

Cooking on an electric stove/oven—Do you have more than one way to cook food without having to rely on fuels that may run out? A propane stove is fine, but what's the plan if there's no more propane?

I use a Global Sun Oven and an EcoZoom Rocket Stove for alternative ways to cook. Look for portable grills or stoves that are multifuel and stock up on charcoal when you can. Stoves such as the EcoZoom are so fuel-efficient they can cook a meal using just five or six briquettes or a few twigs.

Cooking over an open fire is an option that has served mankind well for many thousands of years. However, make sure you have a long-term supply of fuel, as well as multiple ways to get a fire going. Rubbing two sticks together is almost never effective. And remember, one of the leading causes of death for women in the eighteenth century was severe burns when their long dresses caught fire while they were cooking. Be sure you have plenty of fire extinguishers and know basic fire safety if you plan on cooking over a campfire.

Microwave—Keep track of how you use your microwave. Would you be able to cook or warm up those foods without one?

In a power-down situation, the loss of a microwave will be an inconvenience, but a relatively small one. However, be sure you have two or more ways to heat up food and water.

Small kitchen appliances: blender, toaster, mixer, and rice cooker—You may or may not miss these appliances, but pay attention to how often you use them and have a backup plan if they ever become unavailable. Marine supply stores sell battery-powered blenders, slow cookers, coffeemakers, and similar kitchen appliances at prices that are quite reasonable. Just be sure to stock up on more batteries than you think you'll need.

If you're counting on a generator to run kitchen appliances, you might be unpleasantly surprised by how much juice these appliances consume.

Grain mill—For convenience and quick results, I have an electric grain mill. If you store wheat, however, you also need a manual, hand-crank mill. Invest in a high-quality mill, such as the WonderMill Junior.

Refrigerator/freezer—This will likely be the toughest appliance to replace or do without. Refrigerators do more than just keep our food cold. They help preserve food and keep it at a safe temperature. Solar-powered refrigerators and fridges that run on propane and butane are available, although pricey. The alternative is to do without. If that's your only choice, be vigilant about preparing only enough food for one meal or one day at a time, unless there's a room in your home, cellar, or some other building that is 40 degrees or cooler. That's the safety mark for ensuring no one in your family gets food poisoning from improperly stored food.

And what if the freezer goes out? If the power goes out, and there's no quick repair in sight, start cooking that thawed meat as fast as you can. If you have a food dehydrator, plug it into a generator and begin making jerky. Sharing it with the neighbors will earn a significant amount of goodwill, which you'll need during a prolonged crisis.

Washer/dryer—There are portable, hand-powered washing machines that sit on a tabletop and are pretty effective when it comes to producing clean clothes. The Wonder Wash has been used by many Survival Moms, and it is what I've used on camping trips. Plenty of clothesline and clothespins will provide a (very) low-tech method for drying clothes, and if the outside weather is too damp and chilly, one or two laundry racks can be set up indoors. Washing small loads of laundry frequently would become the new norm, at least until power is restored.

If there must be trouble, let it be in my day, that my children may have peace.

—THOMAS PAINE

Perhaps the most unusual method of washing clothes involves two 5-gallon buckets with lids and two new toilet plungers, as described in Chapter 2. Glamorous it ain't, but it *will* get those clothes clean, and it is much easier to use than an old-fashioned washboard.

Vacuum—When the power goes out, the luckiest moms might be those with all tile, concrete, or wood floors. They're used to using a broom and a mop. Homes with wall-to-wall carpeting won't fare as well. Of course, if you have a generator (see pros and cons starting on page 156), you can use it for vacuuming. Just remember that you're burning fuel that could be used for powering the refrigerator, the heater, and other appliances vital to your family's survival.

Battery-powered handheld vacuums are an option for smaller jobs, but the best option for decreasing your use of a vacuum is to reduce the amount of dirt and dust that enter your home in the first place. If you haven't already done so, place floor mats both inside and outside every exterior door. These will be much easier to clean than carpeting and will greatly reduce the spread of dirt and debris. Another tip is to establish and enforce the rule of no shoes in the house and allow food and drink only in a designated area, preferably one that isn't carpeted. These three strategies will greatly decrease the need to vacuum.

Action is the antidote to despair.
—JOAN BAEZ

Computer for banking, blogging, entertainment, and education—I'll go ahead and say it: I rely way too much on my computer. I'm a fish out of water without it. If the power goes down, though, so does my online banking. In fact, ATMs will no longer work, and banks will shut down. That's a good reason to have a supply of cash hidden in your home.

If your only computer is a desktop, replace it with a laptop when you can. Laptops run on batteries, which are much easier to keep charged than running a desktop computer with a generator. Important information that might help ensure your survival should be printed out and stored in your Survival Mom Binder.

Homeschoolers should have hard copies of textbooks and other reference books. Sorry, kids, just because the power is out doesn't mean an end to your education! Some Survival Moms even stock up on textbooks and other school supplies for future grades in anticipation of a long-term power outage. We may have to live like Stone Age families for a time, but we can still provide the next generation with a first-class education!

Heater or the home's heating system—A lack of a toaster oven isn't a matter of life and death, but a home without heat in the dead of winter is. When the electricity goes out, how will you and your family stay warm in a home that's getting chillier by the moment? If you live in a part of the country prone to extreme winter weather, an alternative way to stay warm is vital. Because this is so important, apply the Rule of Three: Have three ways to stay warm in the winter and the supplies and fuel to go along with them.

Lighting—Is there anything we take for granted more than Thomas Edison's greatest invention, the lightbulb? We have never known what it's like to rely solely on candles or lanterns, but when the power goes out, it gets dark—really, really dark. Candles are an obvious solution, but open flames are a significant danger.

Dollar stores and grocery stores sell devotional, or patron saint, candles in tall glass containers. These candles are long-burning, inexpensive, and will provide a safe source of light.

Lanterns using various types of fuel, flashlights, headlamps, and oil lamps are effective sources of light. Whatever you have on hand or decide to purchase, invest additional money in the fuel or batteries required. Rechargeable LED lanterns will give you the longest amount of light on a single charge. Homemade solar lanterns are easy to make out of solar-powered outdoor garden lights—the kind you stake into the ground. Leave these lights outside in a sunny area during the day and bring them inside in the evening, and place them in a glass jar and use for indoor lighting.

Most families will probably choose the early-to-bed and early-to-rise option instead of trying to amass enough candles, lanterns, and fuel to maintain the nighttime lighting they've been accustomed to. Taking care of all important chores and business during the day will be a lifestyle until power is restored.

A brightly lit home attracts all kinds of attention when everyone else is in the dark. One of my readers tells of neighbors becoming angry with her when she didn't have enough oil and lamps to share during a blackout. Even strangers came to her door wanting candles and lamp

fuel. Minimizing the use of light sources at night and putting up black-out curtains, or something similar, may keep your family safe from desperate people.

Fans—Staying cool is a high priority in hot weather. Later in this chapter I provide sixteen easy, low-tech tips for staying cool. If you must operate a fan, purchase small handheld versions and then load up on batteries, especially if you live in an area with long, severe summers.

Entertainment: music and TV—As miserable as you may be with-out electricity, your kids will suffer even more. Gone are the lazy after-noons and weekends of watching TV and spending hours on the Wii or the PlayStation. If you've ever thought of trying to wean them off all of their electronic sources of entertainment, now would be a good time.

In the meantime, stock up on board games, jigsaw puzzles, playing cards, and books. I spend hours every month reading aloud to my kids. What's funny is that my husband eavesdrops and soon gets as involved in the story as everyone else! (Don't wait for a power outage to begin this great family tradition!)

Life without electricity doesn't necessarily mean life without music. A solar charger for an iPod is worth every penny and don't forget bat-teries to power up CD players. If your family is musical, you might as well start learning to play musical instruments now so you can enjoy family jam sessions later. Banjos are optional.

No Lights + Boredom = Kids

No kidding. Population explosions happen about 9 months following power outages. Unless you want to add another sweet little mouth to feed, stock up on birth control!

Automatic garage door opener!—In our home, the electronic garage door isn't just a luxury: It also helps keep our home secure. However, if you've ever tried to open an electronic garage door by hand, by pulling a cord or a release lever, you know it's not the easiest thing to do. Parking your car inside the garage only at night will be easier than heaving that big door open and closed each time you need to run an errand.

Home security system—Without electricity, your home security system is worthless, and it's highly likely that the security company has closed its doors as well. I have some great tips for securing your home in Chapter 8.

Telephones—Some families have given up their home phones in favor of cell phones, and many others own a set of cordless models and nothing more. When the electricity goes out, so will all cordless phones. If you have a regular landline phone, make sure there is at least one corded phone attached to the wall.

Telephone companies have backup generators, which require fuel. It's possible that a long-term power outage would shut down phone service over a widespread area, although this situation is unlikely.

As long as there's cell phone service, a cell phone will be handy in a power-down situation. Be sure to have at least one solar-powered battery charger for your cell phones.

Medical equipment—If someone in your home relies on a piece of medical equipment to stay healthy and alive, you already know that finding a way to keep that equipment running is a top priority. This need alone justifies the purchase of a fuel-efficient generator.

Despite all backup plans, the fact remains that life changes drastically when the power goes down. Rather than load up on battery-powered gadgets, prioritize what your family needs for basic survival and don't worry about anything else. Staying healthy trumps being entertained, and your physical safety is far more important than having a battery-powered blender. There are many ways to minimize your dependence on tools, toys, and appliances that rely on fossil fuels.

Another way a loss of power will affect us is time. Washing clothes by hand and then hanging them up to dry takes far more time than using a washing machine and dryer. Heating up water for bathing is time consuming and so is cooking food over a campfire. When the power goes out, plan on simplifying your life in every way possible just to get

A prudent person foresees danger and takes precautions. The simpleton goes blindly on and suffers the consequences.

—PROVERBS 27:12 (NLT)

Showers for everybody!

After the power goes out, the water in your hot water heater should stay warm for a few hours. Take advantage of that by having everyone run through the shower, 5 minutes at a time, to freshen up. This should make life pleasant for everyone for at least a couple of days. After that, it's either cold showers, dips in the pool, or sponge baths with water warmed over a camp stove.

done everything that needs to get done. Who knows? You may decide to have four or five more kids just to help with all of the extra work!

Even with the power in full force, now is a good time to analyze your lifestyle and see where you might be able to minimize your dependence on fossil fuels. No, this isn't a lecture on carbon footprints. It's just a suggestion to look for ways to be more self-reliant and less overwhelmed when you might have to live without power for hours, days, or weeks, or when you might have no choice but to conserve due to the skyrocketed price of energy.

Life without electricity is a sobering thought. We're used to power companies rushing to make repairs and ensure that power is restored, but the fact is, in a massive crisis you would be on your own, and help might be very slow in coming.

Power's Out Emergency Kit

When the power goes out, there's no need to fumble around for flashlights and wonder where you can find fresh batteries. Put this kit together, all in one location, and you and your family will be ready:

- Assortment of light sources:
  - Handheld flashlights
  - Headlamps
  - FlashLantern (available at www.flashlantern.com)
  - Other battery-powered lanterns, LED preferred
  - Light sticks
  - Coleman lanterns with fuel
  - Candles
  - Oil lamps
- Extra set of batteries for each light source
- Manual can opener
- At least 3–4 days' worth of food that doesn't require heating or refrigerating. If you live in an area prone to frequent power outages, hurricanes, tornadoes, or blizzards, have additional food on hand.
- Food thermometer to check the temperature inside the fridge. If the temperature is 40°F or higher for more than two hours, the food may not be safe for consumption. Throw it out to be on the safe side.

- Matches, a lighter, or another fire starter
- Battery-powered or wind-up clock
- Cell phone charger that plugs into your car
- First-aid kit
- Small rocket stove with fuel
- Read-aloud books
- Deck of cards
- Coloring books and fresh, new crayons
- Hand sanitizer
- Hand-crank weather radio with extra batteries
- Hand tools: pliers, screwdrivers, and a multipurpose tool
- Sturdy pocketknife
- Battery-powered fan, or two, with extra batteries
- Phone number for the power company
- List of appliances and electronics that should be unplugged. When the power resumes, they could be damaged by a power surge.

Know where to find:

- Sleeping bags, camp stove, and fuel
- Tent, in case it's too hot to sleep inside the house
- Enough stored water to last 2 weeks
- Firearm, if you own one, and ammunition
- Extra blankets
- Firewood and tinder
- Extra fuel for a generator or a cook stove
- Generator
- Board games
- Cooler or ice chest for storing food or medication that must be kept cold. If the power outage lasts more than 48 hours, put these items in the cooler and surround with ice.

If the Apocalypse comes, beep me.

—BUFFY THE VAMPIRE SLAYER

Staying Cool When It's Hot

One of the most critical uses of electricity is staying cool in very hot weather. Our bodies can become quickly overheated, with young children and the elderly being most susceptible. I was in Chicago during one of its worst heat waves in 1995. Employees of the Hyatt Hotel where I was staying had to stand on the roof and hose down giant air-conditioning units with water in order to keep them running. In a matter of days, more than 700 people died because of this heat wave.

How did our ancestors survive, then, without air conditioning? I've spent my entire life in the American Southwest, and as you might expect, I have a few tricks up my sleeve when it comes to staying cool:

1. Keep spray bottles of water around and spritz faces and wrists to stay cool.

2. In the earliest morning hours, open windows to let in all that cool air. Be sure to close them again, along with all blinds and curtains, once the day begins to heat up.

3. Just before bedtime, spray bedsheets with plenty of water, aim a battery-powered fan toward your side of the bed, jump in, and go to sleep, quickly!

4. Wear bathing suits around the house.

5. If you'll be outside, wet a bandanna, place a few ice cubes down the center, diagonally, roll it up, and tie it around your neck.

6. Check doors and windows for incoming warm air and install weather-stripping if necessary. This will do double duty in the winter, when cold air is the enemy. Duct tape can substitute for weather-stripping if you're desperate.

7. Check the western exposure of your home. If you have windows that face west, check into inexpensive blinds from Home Depot or Lowe's. Even aluminum foil taped over your windows (gasp!) can help keep your home cooler.

8. If you need to do outside chores, do them in the morning when the sun rises or even earlier.

Symptoms of overheating (hyperthermia):

- Strong, rapid pulse
- Elevated body temperature
- Excessive thirst
- Hot, dry skin
- Dilated pupils
- Dizziness
- Nausea and vomiting
- Headaches
- Confusion
- Seizures
- Coma

9. If you must, douse your naked body with water and stand in front of a battery-operated fan. Stock up on these fans and make sure you have plenty of batteries—and please close the blinds!

10. Take a slightly warm bath, as long as there is water in the hot water heater. It will lower your body temperature, making you feel cooler longer once you get out of the tub.

11. Drink those 8 glasses of water per day.

12. Plant fast-growing shade trees, particularly on the west side of your home. If they provide shade for outside windows, so much the better. Shade = cool.

13. Most of the hot air that enters your home comes through the windows. Thermal curtains may be the solution if your home has lots of windows. If that's not an option, try using pushpins to hang blankets over each window.

14. If you long to be outdoors, fill a kiddie pool with water, sit down, and relax. Be sure to wear sunscreen! When the water gets too warm to enjoy, use it to water the plants.

15. Don't overexert yourself. Avoid working up a sweat, if possible. Save physical labor for the cooler parts of the day. Take a lesson from desert animals: They rest in the shade or underground during the day and come out at night.

16. Fill a tub with a few inches of water and dangle your feet in it while you read a book.

Your clothing choices during hot summer days can cool you down or make you completely miserable. Watch the landscape workers in your town. You'll find they always wear wide-brimmed hats, long sleeved shirts, and long pants. They know what they're doing. It sounds counterintuitive, but that extra fabric will protect your skin from the sun and act as an insulator from the heat. Make sure the fabric is lightweight and breathable, such as cotton or linen. Wicking fabrics are an even better choice since their fibers actually wick away sweat from your body, keeping you dry and cool.

Above all, keep an eye on young children and older friends and loved ones. They are far more susceptible to heatstroke. Be sure they're getting plenty of water to drink and are spending the hottest part of the day in the coolest part of the house.

For peace of mind, resign as general manager of the universe.

—AUTHOR UNKNOWN

If the heat continues and there's no telling when the power will be up and running again, keep in mind that it takes the human body about 3 weeks to become acclimated to a change in temperature. I can vouch for this. When I lived on that kibbutz in Israel, living quarters were pretty rugged, and a small oscillating fan was my only source of cool air. I used some of the techniques listed above, and sure enough, I was soon used to warmer temperatures. Sure, air conditioning felt great, but I was just fine without it, even when days hit 110 degrees.

Decide which of these tips work best for you and then make sure you have everything on hand for a power-out summer season. By the way, applying these tips will also allow you to crank up the temperature of your air conditioning and save some money on your summer power bills.

||||||||||||||||||||||||||||||||||||||||||||||||||||||||||||||||||||||||||||||||||||||||||||||||||||||||

If There's a Summer, There's Gotta Be a Winter!

Cold temperatures are as big a killer as ultra-hot days. Staying warm is vital, and without electricity this will be a challenge but not impossible. Here are some tips for staying sane, safe, and warm:

1. Wear a thermal cap, even inside your home.

2. Buy winter clothing when it's on clearance. If you have kids, stock up on larger sizes of clothing for future use. Look for fabrics that are easily layered, such as silk and wool, as well as brand names GORE-TEX, Polartec, WINDSTOPPER, and DRYline. They might be more expensive, but in the long run, they're worth it. I have a pair of silk long johns I purchased 25 years ago, and they keep me as warm and cozy now as they did when I was, ahem, much younger! Cotton is *not* a good choice for winter wear.

3. Stock up on blankets. They can be used as room insulators and come in handy for bedding when unexpected visitors show up. Look for good-quality blankets at garage and estate sales.

4. Flannel sheets are cozier than cotton sheets in the winter.

5. Cover windows with bubble wrap. Buy it in large rolls from home improvement stores. Cut the wrap to fit each window and tape it

into place using duct tape. It's a good idea to have those pieces already measured, cut, labeled, and stored.

6. If someone in the family will be out and about in the car, make sure it's stocked with a heavy-duty sleeping bag, food, water, and other survival supplies.

7. Remember the needs of outdoor animals. Bring them inside if you can. I've seen photos of horses and buffalo inside (crazy) people's homes. If horses and buffalo can be accommodated, then certainly old Shep and the pack of hunting dogs deserve a bit of warmth and protection on the coldest days and nights of the year. On cold nights, I'm grateful for my little Basenji, Mouse, who burrows underneath the blankets to sleep at my feet.

8. Exercise! Rev up not only your body temperature but your metabolism as well! This will help housebound kids work off energy, and you may lose a few inches around the hips as well!

9. Stock up on hand and foot warmers. You can buy them by the case at Amazon.com.

10. Stock up on wool: wool blankets, wool socks, wool mittens, wool sweaters, wool caps, wool gloves—you name it. It's one of the best fibers to wear in cold weather.

11. Close off all rooms and parts of the house that you're not using. There's no point in wasting valuable energy heating up rooms that aren't occupied.

12. Keeping the icy wind out of your home is essential. Try covering the side of the house facing the wind with clear Visqueen, a plastic sheeting readily available from home improvement stores. Bales of hay piled against the house and even snow shoveled around the foundation and up against the outer walls act as insulators.

If you live in an area prone to severe winters, planning one or two backup sources of heat is an absolute necessity. Freezing temperatures kill, and freak winter storms are a possibility just about anywhere. Without heat your water pipes will likely freeze, and that will leave you stranded without running water or flushing toilets. Avoid this disaster by making a secondary source of heat a top priority. My choice is a fuel-efficient wood/coal stove. When I lived alone up in Arizona's high

Everyone knows that a flashlight, with extra batteries, is a must at home and in the car, but did you know that there's an alternative that you may like much better? If you've ever tried to do something with both hands while trying to hold on to a flashlight, you'll appreciate the quirky-looking headlamp. It takes just a few seconds to pull it over your head, and it lights up a path or a work area perfectly. As an added bonus, these generally require just two AAA batteries, which are a whole lot easier to tuck into a pocket or a backpack than a slew of those much larger C and D batteries.

country, this was all I used for heat, even on the coldest, windiest days. When I could get my hands on a few lumps of coal—and no, they weren't in my Christmas stocking!—I was thrilled. A small piece of coal would keep my stove piping hot through the night and made it much easier to start a fire the next morning.

Whatever backup heating system you choose, make sure the necessary fuel, such as wood or coal, is easily available or safe to store. It's impossible to store all of the fuel you will ever need, so conserving energy will be not just a trend, as in "going green," but a matter of life and death.

Wildly cold days and nights may require you to move everyone into a single room, along with food, water, and the most basic supplies. Seal out the rest of the house by putting up Visqueen or a tarp. Your goal is to keep as much warm air in a small area as possible. Keep out cold

Winter sanity survival tips

1. Don't underestimate the lighting power of a single candle. It can provide enough light for a family game of Monopoly or a family reading night. Plumber's candles can be purchased at home improvement stores. They're dirt-cheap, and each candle lasts about 8 hours. Just be sure to keep *any* open flame away from children and never fall asleep while it's still burning.

2. If you're snowed in, create a daily schedule of chores, school, playtime, and even a few surprises. Try to stick with established routines as best you can. This keeps the household running smoothly and gives everyone something to look forward to. Surprises might be sweet treats that have been stashed away, small gifts from a dollar store, firing up the generator to watch a favorite family movie, or Family Talent Night. Be creative!

3. Keep an eye out for symptoms of stress. I discovered that my husband gets very fatigued when he's under a lot of stress; my daughter begins to need extra time alone; my son needs more physical activity and socialization than usual; and I need mental breaks via a good book or a knitting project. Look for ways to handle stress symptoms unique to each family member.

4. Have plenty of No-Cook Foods available, but if you must cook off the grid, make sure it's done out in the garage or in a very well-ventilated area. The carbon monoxide from lighted charcoal, gas stove, or propane cooker can be deadly in a sealed area.

5. Don't underestimate the magic of the light stick! They're magical to young children and can provide extra light when two or three of them are hung in front of a mirror. At about a dollar per light stick, go ahead and buy a case or two at Amazon.com or eBay.

Get the most out of your generator

- Place an extra spark plug, a wrench, the generator's instructions, a small flashlight, and a small can of oil in a waterproof bag. Tape the bag to the frame of the generator.

- Use a heavy extension cord and a spike protector with a ground fault interrupter (GFI).

- Change the oil once a year, even if you haven't used the generator.

- Never use the generator indoors.

- Many owners prefer the Honda brand because its generators are easy to start and quieter than others. The spare parts for the Honda generators are also easy to find.

- Determine which devices are most essential to your family and the amount of wattage needed and then buy a generator according to those needs.

- A multifuel generator is preferable.

- Always check the fluid levels before starting it.

- Be sure that *you* know how to start it, how to use it—including its refueling, safety, and maintenance requirements—and how to shut it down.

> *Everyone dies, but not everyone lives.*
>
> —WILLIAM WALLACE

air by hanging up blankets or putting cardboard on the windows. One creative—and desperate!—Survival Mom cut pieces of insulation from a roll, pushed them into black plastic trash bags and taped them against each window. (If you try this, be sure to wear long sleeves, gloves, and a face mask to protect yourself from the fiberglass.)

Above all, if you must hunker down at home and indoor temperatures are reaching freezing, beware of the silent danger of carbon monoxide poisoning if you're tempted to use an indoor space heater or any heat source that relies on a flame. It's far better to huddle under a dozen blankets with your kids, hubby, and dogs than for the whole crowd to succumb to carbon monoxide poisoning. Crack open a window or two by at least an inch to allow for ventilation and make sure you have carbon monoxide detectors installed throughout your house.

Is a Generator Really All That?

Ask any survivalists if they own a generator and their response will be: "Of course! Now get off my property!" According to a popular list of the Top 100 Things to Disappear First in a Disaster, generators are

A Survival Mom's Story

Pam Staples, North Carolina

In 1993, Pam Staples and her family lived in a rural area of the foothills of western North Carolina. That particular spring held a nasty surprise for the Staples family. In March they received about 16 inches of snow and ice in a 24-hour period. The snow, along with high winds, brought down power lines, and suddenly the Staples were without electricity for 7 days. Later this storm would be called "The Storm of the Century" for its hurricane-force winds and record-cold temperatures.

Pam recalls, "There were a dozen or so trees down across our driveway, and power lines were down everywhere." Fortunately, her parents lived nearby and regained power after only a couple of days. The two families shared a well, which was operated by an electrical pump, so the Staples' house had running water for most of the duration.

Pam's three children, then about 10, 8, and 6 years old, were out of school for many days. Pam says: "They had a ball! They never wanted the power to come back on!"

"We had a wood stove, which we used for heat, and during the power outage, that's what we cooked on. I made lots of one-pot meals, like chili, spaghetti, and pinto beans. I fried bacon and eggs for breakfast in a cast-iron frying pan set on top of the wood heater. My kids said we ate better in those days than we normally did."

Pam's attitude remained positive, although her work load just about doubled. The family heated kettles of water on the wood stove for bathing and washing dishes, even though it was hard work. "It pretty much took the entire day just to take care of the basics of survival—carrying in water, heating the water, preparing and cooking meals, and then doing what little housework we could during the daylight hours."

Pam says that the worst part was carrying in the wood from the snowy outdoors and keeping the fire going throughout the nights. Temperatures remained below freezing, and the family couldn't risk allowing the severe cold to invade their home. "We usually just banked the fire at night, raked the coals in the morning, added kindling and started a new fire." Keeping her house warm became her new part-time job!

Pam and her family actually have fond memories of the ordeal. "I really enjoyed the fact that we were able to survive quite nicely. We played a lot of board games and card games, sang, read books out loud, made up games, and, of course, the kids had lots of time to play in the snow!" When nighttime came, they wrapped up in blankets and headed to bed almost as soon as it got dark. The hard work took its toll by the end of the day, but Pam says: "I feel like we had more quality time together than usual. To this day my children talk fondly about that week the power was off. They loved it!"

A power outage doesn't have to spell disaster and misery. With a little advance planning and the right attitude, it can spell adventure.

Number One. But a generator is no genie in a bottle. Sure, it may provide enough energy to power up the fridge, keep that frozen food cold a bit longer, and allow for some TV time, but it has its disadvantages.

Most generators are very noisy, give off noxious fumes and have to be kept outside. Are you sure you want the entire neighborhood and passersby knowing that yours is one of the few homes with power? They may wonder, "If they have power, what else do they have?" In a true disaster, you want to blend in with everyone else and not draw attention to what you have that others may not have. We all want to believe in the inherent goodness of humanity, but desperate people often do desperate things.

During a recent hurricane in the Gulf of Mexico, clever thieves targeted portable generators by parking a running lawnmower next to the generator and then stealing the generator. The homeowners were none the wiser because they could still hear the sound of a motor outside. It wasn't until their new "generator" ran out of gas that they discovered the theft. Ideally, a generator should be kept in a locked, vented shed or secured against theft in some other way. In a long-term power outage, a generator is your only connection to normal life.

Like any other appliance, generators need fuel, and that fuel is gasoline, natural gas, diesel, or propane. It would be lovely if generators ran on enchanted fairy dust, but they don't. Whatever the fuel, it will have to be stored safely, and when it's gone, there may be none left anywhere. If you've ever tried to find a propane tank over the Fourth of July weekend, you know how quickly they disappear.

Gasoline isn't the answer either. The pumps at gas stations are powered by electricity. Did you know that? The underground tanks might be filled to the brim, but without electricity, that fuel isn't going anywhere. Storage is another issue. Gasoline *can* be stored for a year or so, but it is definitely not the fuel of choice because of its volatility and relatively short shelf life. If you choose to store gasoline, keep in mind that the fumes are flammable, not the liquid itself. Use a stabilizer, available at Walmart and auto supply stores, to lengthen its shelf life a bit, and be sure to rotate it. Always store gasoline in an airtight container, away from sunlight. Label the container with the date it was stored and use the fuel within 12–18 months.

When you teach your son, you teach your son's son.

—THE TALMUD

Diesel is much easier and safer to store than gasoline. It has a much longer shelf life, up to 10 years, and is not nearly as volatile. A diesel-powered generator gives off some pretty strong fumes, though, and it's important to buy the correct grade of fuel and store it in an airtight container, away from sunlight. Maintaining a constant temperature will help prolong the life of diesel *and* gasoline.

Propane and natural gas are two other choices when it comes to fuels for generators. They are both fairly inexpensive, and tanks of these can be stored indefinitely. If you're tempted to rush out and stock up on propane and/or natural gas, there's a significant downside you should be aware of: Both fuels are *extremely* dangerous when leaked. All it takes is a spark or even a bit of static electricity, and they ignite. If you smell the tiniest hint of natural gas—it smells like rotten eggs or sulfur—get your family far, far away. Even the use of a cell phone can spark an explosion. However, with proper storage and keeping a diligent eye, and nose, out for leaks, propane and natural gas are very good fuel choices. If noise is an issue, generators powered by these two fuels tend to be quieter.

Every mile is two in winter.
—GEORGE HERBERT

I'm not trying to talk you out of purchasing a generator. Just be very aware of the drawbacks so that you can plan around them. When making the decision to purchase a generator, ask yourself these questions:

- What type of fuel, or fuels, does it use?
- Will that fuel be easy to store and readily available?
- How expensive is the fuel?
- How much power will the generator produce?
- How much power do I absolutely have to have?
- How noisy is the generator?
- Considering the price of the generator and fuel, is it really worth the cost just to have a few electrical luxuries running?

Once you've decided to make the purchase, do lots of research and compare prices. A good rule of thumb is to buy the best and most fuel-efficient generator you can afford.

Worst-Case Scenario: Something to Keep You Awake Tonight!

What is an EMP and should I be afraid of one?

I'm not ashamed to say that reading *One Second After* by William Forstchen scared the living daylights out of me. For weeks, I didn't want to travel more than 15 or 20 miles from home. The novel details life in a small North Carolina town following an EMP, an electromagnetic pulse. An EMP can be caused by the detonation of a large bomb, nuclear or otherwise, in the atmosphere, miles above land. Its pulse wave can easily cover a continent and destroy electronic components in computers, engines, power plants, and solar panels alike. An event like this has never happened on a large scale, and there are differing opinions as to the exact consequences, but one thing is certain: In a matter of moments, life as we know it would be gone forever. Our closest star, the sun, could also do extensive damage in the form of a Coronal Mass Ejection (CME). The results would be similar.

This chapter has provided dozens of ideas for managing life without electricity, with the assumptions that the power company is working on repairs and that this is a temporary condition. An EMP hits without warning and would destroy our nation's power grid and everything connected to it. There would be no quick repairs, and phone calls to the power companies would be futile because all phone lines would be dead. Convenient transportation as we know it would cease to exist. Engines in many modern cars and trucks, as well as in airplanes, trains, ships, and farming and medical equipment, would no longer function.

The consequences would be devastating and casualties would, eventually, be in the millions. (Remember, this is the worst-case scenario!) Communities would have little protection of police and fire departments. Prisoners would easily be able to escape, and it wouldn't take long for hospital generators to run out of fuel and no longer be able to care for patients. Much of the military's equipment and transportation would be rendered useless to a large degree, unless the machinery has been hardened to be either EMP-resistant or EMP-proof.

Backup generators for electrical plants, including nuclear power plants, and city water and sewage systems would run out of fuel in short order. In fact, there's a good chance the generators themselves would be of no use because they, too, contain electronic components. We saw something similar happen in Japan after the calamitous earthquake and tsunami in 2011, when fuel for backup generators didn't arrive in time to prevent a meltdown.

If you happen to be on vacation when an EMP burst happens, you would likely never be able to return home. How does a family of four walk from Disney World to Richmond? It's likely you would never hear from loved ones again, unless they lived within walking distance and traveling that distance by foot was safe, which is doubtful. That Emergency Broadcasting System that interrupts your favorite TV programs would be just as dead as your cell phone and laptop computer.

Appliances, large and small, would become museum artifacts without a source of electricity, and if you rely on an electric can opener to open all those cans of food, you'll be out of luck. Even clocks and battery chargers would no longer work. Solar power systems, both large and small, would also be impacted; each system contains computer chips that would now be fried by the EMP.

With little law enforcement, criminal gangs will likely band together and raid apartments, homes, and farms. The armories of police and sheriff departments, military installations, and the National Guard could be emptied, with thousands of weapons getting into the hands of malicious, dangerous people. Well-armed citizens will be the last best hope for most communities. See what I have to say about firearms and ammunition in Chapter 8.

Some might describe a post-EMP world as going back to the nineteenth century, but I think in some ways it would be far worse. We no longer have the tools, skills, knowledge, and, in some cases, raw materials to make the most basic tools for survival. How many blacksmiths do you know? Do you happen to own a pair of oxen and a wagon for transportation? You might know how to sew, but can you create cloth from raw cotton or sheep's wool? The moment of an EMP burst freezes time. The food, medications, supplies, and tools in our homes may be the only ones we have for a long time. If you have 9 bottles of Advil, that's all you may ever have. It's a disquieting concept, isn't it?

Could a Faraday cage be your new best friend?

A Faraday cage is a container that is designed to be impervious to the effects of an EMP. These containers can be purchased, or you can make your own. Tech Protect sells heavy-duty Mylar bags that serve as protection for electronics. Your Faraday cage could contain electronics such as a watch, a radio, batteries, or a solar battery charger and larger items like laptops, kitchen appliances, or even a generator.

The shortwave receiver

Every home needs a shortwave receiver or radio, preferably one that runs on both batteries and a hand crank. These radios can pick up broadcasts from around the world—in English and in real time. Most shortwave broadcasters are on the air round the clock. One of the casualties of an EMP will be information. At the very least, a good shortwave receiver (AM/FM) will keep you informed of current events.

Is there any way to prepare for an EMP? Just knowing what one is and how to quickly identify it is a huge step toward survival. While most people will spend precious, critical hours at home waiting for the power company to show up, you'll notice all the signs of an EMP: stalled cars, dead telephone lines, and a power outage that is longer than usual. If that happens, jump into action.

Make sure that every vehicle is supplied with everything necessary not only to survive but also to get home, if at all possible. If your minivan relies on electronics, and all vehicles built from about 1980 forward do, it will probably stall right where it is without warning. You'll need to hike home, along with your kids and whatever survival supplies you think you might need. Store comfortable walking shoes in the trunk for everyone in the family, along with socks and moleskin. I have complete directions for preparing your vehicle for emergencies in Chapter 11. The number one goal of each member of your family is to get home, no matter what.

In this worst-case scenario, store shelves will empty in a matter of hours once the unprepared figure out they're in for a long-term crisis. Get to stores ahead of the panicked crowd. Warehouse stores, such as Costco and Sam's Club, have pre-packed cases of food and large containers of supplies ready to load on a pull cart. You will probably have less than 36 hours to make this move. Have cash in hand and grab anything to shore up your own supplies. If you have an inventory sheet of your food storage, take it with you as a shopping list. Visit your pharmacy to get refills, if possible. The entire electronic financial system will be down, so cash will be king.

Products like diapers, baby formula, over-the-counter drugs, cigarettes, and toilet paper will become priceless in a post-EMP world. If you have extra money, buy these and similar items to use for bartering or to simply have extra to help a desperate family.

If you're stocked up on water, food, and essential supplies and have a firearm or two, with training to go along with it, your family has a fighting chance to survive. Add to that some medical training, a very well-stocked first-aid kit and, hopefully, a few months' worth of prescription medicines. An established garden will provide your family with fresh produce—hopefully enough to share with others. A growing number of urban and suburban families have begun raising their own chickens for meat and eggs, a smart move whether the future holds an EMP or not.

One smart, relatively simple step is to prepare Faraday cages to store essentials, such as a watch or two, crank flashlights, AA and AAA batteries, solar battery chargers, walkie-talkies, and a hand-cranked shortwave radio. Why do you need the radio? It may be possible to get news and information from foreign sources if all local and national TV and radio is off the air. If you have an old laptop, begin using it to store digital information, although you should have hard copies of everything related to preparedness and survival. Store the laptop and a small printer in a Faraday cage. This will give you the ability to retrieve information and disperse it to others.

For transportation, good sturdy bicycles and strong bodies capable of pedaling many miles will be invaluable. Trailers designed for use with bicycles will be worth their weight in gold, which, by the way, may be of very little value. Durable vehicles built prior to 1970 or so might be worth purchasing, especially if someone in your family is a mechanic by trade or hobby. You already know that storing gasoline is an issue, so a diesel engine is a better choice. Be forewarned that owning one of the few operating cars around might put you in jeopardy, and your car could also be confiscated by a law enforcement agency.

Do you know who has been coping without the luxuries of electricity for generations? The Amish. They use gas-powered refrigerators, oil lamps, and wood-burning stoves. Lehman's, a retail and online store

> *I am not afraid of tomorrow, for I have seen yesterday and I love today.*
>
> —WILLIAM ALLEN WHITE

based in Ohio, caters to the Amish and Mennonite communities and just might have the post-EMP tools and appliances you're looking for.

The possibility of an EMP presents a horrific and depressing scenario, but how likely is it, really? There is no definite answer to that question. The people in government who might know aren't talking, but a 2004 report presented to Congress, "Report of the Commission to Assess the Threat to the United States from Electromagnetic Pulse (EMP) Attack," takes the possibility very seriously. This 208-page report can be downloaded from the Internet, and the warning comes through loud and clear:

> The Commission has concluded that even a relatively modest- to small-yield weapon of particular characteristics, using design and fabrication information already disseminated through licit and illicit means, can produce a potentially devastating E1 field strength over very large geographical regions . . . Indeed, the Commission determined that such weapon devices not only could be readily built and delivered, but also the specifics of these devices have been illicitly trafficked for the past quarter-century.

No country has ever experienced an EMP attack. It's unclear exactly what the results would be. At this point it's mostly theoretical, and the results may not be as dismal as I've described. If you put a few precautionary measures in place, however, they will be useful and practical in the case of other disasters as well.

One day I was getting a little too paranoid about this and noticed that I didn't hear any traffic outside. Fear gripped my chest, and I did the smartest thing I could think of: I called my husband and asked if he could see any cars driving on the street. He laughed when I explained the reason for my question and reminded me that an EMP would take out the telephone lines. What's the takeaway lesson? Plan for tomorrow but enjoy living *today*.

☑ Schedule a "Pioneer Weekend" and plan to live at least 2 full days off the grid. Have everyone take part in the planning because that's an education in itself. What foods will you cook and how? How will you stay warm or cool? When boredom sets in, what activities will keep everyone from going stir-crazy? And what about transportation?

The weekend will be an amazing learning experience for everyone. Be sure to spend some time on Sunday night talking about what happened and what everyone learned from the experience.

☑ Do your kids realize how much they rely on electricity? Assign them the task of making a list each time they use electricity during the day, from the alarm clock in the morning to their video games in the afternoon and their nightlight at bedtime. Together, review their list and ask, "What if our electricity went out for a week?" Kids are creative and this activity will help them start thinking of ways to be more self-reliant and become better prepared for power outages.

☑ Staying cool when it's hot and warm when it's cold are basic survival skills. Teach your children some of the strategies on pages 151-156 so they'll be equipped with important information and skills if they ever have to cope with the elements on their own.

The Prepared Family

Family Preparedness Plan: Home Emergencies

A Power's Out Plan for everyday appliances:

APPLIANCE	SUBSTITUTE WHEN THE POWER'S DOWN
Hot water heater	_____
Stove and oven	_____
Microwave	_____
Small appliances:	
_____	_____
_____	_____
_____	_____
_____	_____
Grain mill	_____
Refrigerator	_____
Freezer	_____
Washing machine	_____
Dryer	_____
Vacuum	_____
Computer	_____
Lamps/lights	_____
Fans	_____
Entertainment	_____
Heater	_____
Medical equipment	_____
Other:	_____

Power's Out Plan:

☐ Make a Power's Out Emergency Kit

☐ Learn how to use our generator

☐ Strategies and supplies for staying cool:

- _____

- _____

- _____

- _____

- _____

☐ Strategies and supplies for staying warm:

- _____

- _____

- _____

- _____

- _____

CHAPTER 8

The Essentials for Safety and Security

If you believe in the inherent goodness of man, you've never been to Disneyland at Christmas time. Sure, the decorations are eye-popping, but tempers can flare in a moment. Crowds, dressed in their holiday finest, mercilessly press against each other to get a better position for the parade. Even the sweet presence of Sleeping Beauty can't hide the ugliness when a mom tries to push her daughter ahead of another's. Walking through Fantasyland one year with our two young children, we heard an ugly epithet behind us, "Stroller people!" There were thousands of us with strollers, but I took that insult personally!

In your own circle of friends and family and among the people you encounter every day, everyone is probably pretty pleasant, at least most of the time. To a great extent, Americans enjoy a secure lifestyle.

One thing is certain, however. Man is, and always has been, the most dangerous animal. Even winning a championship basketball game can bring out the worst in people, as they break windows, attack police cars, and start fires. It makes you wonder what their reaction will be when grocery stores have been emptied of food for days and law enforcement is nowhere to be found. The time to think about your family's security is now, not then.

When 911 Is Out of Commission

It's important for a Survival Mom to make plans with the assumption that no one is coming to the rescue. There are too many examples of disappearing or overwhelmed law enforcement and first responders to think that you and your family will be at the top of their list in a crisis.

Who can forget the poor souls stranded in New Orleans in the messy aftermath of Hurricane Katrina and one woman saying into a television camera, "Come get me, come get me!"? There's something about victimhood that just rubs a Survival Mom the wrong way, and you have probably said to yourself, "That will never be me!"

Preparedness requires you to be ready to survive on your own. Are you up to the challenge?

- Do you know what danger signs to look for?
- What could you do to protect your family and your home if no police were available?
- What steps could you take to protect your family from a home invasion?

Women are incredibly creative and resilient. Men say they need the right tool for the job. Women say: "If I have a shoe, I can hammer that nail! If I have a butter knife, who needs a screw driver?" Apply that same creativity to preparedness, along with a good amount of determination and focus. Make lists and plans and then take action.

|||||||||||||||||||||||||||||||||||||||||||||||||||||||||||||||||||||||||||||||||||||||||||||||||||||||

Security Without a Gun

You may be surprised to hear that the most important weapon isn't a gun or a knife. It's your brain. Recently I asked an agent who works for Homeland Security as an anti-terrorist specialist how he keeps his family safe. I was certain that he had gone to great lengths to conceal his name and identity and made drastic changes to ensure their security. His surprising answer was that he hasn't done much out of the ordinary: They have a home security system, as do millions of families. However, he also made the statement, "Pay attention to your surroundings." The official name for this is situational awareness.

Moms have so many distractions, both at home and when we're out and about. We keep track of where every kid is, whose diaper needs to be changed, how many minutes are left 'til lunch, and whether it's too late in the day to give little Johnny a Tootsie Pop to keep him quiet while we figure out what's for dinner. Outside the house, it's just as bad:

"Where did Cameron run off to?"

"I don't care if a Happy Meal will make you happy. We are not stopping at McDonalds!"

And then there's the shopping list, bank deposits, kids to pick up, and kids to drop off. It's a wonder that most bad guys don't solely target moms running errands. We are such an easy mark!

In spite of all those distractions and mental static, here is what else we're thinking:

"Who's that strange man talking to my kids?"

"Lily's been in the bathroom for 3 minutes. Thirty seconds and I'm going in."

"Where is he? Where IS HE? WHERE IS HE?"

All moms think those thoughts, and it's the smartest thinking you'll ever do. *That's* situational awareness, or at least a mom's version of situational awareness.

A report from Homeland Security defines situational awareness as:

- Knowing and understanding what is happening around you
- Predicting how it will change with time
- Being unified with the dynamics of your environment

I call it being a Survival Mom.

Most people drift through life pretty oblivious to their surroundings. By the time they recognize danger, it's often too late. A brilliant man, Jeff Cooper, developed an easy-to-remember color code to define your own situational awareness and any possible dangers:

Level White—oblivious and only slightly aware of surroundings, people, or events

It's actually rather pleasant to live at Level White. Your heartbeat and blood pressure are at resting levels. Shapes, colors, shadows, and noises move by you, but your tranquility isn't disturbed. You're the perfect target.

Level Yellow—relaxed but alert

At Level Yellow you're still relaxed and enjoying life, but your eyes and ears are at DEFCON 3. You're aware that danger could be lurking anywhere. You notice suspicious characters at the mall and the fact that the house across the street has a steady stream of visitors on Friday and Saturday nights. You're a drug dealer's, or a cheating husband's, worst nightmare.

Level Orange—alert and focused on a specific person or event

If your mind begins rehearsing what you'll do if X happens, you're at Level Orange. There's a specific threat you're aware of. Maybe something or someone is making you feel uneasy. It may be just a feeling, a hunch, or intuition, but something isn't right, and you know you'll take action if you have to.

Level Red—Touch my kid and I'll kill you!

At Level Red a Survival Mom gives no quarter. A very real, present danger is happening *now*. You've hoped this moment would never come, but it has arrived. Your finger is on the trigger, you're gripping the handle of a knife, a hammer, or some other lethal (you hope) weapon. You're ready, consequences be damned. Do you feel lucky, punk?

I love talking warrior talk.

Be a gopher, not a rabbit

You can teach your kids about situational awareness and Jeff Cooper's color code without overly alarming them. The lessons may come in handy at school when faced with a bully or a neighborhood gang, and it just might save your kid from a beating or worse.

Not long ago I subjected my kids to one of my Tahoe lectures. Although undocumented, I become a brilliant orator behind the wheel of my Tahoe. What caught my attention that particular day was a teenage girl walking slowly on the sidewalk, cell phone glued to her ear. Since I believe in the power of the object lesson, I pointed her out to my kids. The lecture went something like this:

Kids, see that girl over there on the sidewalk? What do you notice about her? That's right. She's talking on her cell phone. Is she paying any atten-

tion to what's going on around her? Nope. Look how she's walking. It's kind of a slow shuffle isn't it?

If I were a bad person, someone looking to hurt someone else, that girl would be my prey. Yep, just as there are predators and prey in the animal world, there are predators and prey in the human world.

Think about wildlife out on a prairie. Imagine a little bunny snuffling along, looking for tender leaves and blades of grass for nibbling. He has his head down, focused on what's directly in front of his little wet nose. Now imagine a gopher not far away. This little guy's back is straight, his ears are perked up, and his head is looking this and that way. If you were a hawk, soaring high above these two little animals, which would be the better prey? That's right, the little rabbit! He's oblivious to danger, just as that girl is oblivious to what is happening around her.

My kids learned the difference between Level White and Level Yellow awareness that day.

Level Yellow is smarter than Level White

If you are used to being at Level White, it's not too difficult to raise your level of awareness. After all, you're at Level White when you're sleeping. When you're out and about, with or without your children, stay unplugged: Resist the temptation to plug into your iPod. Music and podcasts are entertaining but quite distracting.

Ignore the ringing cell phone until you're in a safe spot where you can sit down and return the call in peace. Nothing makes a woman more vulnerable and distracted than chatting or texting on a cell phone, and an attack on you or your children just isn't worth it.

Make the switch from carrying a heavy, bulky purse to either only carrying the essentials in a pocket or wearing a small bag across your chest. I have a very nice collection of beautiful handbags, too, but when I carry one, I'm always focused on that darn bag. I stopped carrying purses a couple of years ago just for that reason. As it turns out, I really don't need a Tide pen, extra tissues, four different lipsticks, breath mints, a calculator, lotion, and a bottle of water. Now when I leave the house, I grab my sunglasses, keys, and a Brighton wallet with a detachable strap that I wear across my chest. My cell phone fits in the wallet, and my hands are free. If I really, truly need that Band-Aid or hand

Staying safe on the street

Here are a few facts that will help you stay aware on the streets:

- Most attacks are committed by young men.
- Most occur mid-evening to early morning.
- Summer is the most dangerous season for street attacks.
- Most common injuries are bruises, black eyes, broken noses, and shock.
- Women, the elderly, and children are the most common victims.
- Being alone increases your risk.

sanitizer, they're in my Vehicle Emergency Kit. (See complete instructions for making your own kit in Chapter 11.)

Unruly, cranky, and crying kids are another big distraction, but sometimes you can outsmart your kids by paying attention to their most basic needs ahead of time. When kids are tired, hungry, frustrated, or uncomfortable (think dirty diapers or shoes that hurt), they are far more likely to act out, disobey, or just throw a fit. Heck, I've been known to do that under those circumstances. If you have errands to run and your kids are along for the ride, be smart about timing, taking along snacks, packing their favorite blanket or stuffed animal in the car, and bringing along plenty of clean diapers. You know your kids and the causes of their meltdowns better than anyone. Be proactive.

Moving from Yellow to Orange

You're alert. Your eyes are taking in the details of your surroundings. The kids are under control, and you've ditched the purse. Suddenly, you notice something odd. Something doesn't feel right, and the thought flashes across your mind: "We may be in danger."

What has alerted your instincts are called "pre-incident indicators." These are small movements, sometimes as miniscule as a glance, and cues that warn the alert mom to watch out. Poker players call them "tells," subtle changes in behavior that give away another player's strategy. These cues give the observer the upper hand in the game. Knowing a few of these indicators will move you into Level Orange and give you the advantage over the bad guys intent on harming you or your kids:

- You notice an unnatural obstacle or delay to your movement—You're walking, driving, or even riding a bike when suddenly something is in your way, causing you to change the direction of your path or slow down. It's possible that you are being steered in another direction for the purpose of an attack.

- You notice that another person's movement matches your own— Strangers walking on the same sidewalk or driving on the same street rarely match paces perfectly. If you notice someone walking near you, matching you step for step, stopping when you stop and turning when you turn, something is up.

- Predatory movements catch your eye—If you begin feeling like you're the prey and there's a predator nearby, that's a cue that you may be in danger. Predators often circle their prey and work in pairs or teams. Keep alert for a pair or group of people who suddenly break apart as you approach. They may be planning an attack from behind or off the side. It's important, at that point, to walk toward a group of people, enter a place of business, or take some other action.

- You notice a change in demeanor—I'm 100% convinced that a woman's intuition was placed there by God. Trust that uncomfortable feeling, even if it's based on subtle changes in a person's stance, tone of voice, or actions.

- You notice sideways glances, as if checking to see who's around—Quick eye movements may be a giveaway that someone is checking for the presence of police or planning an avenue of escape. Those glances can indicate that a criminal is sizing you up. If you see those glances exchanged between two or more people, they may be working as a team, giving the go-ahead to proceed with an attack.

- You notice hidden hands—Watch for hands that are in fists, shoved into pockets, or reaching into a jacket. Criminals try to conceal a weapon as long as they can. If it's a very cold day and everyone has their hands in their pockets, this may mean nothing. But if it's accompanied by another indicator or two, regardless of the temperature, be extra cautious.

- You see someone approaching at an angle that will intercept your path—A person may be trying to stay in your blind spot for as long as possible before they attack.

- Any bump or shove is another warning sign—This may be an attempt to provoke a fight, pick your pockets, or focus your attention elsewhere. This is where it really pays to be carrying as little as possible.

- You become aware of the absence of other people—Criminals are most likely to attack when it's advantageous to them, not you. If there are no police and few people around, you may be a sitting duck.

A single pre-incident indicator may mean nothing. After all, I've accidentally bumped into people plenty of times. When I've traveled in foreign countries, the first words I wanted to learn in their language

Safety is a cheap and effective insurance policy.

—AUTHOR UNKNOWN

were, "Excuse me!" Pre-incident indicators become significant, though, when there's more than one or if you feel your hackles start going up. Again, a mom's intuition is something I trust every time. Always listen to yourself!

When you notice one or more indicators, you're at Level Orange. There's a specific person, group, or situation that causes you to realize, "This might be it." The smartest choice may be to immediately move toward other people, take a few steps in a different direction, or run. Retreating *is* a form of self-defense. Your top priority is staying safe, not showing off your kickboxing skills.

You're at Level Red. Now what?

Long before reaching Level Red, when adrenaline is gushing through your bloodstream and options are few, you need training and self-defensive weapons you are comfortable with. Deciding whether to sign up for a martial arts class, get shooting instruction, or buy a Taser is very personal. Handguns may be all the rage in your circle of friends, but if you don't have the training, either get it or explore other options.

A choice that is popular with a lot of moms is learning a form of martial arts. It's a way to get and stay fit while becoming mentally and physically equipped for confrontation. One good choice is Krav Maga, the official self-defense system used by the Israeli Defense Forces. Its techniques are based on street-fighting moves developed by Imi Lichtenfeld, who wanted to develop "natural" and practical fighting skills for life-or-death situations.

Massad Ayoob, renowned expert in personal defense, recommends and prefers Judo. He says Judo downplays physical strength in favor of skill and speed, which is highly strategic if a woman has to face a man in a physical fight. Judo instructors must be thoroughly trained and vetted in order to become certified, and when you're ready to move on to a different martial art or advance to a higher level, your instructor should be able to refer you to other high-quality instructors. Remember, martial arts schools are in the money-making business, so as long as you're writing the checks, seek out the most authentic and effective schools and instructors available.

Whatever martial art you explore, here are six questions to ask the owner of the school and/or the instructor:

- How physically fit do I need to be?
- Is this method primarily for sport or self-defense?
- Besides training to fight, how else will this method teach me to survive?
- Do you have classes for women only? (This may or may not be important to you.)
- Do you allow a one-lesson visit, so I can observe how students are taught?
- Are there current or former students I can contact for a recommendation?

The best way to avoid a Level Red situation is to steer clear of it at the Yellow or Orange levels. Your response at Level Red is when a confrontation has been forced upon you and you must either react with enough force to survive or become a victim. When you decide to react, it must be an all-out fierce offensive. A "warning shot" won't do. Your goal is to *stop* those who would cause you and your family great harm, and once your effort has begun, there's no going back.

. . . and Then There Are Firearms

The Second Amendment to the Constitution gives us the right to bear arms. There are millions of firearms in homes across the country and millions of women who can shoot. Often these women are better shots than men.

When my son was a toddler, I decided to keep all toy guns out of the house. My husband owned handguns that were stored away and never used, and our household was virtually gun-free. Touring Disneyland one year, my little guy begged me for a Buzz Lightyear Space Shooter. Naturally, I said no and felt quite certain that I was protecting him from a violent future. Not 2 weeks later, though, he managed to transform a partially eaten pizza crust into a small handgun and proceeded to aim it at the waitress. That's when I gave up the fight and bought that Space Shooter.

I wasn't against guns, exactly. I just honestly thought I was doing the right thing to protect my kids. After all, if our home were gun-free,

TheSurvivalMom.com

Check out my handgun reviews written just for women on my blog, www.thesurvivalmom.com.

we would be safer, right? In retrospect, that doesn't make a lot of sense. Bad guys will always, always have loaded guns. They will bring the most firepower they can get in order to give themselves the advantage. I want to be on at least equal footing.

Most experts suggest a home be equipped with three different types of firearms:

1. Rifle
2. Shotgun
3. Handgun

Each weapon has a different purpose when it comes to home- and self-defense, as well as hunting. The key is to go for versatility and common calibers.

Rifles

I love shooting a rifle, from a .22 plinkster to a hefty AR–15. I love the way I look when I'm shooting a rifle— kind of like an older, chubbier Sarah Connor, with barely discernable biceps but intimidating nonetheless.

Rifles are your go-to weapon for hunting and long-distance shooting. Even if your family isn't into hunting, a rifle is valuable as a defensive weapon because it shoots farther and with more velocity than a handgun. Because of that power, you need to always be aware of what is behind your target. A .30–30, for example, could fire a round that not only goes through a bad guy but also through the wall behind him and even further. For that reason, a rifle is better used for defense in outdoor settings, like when a band of roving zombies is heading toward your cul-de-sac.

A .22-caliber rifle is a particularly useful firearm and can be purchased for less than $300 or so. The ammunition for this caliber is extremely inexpensive, which makes this rifle a terrific weapon for target practice. Should you ever need to hit the hills in search of game, this weapon is just right for shooting the occasional rabbit or another small mammal.

As you might expect, rifles come in all shapes and sizes, from the militaristic AR–15 and AK–47 to the common .30–30 and .30–06 hunting rifles. Versatility is important in choosing any firearm, and for that, you can't beat the .30–30 or the .30–06 (pronounced "thirty-ought-six").

Know the law!

Each state has its own requirements for the purchase and licensing of firearms. Go to www.nraila.org/gunlaws/ or www.handgunlaw.us for a summary of the laws in *your* state and follow these laws closely.

One budget-friendly training program, guaranteed to deliver a fun weekend for everybody, is The Appleseed Project. If you would have told me the day before our family's Appleseed weekend that in less than 24 hours I'd be lying on my stomach, sniper-style, and shooting a rifle, I wouldn't have believed it. However, that's just what happened! I also learned how to shoot a rifle in standing and seated positions and how to change out magazines without losing my focus on the target. Believe me, by the end of the day, I felt nearly invincible!

Shotguns

If you've wrapped your brain around the idea of having defensive fire-arms in the home but you're not exactly Annie Oakley, a shotgun is the gun for you. In fact, many security experts consider it the gun of choice for home defense, and one reason is that it's a little more forgiving when it comes to precision-shooting than a rifle or a handgun.

Yes, the shot does have a spread when it hits its target, but the spread will be approximately 1 inch per foot from the target. So if the bad guy is 8 feet away, the spread of the shot will be 8 inches. Range practice with a shotgun is necessary if you're counting on this weapon for home defense.

While a 12-gauge shotgun is most often prescribed, a 20-gauge one is worth a look. It will have less of a kick when fired, and I know from personal experience that I'm a lot less likely to fire a gun if it's so pow-erful that it bruises my hand or shoulder. A moment of hesitation at a critical juncture could cost you your life, so if you're going to have a gun for self-defense, it must be the one you're comfortable with.

baby step

If you've never before shot a gun, try out a .22-caliber handgun at a gun range. It's a great way to learn basic shooting skills, gain accuracy, and learn about gun safety, using a gun that has a very light recoil.

The Appleseed Project

Volunteers around the country spend several weekends each year teaching "every American our shared heritage and history as well as traditional rifle marksmanship skills." The 2-day program costs less than $50 for men, and women and children participate nearly for free. You can expect expert-level shooting instruction, a history lesson or two, greatly improved shooting skills, and sore muscles! The program is ideal for families and kids over the age of 8 or 9 years. You can find out more at www.appleseedinfo.org.

A shotgun shell contains many tiny projectiles, from a few to hundreds, depending on the type of shot you use. For home defense, most experts recommend using the #4 buckshot. When the trigger is pulled, those metal pellets go flying. Aim for the chest area of the nearest bad guy, and he's likely to stop in his tracks.

Some say that the sound of a double-action pump alone is often enough to deter bad guys. If you've ever watched a *Terminator* movie, you know the sound I'm talking about. However, don't count on the sound alone to save you. If you're cocking that shotgun, you'd better be ready to pull the trigger.

A shotgun can have one heck of a recoil, especially if you're not ready for it, and because it's not exactly a handgun, it's really difficult to conceal if you're hoping for the element of surprise. A shotgun with the shortest barrel possible will give you better maneuverability around the house and will be overall easier to handle. Avoid sawed-off shotguns, unless you want to spend some time in the slammer for ownership of an illegal weapon!

Shotgun shells (ammo) are inexpensive, but not every shooting range is equipped for shotgun practice. Call your local range first before heading out. Plenty of practice will condition your eyes, ears, and body to this powerful, effective firearm. Do not depend on a shotgun for self-defense until you have had plenty of practice loading and firing it.

Handguns

The first gun I ever shot was a handgun—a small .22-caliber Ruger. I was 48 years old and had never fired a gun before in my life—not even

INSTANT SURVIVAL TIP

Guns can be loud! I guess that's hardly breaking news, but when you go to the range, you'll need good ear protection. I always use foam ear plugs and earmuffs. In fact, I find that when I wear those around the house, I experience blissful, peaceful days, and my mood improves considerably.

a BB gun—but there I was standing in front of a target at an indoor shooting range, firing that baby like my life depended on it.

To this day, I love handguns. Compared with rifles and shotguns, they are smaller and lighter but don't have the long-range firepower of their big brothers.

There are two categories of handguns: revolvers and pistols. Think John Wayne, and you're likely thinking revolver. It's the classic six-shooter: easy to load, easy to use, and easy to clean. Many firearms experts recommend a revolver for beginners for those reasons.

Trained law-enforcement officers have a 25% success rate when it comes to hitting their target in a gunfight, so you can imagine what your accuracy rate might be as a relatively untrained civilian, loaded with adrenaline and scared out of your mind. A revolver doesn't require much thinking in order to shoot. Each time the trigger is pulled, a single bullet in the cylinder is fired. However, you need to be able to count to six under a state of duress, because once you're out of those six bullets, you're also out of luck. Be aware that some revolvers have a very heavy trigger pull, which means you have to exert more effort to pull the trigger.

The pistol belongs to the second category of handguns. Nearly all pistols are semi-automatic, which simply means that a bullet is auto-

What to expect from a handgun class:

- Basic safety rules and the reasons for them
- Parts of a pistol and a revolver
- How to load a revolver and a pistol
- How to store a gun safely in the home
- Laws and responsibility of owning a handgun
- When to shoot and when not to shoot
- Proper shooting stances and identifying your dominant eye
- Shooting techniques
- Comparison of handgun calibers and their proper ammunition
- How to clean and care for your handgun
- Hands-on practice at a shooting range
- Trying different types of guns and calibers

How should a lady carry her gun?*

There are some very, very nice purses on the market with hidden pockets designed to carry a handgun. If you always, and I mean *always*, have your hand on your purse, this is an acceptable way to carry a gun. The downside to the holster purse is that too many moms aren't always 100% in control of their purses. If you've ever looked around in a panic for your purse, maybe a purse isn't the best way for you to carry a gun. I favor a small holster that I clip to the waistband of my jeans or slacks. It can easily be covered by a shirt or a jacket, if your state allows carrying concealed weapons and you have a permit.

Another great option for women is the Flashbang holster, which clips to your bra.

*This advice is only useful if you live in a state that allows its citizens to carry a concealed handgun.

matically loaded after each shot, until the magazine is empty. Ammunition is loaded in a detachable magazine, which is typically inserted into the handle of the gun. These magazines usually hold ten rounds (bullets) or more. However, until the slide is pulled back manually, there are no rounds in the chamber. Depending on the individual pistol, it can take a good deal of hand strength to pull back that slide. Practice makes this easier.

After each round is fired, a spring in the magazine pops the next round in place. There's no need to cock a pistol after each shot, which is sometimes required with a revolver. It's one less thing to worry about if you ever have to shoot in self-defense.

If you decide to buy a gun, any gun, buy something that uses commonly found ammunition. Keep in mind that a firearm is going to be useful only as long as you have ammunition. Otherwise, it's kind of like a car that runs out of gas, and beating someone over the head with an unloaded Glock isn't my idea of a good self-defense plan.

Gun enthusiasts will tell you that any gun is a good gun, but when you buy the most popular guns in the most common calibers, ammunition will be easy to come by. One experienced hunter told me, "If you're out hunting and you run out of ammo for your .30–06, it's such a common round that someone nearby is certain to have extra bullets to share." Sharing ammo—I wonder, is that something I should have learned in kindergarten?

Generally, it's quite easy to pick up a box, or ten, of ammunition for the most common calibers of rifles, shotguns, and handguns. The most common calibers of handguns are .22, 9mm, .357, .38, .40, and .45. Stick with a 12- or a 20-gauge shotgun, and you'll almost always find stacks of boxes of shotgun shells at sporting goods stores. The most common calibers of rifles are .22, .30–30, .30–06, .223, and 7.62x39mm (AK–47). My advice is to use a .22 handgun or rifle to perfect your shooting techniques in frequent target practice. You can pick up a box of 500 rounds for less than twenty bucks, and believe me, 500 rounds is a *lot* of shooting!

Don't be afraid of the word "semi-automatic," by the way. If you've ever used a single-shot firearm, you know how time-consuming it is to load another round into the chamber of the gun after every shot. Semi-automatic is *not* a machine gun! The machine guns you see on TV and in movies are *fully automatic* and are extremely expensive and

Know the rules!

- Assume that every gun is loaded and handle it accordingly.
- Always keep the gun pointed in a safe direction.
- Keep your finger off the trigger until you're ready to shoot.
- Know what you're shooting at *and* what is behind that target.
- Be familiar with your gun.

difficult to purchase. As long as your finger is holding that trigger down, an automatic gun will continue firing. I have to admit, I would love to shoot an automatic weapon and will if I ever get the chance, but the semi-automatic feature of a pistol is just a convenience and a time-saver. If you're ever standing between a bad guy and your kids, you'll be grateful that the gun in your hand holds more than six bullets—but that's only if you're willing to pull the trigger.

Part of the responsibility of owning a gun and then becoming trained to shoot it is having the confidence to use your weapon if your life or the lives of your kids are ever on the line. If deep down inside you know you could never shoot another person, gun ownership isn't for you. Criminals will sense your hesitation, but *they* won't hesitate in grabbing your gun and using it against you if they can. Carefully consider how far you're willing to go to protect what is most important to you.

The safest place in the house: a safe-ish room

If your home is the eye of the storm, a safe room is its pupil. Have you given any thought to where your family might take shelter during an especially violent storm or a home invasion? Large-scale disasters, both natural and man-made, usually spawn a higher level of criminal activity, and a Survival Mom would be smart to consider where her family could take shelter in the face of real and present danger.

If you have a concrete, windowless room that is reinforced with steel rebar, you're good to go; however, few modern homes and apartments are equipped with such a room. In many parts of the country, the building code requires a window as a second point of egress, or exit, in every room of the house, which makes for a handy fire escape but increases your home's vulnerability at the same time. Still, you and your family need a safe place within your home. If your kids are ever home alone and need to run to safety, they should know which room of the house is the safest, in case going to a neighbor's house is out of the question.

Assess each room or space in your home. A windowless room is ideal, but if every room has a window, then consider other factors. In case of a fire, is one room easier to escape from than the others? Is one of the rooms equipped with a telephone outlet and connected to a bathroom? Both features are desirable. Is one of the rooms better ventilated than the others? You definitely don't want to run out of oxygen, hunkered

Do you have an early warning system?

Safe rooms are great ideas, but you have to *get* to the safe room first! Don't let weather, a natural disaster, or bad guys catch you by surprise. Pay close attention to weather reports for tracking hurricanes, severe storms, and tornadoes. Even an inexpensive, DIY home security system will sound an alarm, giving you time to sequester your family in safety or, depending on the circumstances, to race to a neighbor's house.

down in a safe room fully equipped with everything but fresh air! In the end, the choicest location may be a bathroom or a closet.

If you have very young children, the best location for a safe room might be their bedroom. It's easier to rush into their room for safety than to run to grab them from their crib and then run to the safe room.

Once a space has been selected, focus on how to fortify it from outside forces. First, the door should be replaced with either a solid-wood door or a steel door, and the wood door jamb should be replaced with either a steel trim or a door jamb made of steel. Use 3-inch screws to attach the door to the frame and set the door so that it opens outward, making it far more difficult for someone to try to force their way in.

This is no time to rely on a measly doorknob lock. Instead, install three evenly placed deadbolt locks and use 3-inch screws to attach the door to the frame. Not many home invaders will want to take the time or have the physical strength to break down such a door. Be absolutely sure that you have keys to every door lock stashed in a secure location outside the room.

A secure door is the first and most important step in shoring up the fortification of your chosen room. Walls are another potentially weak point. A really angry mom can make a dent in one of these with a coffee mug. I know that from personal experience. Interior walls are generally wood-framed with drywall, or gypsum-board, panels covering wires and insulation. Depending on your budget, there is a product called Sure-Board that can make your interior walls non-combustible, safer against hurricane-force winds and earthquakes, and even bulletproof! Sure-Board merges together gypsum board with steel, and although this product seems nearly miraculous, it comes with a hefty price. Eighty square feet, enough to cover one wall in an 8-by-10 room, will cost several hundred dollars. Sure-Board offers free instructional videos, so this can be a DIY project with the right tools and a little know-how.

Sheets of Kevlar, fiberglass, or steel sheathing are other options for making the walls more secure. This is an expensive step, and you may feel that your family will be fine without these extreme measures. It all comes down to assessing the likelihood of a given threat, weighed against the expense, the level of difficulty, and the inconvenience of putting any type of security measure in place.

When you gamble with safety, you bet your life.

—AUTHOR UNKNOWN

Technology has come a long way in the security department, and there are numerous options for making windows more secure. Laminated, tempered, and wired glass can make your windows less vulnerable. The entire window, frame and all, can be replaced with a security window. You can put up security bars if you're going for a neo-prison look or take the simple step of covering the window with security film. Security film makes it far more difficult for someone to break a window and will probably be your cheapest option. If you make a change to the glass in your windows, just be sure you still have the ability to exit in case of a fire or another emergency.

It's also important that the window have either heavy curtains or blinds to prevent intruders from knowing exactly who is home or possibly targeting individuals with a gun.

Depending on your risk assessment, your budget, and the steps you're willing to take, you may decide to leave your walls and windows alone and buy a second shotgun or a better-quality home security system. Remember, there's nothing about preparedness and survival that is "one size fits all."

If money is no object, check out the highly detailed FEMA-approved plans for safe rooms on the agency's website. There are also contractors who specialize in building safe rooms. Again, only you know your family's unique circumstances. You can go all-out and have a state-of-the-art room that Jason Bourne would envy or do the best with what you have. A safe-ish room is far better than nothing.

Once you're satisfied that your safe room is as fortified as your space, time, and budget allow, you'll need to equip it with some basic supplies. Keep in mind that the purpose of a safe room is to be safe for a few hours or maybe a day or two. It's not your new vacation home! A few essential items are:

- A few gallons of water
- Several nutritious snacks per person
- Portable toilet and toilet paper—the GottaGo Toilet is hard to beat (see page 38)
- First-aid kit
- Defensive weapon, or two, and plenty of ammunition
- Landline phone and cell phone

- Dual-powered radio
- Flashlights with extra batteries
- Small, silent distractions for the kids, such as coloring books with crayons
- Fire extinguisher
- Smoke detector and carbon monoxide detector
- Respirator for each person, in case of a fire or poisonous fumes
- Blankets
- Hand and foot warmers
- Prescription medications
- Battery-powered fan with batteries
- Megaphone or air horn to attract attention or call for help
- Keys to the room's locks and the outside doors
- Emergency kits (details in Chapter 11)

baby step

Decide which room will be your safe room and begin collecting items on this list. Store them in a container and add to it whenever you can. Replace the room's door as described, and at the very least you'll have a well-equipped safe room with a sturdy door.

Small, inexpensive security cameras can be purchased online and would be an excellent method of keeping track of intruders and other happenings outside your safe room. Experienced burglars know where to look for these cameras, so give careful consideration as to their placement. A crime prevention officer from a police or sheriff's department will be able to give you sound advice.

Your kids will be fascinated by the safe room—this I can guarantee. I can also guarantee that sooner or later they will make incursions into the room to investigate its contents and sample one or two granola bars. Actually, this is a good sign. They're aware there's something different about this room and explaining to them that it's a cocoon where the family can go to be safe makes sense. Hold a family meeting and talk about the safe room—what it's for and when to use it. Older kids should learn how to lock the room from the inside, close the blinds or curtains, and call 911. Emphasize the fact that the room will likely never be used as a safe room but is there just in case. The novelty will quickly wear off, but the seeds of information will have been planted.

What can an apartment dweller do? Obviously replacing doors and windows is out of the question, but your landlord might allow you to replace the screws in the door hinges, as well as lock strike plates of your front door and the door to your safe room, with 3-inch screws. The lock strike plate is the piece that holds the latch or lock bolt in place and is usually only secured with very short, weak screws. You can still select the most easily secured room, even if it's the bathroom. There are numerous security gadgets available—such as door-stop wedge alarms, door-handle alarms, and glass-break alarms—if installing anything more isn't possible.

Home Security Systems: A Scam or a Life-Saver?

Consider these statistics:

- Seventy-three percent of burglars say they would still rob a house if it had an alarm.
- A home without a security system is two to three times more likely to be burglarized.
- Sixty percent of burglaries attempted on homes with security systems are unsuccessful.
- Fifty-four percent of homeowners with security systems are unsure how to operate their systems!

Based on these varied statistics, it may be hard to decide if a home security system is worth the money. When you apply the concept of layers, though, a system makes a lot of sense. On its own, it may or may not deter a specific criminal on a specific day; however, that alarm system teamed up with security lights, a watchdog, and other measures can make your home a veritable fortress in the eyes of a bad guy.

No security measure is 100% bad-guy-proof, but security systems sometimes fail because the homeowners forget or decide that it's too much of a bother "just this once" to activate the alarm. Even the activation of a door chime will let you know when the kids go in and out of the house. Trust me, that's worth a bundle of money right there.

Security companies offer motion detectors, glass-break alarms, door chimes, video surveillance, remote security devices, flood detectors, panic buttons, wireless technology, and carbon monoxide detectors. If your home or property is large, it's best to consult directly with a home security expert who can put together a customized package for you. All the major security companies, such as ADT and Brink's, have ready-made packages for different budgets and offer their monitoring services for a monthly fee.

If you decide to install security devices yourself, you can shop online or at retailers such as Costco, Radio Shack, and Home Depot. Be aware that while you'll probably save a lot of money if you do your own installation, you'll be on your own when it comes to monitoring the alarms. Fortunately, advances in technology allow you to do this with your cell phone, and that can bring some peace of mind, especially when you're out of town. Cell-phone and alarm-system batteries die, though, and if an alarm goes off, you may not hear it, especially if you happen to be snorkeling or riding a roller coaster at a Six Flags amusement park! A professional monitoring service is worth the money, if your budget allows.

Once a home security system is installed, it's time for some training! Everyone in the family should know how to arm and disarm the alarm system, what to do if it should go off accidentally, and what to do in a true emergency, such as a home invasion, burglary, or fire.

If your alarm system goes off or you hear a noise that would possibly signal an intruder, have the children stay in their bedrooms or head to the safe room. If there are multiple children in separate rooms, designate one child's room as the "safe room." Once inside that room, lock the door and stay on the phone with the 911 operator until officers arrive. Keep a spare door key in that room, so that it can be thrown from a window to the officers for entry into your home. Let the officers clear the home and make their way to you.

Honesty Isn't Always the Best Policy

In survival circles you will often hear the term "OpSec," or Operational Security. Even if your only "operation" is stocking up on a month's worth of rice and ravioli, you still need to keep that information to yourself. In case nosy neighbors, burglars, or an angry mob with pitch-forks invade your living space, there are three principles that will help keep your stored goods and supplies safe:

1. Inaccessibility
2. Camouflage
3. Silence

Unless home invaders have an unlimited amount of time and are unconcerned about law enforcement, they are in a hurry. Their goal is to grab anything of value, as much as will fit in their pockets, and then leave. If your firearms, vital documents, valuables, and even stored food are difficult to access, it's likely they will leave empty-handed. A wall- or floor-mounted safe is a deterrent, but so are many sneaky hiding spots. Just make sure you keep track of what is hidden—and where!

Some of the more clever hiding places a Survival Mom can stash her valuables are:

- In battery cases, like the ones on the back of every remote control. They're good for hiding tiny valuables.
- Behind framed photographs. This is an especially good location for valuable documents.
- Inside a "dummy" VHS tape inserted in an old VCR.
- In a "dummy" electrical outlet. The outlet is there, but when unscrewed from the wall, an electrical box, empty of wires, waits to be filled.
- Inside an empty package of frozen food filled with valuables, re-glued shut, and then stored back in the freezer.
- Inside a used toy, tucked away in a toy box.

It takes a lot of time for thieves to look for false walls and check every floorboard. Their main goal is almost always to grab and run. The more you can conceal, the safer your stored goods will be from greedy hands.

Camouflage doesn't only come in shades of green and brown! An old beat-up storage bin labeled "Extra Cords" will certainly not appeal to thieves, but it is a perfect way to store important tools or your stash of brown rice. "Old Toys" or "Extra Yarn" won't even get a second glance from most intruders. One friend camouflages her important receipts in a small box labeled "Extra Tampons." Even her husband won't go near that box! Keep in mind, thieves can't steal what they can't see or find.

One final layer in keeping your stored goods secure is to remember the adage, "Loose lips sink ships." Your friends may be completely trustworthy, but whom might they tell? And whom might their friends tell? If grocery store shelves are ever emptied and remain that way for more than 3 or 4 days, it won't be long until someone somewhere remembers *you*!

Give Your Property a Security Scan

If your home is the eye of the storm, you must be sure there is a high level of protection around it. Systematically scan your home from the outside, doing a complete, 360-degree scan of your home and property. If you live in an apartment, scan the walkway from your car to your apartment. Become aware of potential hiding places for bad guys and get to know your apartment complex thoroughly, so if you need to make an escape, there are numerous routes you're familiar with.

I tend to be pretty methodical, so when I made a security scan of our property, I started at one corner, walked around the perimeter of our backyard, and made notes of how we could "harden" our home. I started at the west corner of our property and contemplated the side gate that opens into our backyard. I thought, "What could we do to make this more secure?" My short list of solutions included replacing the gate with something sturdier and with more mass and purchasing a much heavier lock. I also thought of making sure that no smaller objects that might provide a step-stool for an intruder are placed against the gate. (I saw my son use an overturned bucket to open the latch, which gave me this idea.)

Once past the side gate, I scanned the side yard. What could be done to "harden" the outside windows? How could we make our backyard look less inviting? Perhaps planting a few cacti against the side fence would be a good idea. I could allow our rose bushes to grow untrimmed and become much larger. (Have you ever had a close encounter with a large, mature rose bush?) What could we do to discourage someone from hopping over our back wall?

The world is filled with violence. Because criminals carry guns, we decent law-abiding citizens should also have guns. Otherwise they will win and the decent people will lose.

—JAMES EARL JONES

Do this scan again after the sun goes down. What can be seen from the outside at night that might endanger your family and property? Are your kids' rooms brightly lit, but their window blinds allow peeping toms to see what's inside? Is your fancy new computer visible from a small, side window? If you have motion-detector or photosensor lights, are they working properly? Are there any lightbulbs that need to be replaced?

If there's ever a time you may want your home completely blacked out at night, be sure to do regular nighttime scans. Even a sliver of light can give bad guys more information than you want them to have.

When the outdoor security scan is finished, do the same thing within your house. Go from room to room and check every window and door to the outside. How could you "'harden'" those entrances, camouflage valuables, and deter criminals?

The survival principle of thinking in terms of layers applies to home security. It's not enough to just have an alarm system. It's not enough to have a big, mean dog or be trained in the use of a firearm. Planting a row of 3-foot-tall chollas (a.k.a. the Cactus from Hell) around the perimeter of your property isn't enough, but all of these elements together create layers of protection. If a bad guy gets past one, there are several more he, or she, has to cope with.

Three key concepts to remember are inaccessibility, deterrence, and camouflage. Make your home a low-value, high-risk target for bad guys. Here are a few commonsense steps to make sure your property is more secure:

It is surmounting difficulties that makes heroes.

—LOUIS PASTEUR

- Every window and sliding glass door should have a lock.

- Pay particular attention to all entry points that are obscured from view. Focus motion lights on these areas and make them difficult to access.

- Install deadbolt locks on all doors that lead outside. Chain and flip locks aren't good choices for security. Talk with a locksmith to determine the best lock for your doors.

- Re-key or change all the locks when moving in to a new home.

- If you sometimes open a window for ventilation, make sure there's a pin or a dowel in the tracks so the window can't be opened any further.

- Install a fence. If you already have a fence, is it sturdy enough and tall enough? Are there locks on all gates?

- Make your home look uninteresting and downright poor. If it already looks that way, you're ahead of the game! If your kids have fancy bikes and scooters and sometimes leave them outside, criminals may wonder what other expensive toys might be inside.

- Re-think using your master bedroom to store your valuables. Burglars often head there first but generally leave the kids' rooms alone.

- Close blinds and curtains in the early evening hours.

- Get in the habit of doing a door and window check every night before going to bed.

- If you have an alarm system, make sure to prominently display the alarm company's window decals and front-yard sign.

- When you purchase an expensive appliance or electronics, cut the packaging into small pieces before putting it in your trash container. A huge box labeled "52-inch plasma TV" sticking out on the top is like putting up a neon sign, "We have valuables! Come rob us!"

- Don't advertise that you have guns, as in those window stickers, "This house protected by a .357 Magnum." Bad guys will either come looking for your guns when they're sure you're not home or they'll have their own guns cocked and ready when they break in. If you have guns and are prepared to use them, the element of surprise should be on your side, not theirs.

Police departments offer free information for citizens who want to make their homes or apartments more secure, and are willing to meet with groups of neighbors to discuss security issues and answer questions. They know better than anyone how safe your particular neighborhood is and security strategies unique to your area. Ask locksmiths and alarm companies for advice, and if you belong to a homeowners' association, enlist its support. After all, home values fall in neighborhoods with a high crime rate.

Safety-Savvy Kids

More than a safe home, I want safe kids. If my home burned down and all was lost, I would feel completely blessed if my kids were unharmed and we were together. However, I know that I can't be every-where 24/7. At some point my kids need to know about staying safe on their own, but that information needs to come in measured amounts and at appropriate ages.

Almost all the security measures discussed in this chapter can be done without alarming the kids. There's no need for them to know why you're installing motion-detector lights outside or replacing a bedroom door with one that is solid wood. Taking Judo or target-shooting lessons is just another way to spend some fun time together. Later, they'll understand the "why" of your actions, but by the time that happens, they'll likely have the maturity to appreciate and under-stand without becoming overly fearful.

It can be a little tricky raising kids who are as wise as serpents but as harmless as doves (a great biblical analogy). We all want our kids to have worry-free childhoods, with plenty of playtime, fresh air, and good times, but as adults, we lost our innocence a long time ago. We know exactly the types of dangers that lurk and all too often prey on trusting little ones. If there's one key we, as parents, hold when it comes to keeping our kids safe, it's this: teaching our kids to *obey*.

Obedience sounds kind of old fashioned, doesn't it? I hope the con-cept doesn't rock your world, but when our kids obey us quickly and without argument, it's easier to keep them out of harm's way. See, parents are a lot like air-traffic controllers: We can spot trouble, threats, and danger that our kids simply can't.

I've taught my kids to pay attention to the tone of my voice, and I've even modeled it for them. I use a completely different tone when I call out, "Andrew, lunch is ready," than I would if I saw a group of menacing people headed our way or noticed a speeding car racing toward him and his skateboard. My kids know that when they hear a sense of urgency, or even harshness in my voice, they'd better obey immediately.

Imagine going through the effort of setting up a safe room in your house, equipping it for emergencies, and ordering your kids to run to the room, only to hear, "In a minute, Mom!" They may not perceive danger, but if *you* do, obedience isn't negotiable.

Add to your obedience lessons a code word or phrase that sends the message, "OBEY NOW!" The one my family uses is, "Where's the black cat?" We don't have a black cat, but if my kids hear those words, they

> *Always do what you are afraid to do.*
>
> —RALPH WALDO EMERSON

know to go to a safe part of the house immediately. That same sentence could be used in public if I sense a threat— my kids would then know that immediate obedience is expected. If I can't give a verbal warning, I've been known to tap my ear twice to send the message, "Listen and obey!"

Games such as "Mother May I" and "Simon Says" provide easy and fun ways for kids of all ages to learn to listen carefully and obey. Play one of these games with your kids and then sit down with them for a discussion about the importance of listening and obeying immediately. Give loads of sincere compliments when they obey the first time, whether they're told to wash dishes, feed the dog, or get in the car and lock the door.

Finally, honor your kids' instincts and teach them to listen to the small voice that whispers, "Danger!" Too often, adults brush aside concerns voiced by their kids, certain that the kids' fanciful imaginations have conjured up another boogeyman. But when we dismiss their fears and warnings, we're teaching them to ignore their own survival instincts and lose trust in the very people commissioned with their safety. If a person, place, or situation makes them feel "funny" or "strange," that's a sufficient warning for mom or dad to step in.

My husband and I decided a long time ago that we would rather risk hurt feelings on the part of some adult, even a family member, than place our children in jeopardy in the name of politeness.

Act as if what you do makes a difference. It does.

—WILLIAM JAMES

Situational safety lessons for kids

When answering the door or phone—A basic safety lesson for all kids is how to answer the phone or the door if Mom and Dad aren't around. We've taught our kids to ignore all phone calls coming from numbers they don't recognize. When they answer the phone, they're to say, "My dad (or mom) is outside right now and can't come to the phone."

A ringing doorbell presents a different dilemma, though. If the person at the door is checking out the neighborhood for a future burglary and no one answers the door at your house, it marks your house as a target. On the other hand, if your kid answers the door and a shady character is standing there, what should be done then? Teach them not to open the door for strangers, ever, but respond with,

"My dad's asleep, and I don't want to wake him up." Most bad guys are looking for easy targets and no complications—and that includes not waking a grumpy dad.

Spend some time role playing these situations with your kids. Even older kids might get flustered when confronted with a real stranger at the door, so a few practice sessions will help everyone know what to do and what to say. These lessons will become particularly important when your kids are old enough to stay at home alone.

Around firearms—The very best firearms training for your kids begins at an early age. When they are as young as 3 years old, you can begin teaching basic safety rules. The Eddie Eagle GunSafe Program, developed by the NRA, teaches these three simple rules if a child sees a gun:

- Stop!
- Don't touch!
- Leave the area!
- Go tell an adult.

This is a good place to begin, but eventually your kids may think they've outgrown these rules. At this point, safe hands-on practice at a firing range is the best option. I like firing ranges because even sassy kids will pay attention to a gruff range officer, and believe me, you don't want to disobey one of these officers—ever!

Believe it or not, one of my goals has been for my kids to be bored when it comes to guns. We've taken our daughter to the range so often that she now carries along a book to read. When she's finished shooting 30 or 40 rounds, she sits on the sidelines with her custom-made ear-plugs and reads. She's bored with the whole gun scene, and I know if she ever encountered a gun at a friend's house, she'd roll her eyes and say: "This is so lame. Let's go and do something fun!"

I'll never forget the time my husband bought a new shotgun. My son was entranced, and as soon as I returned from a business trip, he led me by the hand to the closet where the unloaded gun sat. He marveled at the design and picked it up in his 7-year-old hands. He was positively giddy when we took it to the range for the first time. My husband crouched behind and supported him, as he aimed and pulled the trigger. That gun kicked like the proverbial mule, and my son hasn't wanted to touch it since. Perfect!

On the other hand, when kids have never seen a real gun but are exposed to the excitement of "shoot 'em up" movies and TV shows, they are far more likely to handle this forbidden object and are less likely to know its power and the damage it can do. After all, shooting a gun looks like so much fun on TV! If they've played with Nerf guns and water pistols, they might think they know all there is to know about guns, but they couldn't be more wrong.

Shooting ranges, Fish and Game departments, outdoor stores, and organizations such as The Appleseed Project and the NRA offer gun safety classes for kids; many times these classes are free. A small investment in time and money will go a long way to gun-proof your kids.

At school or away from home—Our kids begin to live at least part of their lives away from us at a fairly early age. They're off to school, soccer practice, summer camps, and scout meetings. When we can't be there with our little darlings, we can still provide them with a few basic pieces of equipment in their own survival kits. They can keep these supplies in large Ziploc bags in their backpacks or school lockers, as well as in their overnight bags. Keep in mind that you're not packing all-inclusive emergency kits, but just enough provisions to help them feel secure and loved until you're reunited. Here are a few suggestions:

> *Courage is knowing what not to fear.*
> —PLATO

Sanitation
- Small package of tissues
- Hand sanitizer or packages of hand wipes

Sustenance
- Hard candy
- High-calorie energy bar
- Chewing gum
- A couple of cans of Ensure or a similar nutritional beverage

Survival
- Bandanna (brainstorm ideas with your child for different ways to use it)
- Water bottle or water pouch
- Plastic poncho
- Hand and feet warmers
- Extra pair of wool socks
- Light stick and/or headlamp

- Small pocketknife (unless having one will get him or her expelled from school)
- Band-Aids and small pieces of moleskin to cover blisters
- Easy-to-read map with routes home clearly marked

Security

- List of emergency phone numbers
- Cell phone
- Sturdy whistle
- Money

Sanity

- Small pad of paper and pencil
- Small paperback or puzzle book
- MP3 player or iPod

If the family will be outdoors camping or hiking, you can beef up their kits with more of these items. It will be important to do some role-playing and/or discussing what is in their kits and how and when to use each item. Of course your kid's kit will contain items that are age-appropriate. Emphasize to your children that their Survival Packs should always be with them.

If your area is prone to extreme weather or natural disasters of some sort, talk with your school administrators about plans they have in place. Don't assume that they have given extreme emergencies more attention than a cursory blurb in a handbook for parents. Moms have told me horror stories of lockdown situations or prolonged fire drills at school in which their kids didn't even have access to the basics such as water. It is really up to you to prod school officials into action if none has been taken. If a blizzard shuts down access to the school or flooded roads make getting home impossible, a survival pack—brought to school by each child, stored in a classroom closet, and containing a change of clothes, a toothbrush, toothpaste, and a small blanket— would make life a lot easier for the kids *and* their teachers.

History is a vast early warning system.

—NORMAN COUSINS

☑ Refer to your home as a cozy, safe nest or refuge. Birds are an excellent example of home safety. They conceal their nests, guard their nests, and run off any potential enemy. As you take steps to do the same with your home, use this example from nature.

☑ Teach the four colors of situational awareness and have your kids identify the level of awareness of characters in TV shows, pets (mine are *always* at the Level White), and family members as you go through your daily routines.

☑ Participate in The Appleseed Project weekend. The whole family will learn a bit of American history and rifle marksmanship skills. Both kids and adults love seeing their shooting skills improve in just a matter of a few hours, and the weekend offers plenty of recognition for improvement and family time.

☑ Make safety drills fun by requiring family members to hop, skip, or jump to the designated safety areas. Do frequent drills until you're confident that everyone knows just what to do in a scary situation.

☑ Make a copy of the list for each kid's survival kit and have your children begin collecting all listed items. Put the kits together, teaching your kids how and when to use each item. The kit should then be kept in a school locker or possibly in the backpack that the child leaves the house with every morning.

The Prepared Family

Family Preparedness Plan: Home and Personal Security

My plan to minimize distractions and improve situational awareness:

☐ Minimize what I carry

☐ Keep my hands free as much as possible

☐ Train children to stay near me or ask for permission before wandering off

☐ Minimize use of cell phone, texting, or iPod when out and about

☐ Other:_____

☐ Other: _____

Errands and locations in which I am most vulnerable:

☐ _____

☐ _____

☐ _____

☐ _____

My plan to improve my personal and my family's safety:

☐ Martial arts training

- My choice: _____

☐ Firearms training

- Rifle
- Shotgun
- Pistol

☐ Firearms training for children

- Yes
- No

☐ Establish a safe room

- Location: _____

  – Strengths: _____

  – Weaknesses: _____

- Strengthen entrances, both doors and windows
- Equip with survival basics
- Family drill

- ☐ Install a home security system
  - Yes
  - No
  - Family drill
- ☐ 360-degree home security scan
  - Fortify these areas outdoors:

  _____

  _____

  _____

  _____

  _____

  - Add outdoor lighting here:

  _____

  _____

  _____

  _____

  - Indoor security
    – Windows
    – Exterior doors
  - Consult local police or sheriff's department for additional security ideas
- ☐ Safer kids
  - Procedures for answering the door and the phone when we are away
  - Firearms safety training (whether we own firearms)
  - Pack a survival kit for each child in the family

CHAPTER 9

Survival Finances

I've been rich-ish, and I've been poor, and let me tell you: Being rich is better. That's probably no surprise. Money in the bank eases worries, smoothes just about any path you wish to take, and allows for fun little splurges and exotic vacations along the way. Being rich gets my vote any day.

In this same life, I've also had to make the decision, "Do I pay the electric bill or health insurance this month?" Those were scary days that extended into weeks and then months. There was no more cable TV or YMCA membership. We limited cell phone calls and canceled piano lessons, and when the dishwasher went kaput, we washed dishes by hand—for weeks. I hated it. Every expense was fretted over, and every dollar was tracked. Trying to make ends meet was my new (unpaid) part-time job.

It was just a stroke of luck that my husband and I had agreed to begin stocking up on food and other supplies a year or so before our family income spiraled downward. One month, when we were hit especially hard with expenses and had almost no income, our "Big Pantry," as we called it, kept food on the table.

It's impossible to stock up on extra food or toilet paper when the money just isn't there. The desire to buy gold or silver as a hedge against inflation isn't enough. You need cash to make those purchases. Families in debt will find it very difficult to add preparedness expenses to an already stressed budget, and if one of the main breadwinners is out of work, the situation is even worse.

Top causes of bankruptcy:

- Medical expenses
- Credit card debt
- Job loss
- Overspending
- Divorce
- Unexpected disasters

Sadly, that's the situation in which many Americans find themselves. I've gone through tough financial times and have dozens of ideas to share with you in this chapter that will inspire and help you to survivalize your family's financial condition.

Financial survival may be the most important factor in determining how well your family is prepared for uncertain times.

|||||||||||||||||||||||||||||||||||||||||||||||||||||||||||||||||||||||||||||||||||||||||||||||||||||||||||||||||||

Pay Off Debt or Save?

This is a question that used to be quite easy to answer but now, not so much. Everything about preparedness and being a Survival Mom is unique to each family's circumstances, but here are the pros and cons of paying off debt versus adding to your savings account.

Pay off debt first

This has always been the standard advice of any financial advisers worth their salt. Life without debt allows a family to choose how *they* want to spend their money rather than have those expenses dictated by creditors. If you enjoy a debt-free life, you know what I'm talking about. It really is financial freedom.

One reason to be debt-free is the very ugly possibility of future hyperinflation. It's not the wild-eyed, extreme scenario it once was; nor is it something that only happens in third-world countries. For years our government has followed the same disastrous financial choices as Argentina, Yugoslavia, and Weimar Germany, where hyperinflation left most of the population living below poverty level. In those countries, printing money out of thin air to cover massive and excessive government spending resulted in out-of-control inflation that increased so rapidly that sometimes prices changed between the time a customer entered a store and the time he or she paid for the purchases! If it happened there, it can happen here.

Imagine a scenario in which someone hands you a check for $50 to pay for a product or service, and by the time you reach the bank the next day, the check is worth only $47.75. In a time of hyperinflation, money exchanges hands very rapidly, because its value is likely declining even as it sits in your wallet or bank account!

Mini-Glossary

Inflation: a rise in prices of goods and services

Hyperinflation: a rapid, out-of-control inflation

Deflation: a decline of prices over a period of time

Unsecured debt: money borrowed without providing any collateral

Hyperinflation is particularly dangerous if you have debt, especially unsecured debt such as credit cards and personal loans, because the interest rates on your debt can increase at any time. That type of debt doesn't have a fixed interest. Since the prices of all goods and services will also increase, you're not left with much extra money to pay those higher payments on your debt.

13 ways to prepare for hyperinflation

A mom could get whiplash trying to keep track of the widely differing opinions of financial experts. Many claim that America is headed toward deflation, others claim that a deflationary depression is on its way, and yet many voices are crying, "Get ready for hyperinflation!" Hyperinflation is particularly dangerous for families because the prices of necessary goods (think fuel, energy, and food) will skyrocket, leaving little money, if any, for anything else.

Here are some commonsense steps that will help you and your family be in a more stable position:

1. Pay off any debt that has an adjustable interest rate as quickly and as soon as possible. Unsecured credit card debt, in particular, is vulnerable to increased interest rates that would demand more and more income from a family already strapped to cover the most basic necessities.

2. While interest rates are low, investigate the possibility of refinancing your mortgage. If your mortgage rate is already low, and fixed, focus debt repayment first on anything that has an adjustable rate.

3. Consider ways to decrease your transportation expenses. Should gasoline prices soar out of control, you may be very happy for a job that is within walking or biking distance. Can you sell that second or third vehicle and pocket the savings in gas, upkeep, and insurance? Be strategic and purposeful in deciding which vehicles to keep, sell, and/or purchase.

4. Never buy new if you can help it. Craigslist, eBay, Freecycle, resale shops, and garage sales offer nearly everything you'll ever need. Refuse to pay full retail and use the savings elsewhere.

5. Have a backup plan for every major appliance in your home. If electricity prices become outrageous, do you have everything necessary for washing clothes by hand and drying them on a clothesline, as well as an old-fashioned dish-drainer or two?

6. Visit local coin shops and become educated about purchasing gold and silver. It's easy to make poor decisions in a panic, and this is no time to lose money making investments in the unknown. As the dollar loses its value, precious metals increase in value.

7. Continue stocking up on food and household supplies. When prices increase, this will give you a much-needed cushion of time. The price of food *always* increases during hyperinflation.

8. If restaurant meals are part of your routine, cutting back is one of the easiest steps you can take to save money and learn how to make more meals from scratch. That will be especially important if you ever need to rely on your stored food.

9. Have a passport for every member of your family, just in case. This isn't paranoia; it's just a precaution if you ever need to leave the country to travel or pursue a job in another country.

10. Discover new ways for your family to earn money. As soon as they're old enough, every member of the family should have a way of earning a little extra money. A side business that involves everyone is even better.

11. Consider how you might establish sustainable sources of food and water. This will involve gardening, planting fruit-bearing trees, and, perhaps, even purchasing land with a natural source of water. There is no survival without food and water, so these should be a top priority.

12. Beef up your home's security and your own personal security. Empty store shelves, scarce resources, and overwhelmed law enforcement are common in countries where hyperinflation is a fact of life. Proactive steps in this area just make sense.

13. Stay positive. The future is unknown, but what *is* known is the importance of family, friends, and positive mental attitude. Survival experts say this is the key to surviving difficult circumstances. You might as well start practicing now!

If hyperinflation never occurs, you'll be enjoying a debt-free lifestyle, with investments in precious metals, stored food and supplies to rotate into your family's daily life, and a secure home or apartment. Being a Survival Mom is being a smart mom, and "smart" means being proactive and postponing that panic attack for another day, when you're not so busy!

When *is* it smart to save?

Prominent financial guru Suze Orman has always recommended, "Pay off debt!" but now with our shaky economy and job market, she has a different take on things. Her advice is that it's more important than ever to have at least 8 months of savings set aside, even if it means paying only the minimal amount on credit cards for a while. The average length of unemployment is now more than 8 months. How many families do you know who could survive 8 months with little to no income?

The bottom line is, if you lose your job and can't pay your bills, mortgage or rent, the best credit score in town won't help you. The bank will begin foreclosure proceedings, the landlord will take measures to evict you, and those darn bill collectors will be calling at all hours of the day. Remember, money in the bank is the difference between desperation and having options.

Should you keep cash at home?

In times of extreme financial crisis, banks have been known to lock their doors and take a temporary "bank holiday." Always keep enough cash hidden at home to cover at least a few days' expenses, such as food, fuel, and medicine.

With money in the bank, your family can continue paying bills while you look for another job. If you've been stocking up on food and supplies, that's even better. Those "hard goods" are an insurance policy against difficult times as well as inflation. Think about it. If you have enough food and supplies to last 3 months, you'll need that much less actual cash saved to cover those expenses during that time frame.

||||||||||||||||||||||||||||||||||||||||||||||||||||||||||||||||||||||||||||||||||||||||||||||||||||||||||||||||||||

The Worst Move You Can Make Right Now: Advice for Every Survival Mom

The truth about me is that I love to spend money. Hoo boy. I love going to an upscale mall and looking for fun, unique things to buy. I adore spoiling my kids, and looking for little splurges that I know will bring smiles to their faces brings me joy.

I don't do that so much anymore, though. I've made a commitment to be smarter with our money. Splurges that turn into money-spending orgies are just plain dumb.

I don't know what your personal circumstances are, how much money you have in the bank, or how secure your income source is, but

A Survival Mom's Story
Karey McKenzie, California

For most of us, a tent is a fun, temporary shelter for family campouts. To Karey McKenzie, 42, of San Diego, it may be her future home. I first got to know Karey in an online discussion about buying a tent. (Which brands are the best? What features should I look for?) Little did I know that she was shopping for her next home and that her family might soon be homeless.

Karey is a manicurist who once had a thriving business and a client list that included some of San Diego's wealthiest women. She and her husband, who owns his own car-detailing company, enjoyed a simple life not far from the beach and had decided that the self-employed life was the life for them. Their son, now 13, is Karey's pride and joy.

In 2009, the family's income hit a downward spiral that forced them into some difficult decisions. Their second car was sold. Karey gave up her cell phone and permanently shut off cable TV service. One step at a time, she deleted every extra expense and determined that her family would somehow survive this setback.

But then, Karey is a survivor. She is a child of divorced parents; her mother had married a man who was verbally and physically abusive. She remembers being held hostage by him one evening when her mother was late getting home from work. "I *know* I am a survivor, and I often wonder if God put these moments in my life to bring me to where I am now," Karey says.

By October 2010, "our eyes were opened," Karey says. "We knew that the economy wasn't going to make a quick comeback and that our devastated businesses would probably remain that way. We were pinching pennies, but it was obvious that our government was not."

This is when Karey morphed into a Survival Mom. Her first step was to research practical ways to survive hard times. She says: "I knew I had to get things right the first time, with no regrets. We don't have the money to make mistakes."

She and her husband decided to put their small tax refund toward the purchase of long-term food storage, a pressure canner, and a food dehydrator. Every little bonus, every cash gift, is turned into something that will make the difference between her family's survival and disaster. She taught herself how to can meat and produce, and one of her clients allows her to garden a small plot of land on the client's property.

Despite these hardships, or maybe *because* of them, her attitude remains positive and her sense of humor is well intact. "My advice for someone who has just realized the importance of preparedness is not to feel overwhelmed. It's wasted emotion. Research, learn, and then do something every day. It all adds up. Above all, don't focus on what you *don't* have," Karey says.

here is my urgent advice: DO NOT SPEND MONEY FRIVOLOUSLY OR THOUGHTLESSLY. Even if you have deep pockets, there are so many critical ways you can help your family's future be more secure. An expensive vacation or other expenses can be canceled or postponed in favor of buying several months' worth of food, precious metals, a fuel-efficient car, home-defense firearms and ammo, water barrels—you name it. You're one of the lucky Survival Moms who has the ability to prepare without crippling the family budget.

On the other hand, if you're on a tight budget, and most Americans are, you're already pinching pennies. You still have options, though, and many of them are discussed in this chapter. What can you sell? What service can you provide? Is there a part-time job that might bring in enough money to go toward debt or food storage? This is the time to get serious about clipping coupons, shopping only at consignment and secondhand stores, and even limiting the amount of driving you do.

There's an increased level of uncertainty and turmoil in the Middle East, where much of our oil comes from. Gas prices are in a constant state of flux. Worldwide food shortages are being reported. The severe 2010 winter in Mexico devastated the region's production of produce, much of which fills the produce section of American grocery stores. We're dealing with a double whammy—rising food *and* volatile gas prices.

Sometimes preparedness is a fun adventure, and there isn't a sense of urgency. That isn't the case anymore. Set your priorities, take a deep breath, and stay focused. Just don't buy that expensive handbag—at least not right now.

INSTANT SURVIVAL TIP

Gifts for birthdays and holidays can really take a bite out of the budget. This year, start giving the gift of experiences rather than things. For Mother's Day, take the family for a long walk or bike ride, followed by a picnic lunch. People will always remember the experience long after the thing has been lost, broken, or thrown out.

Between a Rock and a Hard Place

So what does a savvy Survival Mom do if she's on a tight budget already? Do you save money first or pay off debt? Pay this month's bills or buy extra groceries for food storage?

These challenges are tough choices, and every family will have to set their own priorities and make a plan that suits their circumstances and goals. Generally, though, you'll have to buckle down and do two things: spend less and earn more.

Spend less

When our family business was circling the drain, I pulled up our bank account records and went through them line by painful line. Nothing was sacred, not even my son's guitar lessons or regular dinners out. We cut our cable TV down to about fifteen channels and kept the Internet connection but nothing else. I discovered that we rarely used the long-distance service on our home phone, so—whoosh!—that was gone with a phone call. I called our insurance agent to find ways to lower our car insurance but ended up adding two more features to our policies. I guess she had eaten her Wheaties that morning. Oh well.

Lessons from the Great Depression

What did survivors of the Great Depression of the 1930s know about survival? Quite a lot, actually. It's amazing how creative you can be when you're down to nothing. For example:

- Depression-era knitters unraveled old sweaters, washed the yarn and then used it to knit something new.

- Lard, bacon grease, and ketchup sandwiches filled people's tummies, even if this food lacked in presentation.

- People worked hard for a single meal as payment.

- Women living in the Dust Bowl region cooked and canned tumbleweed.

- Families moved in with each other.

- People raised most of what they ate.

- Bartering for goods and trading work for goods was common.

- Nothing went to waste. A newspaper or a Sear's catalog was sometimes used in place of toilet paper.

- People simply didn't own much.

- Moms took old clothes and remade them into new outfits in smaller sizes.

- Vacant lots turned into productive gardens by hard-working people.

- Kids got one pair of shoes each fall. When their shoes wore out or became too small, they just went barefoot.

- People hitched their Model Ts to a horse when they couldn't afford gas.

- People walked the railroads looking for coal that had fallen out of coal cars.

- They bought discounted stale bread at the end of the day from bakeries.

- People went door to door selling things.

- Neighbors held "rent parties" to collect money for an especially needy family who couldn't pay the rent that month.

- Every bit of fabric was saved to use as patches on clothing or quilts.

- People rented out spare bedrooms for extra money.

As you dig through your financial records, you'll likely find areas of waste and expenses you didn't realize were there. When I went through our cell phone bill, I discovered we were paying over $7 a month for a game my son had downloaded and subscribed to. Then, imagine my surprise when I found a monthly charge of $14.95 for a credit report service we didn't even use. I used to think these little expenses didn't matter, but they add up. Those two charges alone would pay for a date night for my husband and me. Trust me, every dollar counts!

Other Survival Moms have passed along their great money-saving tips to me:

- When you're at the grocery store, ready to check out, look over everything in your cart and take out five items you really don't need after all.

- Buy food in bulk but be sure to check the price per unit to make sure you're getting the best deal. When you buy something in bulk, you won't need to go to the grocery store and be tempted to make unnecessary purchases as often.

- If your kids like juice drinks, water these drinks down. It's less sugar for the kids, which is a good thing.

- If you can't pay for something with cash, it's a serious warning sign that you don't really need it.

- Stash surprise money and let it accumulate to help with your savings or to make a big purchase.

- Get the most basic plans you can for cell phone, telephone, cable, and Internet services. It won't be long before you don't miss the bells and whistles.

- Don't let food go to waste. Track how much food is thrown out because it rots or because leftovers are never eaten. It's appalling!

- Don't allow yourself to make impulse buys at the grocery store. Make a menu, shop the menu, and then make the meals on the menu! You'll be surprised by how efficient that system is!

- Go out only to restaurants that are offering a discount or coupons and then stick with the basics. Forget the appetizer, dessert, and wine!

- Use the dollar movie rental boxes instead of going to the movie theater. Pop your own popcorn, turn off the lights, and snuggle. It's a lot more fun!

If you want children to keep their feet on the ground, put some responsibility on their shoulders.

—ABIGAIL VAN BUREN

- Give up cable TV altogether and buy an HD antenna. You'll be amazed at the picture! These antennas really work.
- If you're going somewhere and know that you'll be tempted to spend what you don't have, leave your wallet at home. Don't even try sneaking a debit card into your pocket! (Can you tell that I've done this?)
- Stay away from the mall and any other store that lures you into buying.
- Grow as much of your own produce as possible. Increase the size of your garden just a little bit each year and plant fruit trees and berry bushes if you can.
- Maintain your car in excellent condition so you won't have to buy another one. In the meantime, try to save up enough money to buy the next vehicle with cash.

Did you know that you can become a coupon queen using just online coupon sites? I didn't believe it until a friend showed me her enormous stash of food she had purchased, along with her receipts. The trick is combining coupons with grocery store sales and double- or triple-coupon days as often as you can. I actually get a rush of adrenaline when I see the tab for my food diminish with each coupon and then hear those sweet words, "You saved 72% today!" Woohoo! Better than two margaritas!

You don't need the Sunday paper to be a coupon-clipper!

Check out these websites:

- TheCouponClippers.com
- SouthernSavers.com
- SmartSource.com
- RedPlum.com
- Kroger.com
- Hip2Save.com

Earn more

Cutting out unnecessary expenses probably won't be enough to make life financially comfortable during tight times. In fact, many families have already eliminated every possible extra and are still struggling. As Dave Ramsey says, you have an income crisis. The second piece of financial survival, then, is developing other streams of income. This is key.

I've been able to be a stay-at-home mom during my entire mom-career for one reason: I had a side business. When I was a classroom teacher, 18 years ago, I found myself signing an agreement form with a direct sales company. Without a single shred of sales or business experience, I impulsively launched what would become a very success-ful venture. Looking back, that blind leap of faith was a brilliant move. I didn't realize it at the time, but I had opened the floodgates to an additional stream of income.

How I built my blog into a source of income

I never dreamed I would make money by writing a blog. That was never my intention. In fact, when I read websites that promised to teach me how to make money from my blog, for the life of me, I couldn't figure out how it was to be done.

Always the simpleton, I decided to follow directions just as they were given. More experienced bloggers told me to start by signing up as an Amazon affiliate. I would earn a whole 6% from any purchases made by readers clicking to Amazon from my site. Since I was garnering a whole hundred readers a day, that didn't sound too promising. However, the day came when I checked my affiliate records and discovered that I had earned $1.72. Some blessed soul had bought four books from Amazon with a click from my site. Tears came to my eyes (no kidding!), and I realized, "*This proves it can be done!*" I was on cloud nine until my daughter said, "Mom, I can make more than that baby-sitting!"

I didn't let that discourage me. Soon afterward, I had my first advertiser! Now I could proudly announce to my family that I was earning a whole $75 per month with my blog, plus those big Amazon earnings, of course! Well, over time I added other advertisers, signed up with more affiliate programs that were of interest to my readers, and my income grew.

Now, I'm no expert when it comes to building a website or a blog, but here are some tips for creating an online presence and income that have worked for me:

1. Decide on a domain name for your site. I purchased mine from GoDaddy, but there are many other companies that offer the same service. Your domain and blog name should be memorable and not too lengthy.

2. Your website or blog should tell others what you have to offer. For example, a website that teaches canning using step-by-step instructions, with photos and videos, will soon attract visitors. If you know how to weld, do the same thing. People *want* to learn new skills. Smart people want to learn practical skills.

Well-behaved women seldom make history.

—*LAUREL THATCHER ULRICH*

3. Are you witty? People love to laugh. If you can combine that with teaching them something, that's even better.

4. If putting a website together is 100% foreign to you (it was to me!), there are tutorials and websites galore. Go out and buy a how-to book *only* if you absolutely must have a hard copy in your hands. There are many smart people whose online businesses teach others how to create websites and online businesses! Go figure!

5. Two sites that have taught me the most about how to create a successful blog are Copyblogger and Problogger. Prepare to learn a lot from these sites! Even if your goal is a website and not a blog, you will still learn oodles from them.

6. Keep it simple. You can always add fancy doodads to your site later. If your website is too cluttered, people will immediately look for another one.

7. Look for affiliate programs that have products related to your area of expertise. Amazon is popular, as is Google AdSense, and there are many, many others. E-Junkie, Commission Junction, LinkShare, and Clickbooth are affiliate networks recommended by bloggers that I know.

8. Write an e-book and offer it for sale.

9. Work hard. Whether you're establishing a real-life business or something online, it requires hard work. I spent hours and hours putting together The Survival Mom.

There's a successful blog out there for virtually every interest, hobby, cause, passion, event, and group. It's just a matter of finding where you fit in and then getting busy!

Some of my favorite, successful blogs:

- FrugalDad.com
- FoodStorageand Survival.com
- HillbillyHousewife.com
- SurvivalBlog.com
- PioneerWoman.com
- SmittenKitchen.com

Streams of Income

Think of additional income as streams of water. Streams come in all sizes and from all directions until they empty into a reservoir. Sometimes they dwindle down to a mere trickle, only to become a roaring river farther downstream. Eventually, many streams empty into a much larger body of water. Think of that body of water as your bank account and of all those little streams as income from a multitude of sources such as Craigslist, eBay, tutoring, selling homemade crafts, etc. Fifty bucks here, $230 there, and pretty soon you're talking about some real money.

With multiple income streams, you have a bit of insurance in case, for example, some of your tutoring students drop out or your hand-knitted bun warmers aren't selling. Each stream of income is a backup to the others. Financial experts tell us to diversify our investments, and it makes even more sense to do the same with our sources of income.

A traditional 40-hours-a-week job will bring in steady and significant income, but when those jobs are hard to come by, a bit of creativity and hard work can pay some nice dividends. Traditional part-time jobs are an option, but they tend to be low-paying with inflexible hours. Fortunately, there are many, many ways to earn money, earn better than minimum wage, and do it on a schedule that is helpful—not a hindrance—to your family's lifestyle.

> *Don't handicap your children by making their lives easy.*
> —ROBERT A. HEINLEIN

How to discover your own streams

Each stream of income starts with determining a need or a want and figuring out how your unique skills and knowledge can meet it. Consider this. People want to know:

- How to save money
- How to become more attractive
- How to be smarter
- How to feel special
- How to earn money
- How not to be afraid (of buying a car, making a decision, homeschooling, etc.)
- How to be safe (physically, financially, and emotionally)

Tap into one or more of these areas, and you may have the start of a successful business, or two, or three!

What skill or knowledge do you possess that would meet one or more of these needs and desires? Are you an expert at couponing? Have you helped your family become debt-free? Are you one of those shoppers who can find amazing bargains anywhere? There are moms out there desperate for that information and expertise.

What experiences do you have that would provide guidance and reassurance to someone's fears? Have you been a longtime homeschooler? Are you an auto mechanic who could give tips on what to look for when buying a used car?

Make a list of everything you know how to do and your areas of expertise. Include hobbies and skills that maybe you take for granted. Then, see if there's a way to monetize them.

Jobs No One Wants to Do

It was a little disheartening to read a recent poll from 2010, sponsored by Nuts, Bolts & Thingamajigs, the foundation of the Fabricators & Manufacturers Association, Intl. This poll showed just how far Americans have come from the days when Dad and Mom could fix or build anything. Of the 1,000 adults polled, 58% said they had never built or made a toy, 60% said they avoid handling household repairs themselves, and, astonishingly, 73% of polled teens said they have no interest in blue-collar jobs.

The same skills and knowledge that, apparently, teens and many adults shun will become more and more valuable in a downturned economy. Hey, if your washing machine isn't working and you can't afford a new one, what are you going to do? Will you call an attorney or a CPA? No, you'll call an appliance repairman! A plumber will come to your rescue when your toddler flushes down a whole package of tampons. In the economy of the future, it may very well be the blue-collar families who prosper the most.

A former employee of ours, Jake, is an example of how well this can work out. My husband hired Jake right out of high school and put him to work as a $9-an-hour helper in an electrical contracting business.

Over a period of 5 years, the company paid for his classes in residential wiring, and he became a very competent electrician. When the construction business slowed and Jake was laid off, he quickly got a job in the electrical department at Lowe's and recently was promoted. In addition to his hours there, he picks up odd electrical jobs. Financially, he's doing quite well, while many of his buddies from high school have been unemployed for months.

Most older teens and young adults earn money in order to buy the latest fads and pay for dates, expensive toys, and, perhaps, their car payments. Unless an income is absolutely necessary for his or her family, it may pay off, in the long run, for a young person to work for a time as an unpaid apprentice, learning electrical wiring, car repair, carpentry, or any number of skills in the trades.

It turns out that blue-collar professions, or trades, may be the best way to earn an income as our economy goes from bad to worse. During boom years, these professions also do quite well. Encourage your kids from an early age to build things, invent things, tinker, and putter. Give gifts of bird-house kits and real, kid-size tools and let them learn the joy and pride of building something with their own hands. You'll soon discover if they, and you, have an aptitude for fixing things and doing the sort of work no one else seems to want to do.

Whip out the calculator!

The financial calculator, that is!

Financial guru Scott Gamm has an online calculator that will assist you in spotting unnecessary expenses and then making a plan for paying off debt *and* saving. You can find his calculator at HelpSaveMyDollars.com.

The Financial Comeback

Is there any hope for those who have crashed and burned in this economy, either by making foolish decisions or from just being in the wrong place at the wrong time? Every financial expert I interviewed said a resounding and encouraging, "Yes!"

Scott Gamm of HelpSaveMyDollars.com recommends a secured credit card, which allows you to rebuild a positive credit history. Payments must be made on time every single month. Even being a day late can affect your comeback. Spending habits absolutely must be changed, with every dollar accounted for. Otherwise, you'll soon find yourself right back where you started, wondering, again, how you got there. Scott says there's one silver lining to our economic crisis: People are re-examining how they spend their money and questioning what is more important, financial security or the latest electronic gadget or high-fashion accessory. He thinks this has led many people toward a path of less materialism—a good mind-set for making that financial comeback.

Other experts stress the importance of setting goals for savings and upcoming big-ticket expenses. Here are two steps to get going in that direction: Have two savings goals.

Goal #1

The general rule of thumb is to have several months' worth of expenses set aside in savings, as mentioned earlier. However, do you know what your total monthly expenses are? It's super easy to figure this out if you use your debit card to pay most expenses. It's a simple matter of going through every item that shows up on your account page on your bank's website. If you pay with cash, checks, and/or credit cards, the accounting process will include gathering more documentation, but it can be done.

As you go through one month's expenses, write each in one of three categories: monthly bills, necessary expenses, and miscellaneous expenses.

Monthly bills—This category will include rent or mortgage; insurance; utilities; credit cards; cable, phone, and Internet; cell phones; medical bills; and all other expense for which you receive bills or have automatic deductions from your account.

Necessary expenses—These expenses are necessary, but you don't receive an actual bill for them. Typically, you pay for them with a debit card, cash, or check. They include things like food, gas, doctor appointments, and school expenses. If you're ever going to build up a savings account, savings also goes in this category.

Miscellaneous expenses—This category is for expenses that are nice, *really* nice, but in a time of financial desperation, just not necessary. Manicures, pedicures, spa treatments, books, subscriptions, restaurant meals, ballet lessons, and entertainment are just a few examples.

Keep these financial records safe:

- A list of your financial institutions, phone numbers, and account numbers
- A list of all your creditors, their phone numbers, and account numbers
- Investment account numbers
- Safe deposit box location and a list of contents
- Tax records for the past 7 years
- PayPal account information
- Banking information for any account for which you're a signatory
- Insurance policy numbers and the names and phone numbers for each insurance company
- Details about any and all assets

Once you've gone through a month of expenses, go through a second month to see if there's anything missing. For example, I don't have the oil in my car changed every month, but it should be included in the "necessary expenses."

Take one category at a time and deliberate whether each particular expense can be decreased. Is it possible to switch to a less expensive cell phone plan? Could you be paying for more insurance than you actually need? Make phone calls to each company or creditor and explain that you're trying to decrease your monthly expenses; they may be willing to offer discounts or other assistance in order to keep your business. When I called to cancel our cable TV service, the customer service rep offered me everything but his firstborn to convince me not to go through with the cancellation. It was really hard listening to a grown man beg, but I cancelled anyway.

The third category, miscellaneous expenses, is the easiest but might also be the most painful to slash. I love nothing more than the idea of dropping my daughter off at a ballet class, taking my son to a private math tutor, settling down for a relaxing mani-pedi, and then going shopping and out to lunch with my BFFs. However, every single one of those expenses can be eliminated, giving a huge boost to any savings account.

I think you'll be pleasantly surprised by how much you can whittle out of each expense category, but don't tighten your belt so much that you're over budget every month because there are expenses unaccounted for.

The final totals of your three categories will give you a dollar amount that now becomes your savings goal. Let's say that your family needs a minimum of $3,200 every month to meet your monthly expenses and allow for a bit of "miscellaneous money." While it may seem daunting, at least you now know what you need to save in order to have just one month's worth of expenses set aside. If you're thinking that there's no way you can ever save that amount, reread the tips in this chapter for starting a side business and earning extra money and make absolutely sure that every dollar that goes out is accounted for!

Goal #2

This goal will likely be smaller than Goal #1, but it's just as important. This goal is for a specific future expense. Dave Ramsey recommends

Keep your Face(book) shut!

It's a fact that potential employers will check your Facebook entries. Private entries about your health, family, personal, and financial issues may come back to bite you if employers perceive you as being a potential liability.

having $1,000 in this type of savings, and that's a good goal—until you realize that you'll have to spend $4,800 to replace your air conditioning unit, and it's the middle of July. If that extra $3,800 isn't there, you'll find yourself pulling out a credit card.

I recommend listing every future expense you can think of that will cost more than $100. Just take a look around the house—at your appliances, your front- and backyards, and your vehicles, as well as medical and dental issues. I imagine you'll end up with quite a list of future expenses that aren't exactly urgent *right now* but that are looming, nonetheless. List the items by priority, identifying which need is most important, and then start saving.

Your total financial comeback will happen when several pieces all come together: cutting out expenses, knowing where every dollar goes, not repeating past financial mistakes, paying off debt, earning extra money, and being prepared for future setbacks by having enough savings in the bank.

Your savings safety net

That $1000 in savings is important as an *emergency* backup. If you know your car is going to need new tires, that's not an emergency. It's a predictable expense. Have a savings plan to cover predictable expenses and keep that $1000 as a fund for a sudden and unexpected crisis.

||||||||||||||||||||||||||||||||||||||||||||||||||||||||||||||||||||||||||||||||||||||||||||||||||||

Have You Caught the Gold Bug?

Other than buying a nice piece of "real" jewelry, the thought of buying gold never occurred to me until recently. With a weaker economy and a dollar that is steadily losing value, suddenly advertisements for gold and silver began popping up everywhere. There are dozens of new, "We buy gold!" shops in town. Women began flocking to home parties where they could sell their unwanted gold jewelry and walk away with cash.

Buying gold and silver has been a big trend, but is that the wisest place for your money? Who should buy precious metals, and what are some first steps for families just now venturing into them?

Whether you jump onto the precious-metals bandwagon is a personal choice that should be made only once you've done your due diligence and have researched all options. Keep in mind that you can't eat or drink gold and silver. I recommend that you first stock up on food, supplies, and water that your family will need for at least 3 months, activate plans to pay off debt and stabilize your financial situation, and *then* begin adding gold and silver to your stash.

What You Need to Know About Gold and Silver

I turned to my friend Chris Slife, president of Howling Coyote Silver, for some answers to my questions about precious metals. At one point, Chris was a high school teacher of history and economics, but 10 years ago his interest in precious metals took a more serious turn. He came to the conclusion that financial security lay in investments in silver and gold, specifically in the physical ownership of these metals. Now he's in the precious-metals business full time.

Chris isn't a trained financial adviser, but his information about gold and silver is helpful.

As a newbie to precious metals, I had quite a few basic questions for him. *Note:* When Chris talks about gold or silver, he is talking about actual, physical coins, not paper certificates.

The Survival Mom: Why is silver your preferred precious metal for the average buyer?

Chris: Silver is a relatively inexpensive hedge against runaway inflation, if that ever occurs. There's also a growing demand for silver in various industries, while, at the same time, the mining of silver is decreasing. Finally, silver is good to have on hand as a good barter currency.

The Survival Mom: How do I know what a real gold or silver coin looks like?

Chris: Begin now to educate yourself. My best advice is to visit a local coin shop and purchase a 90% silver dime, quarter, and half-dollar. Compare those to their more modern counterparts. Immediately, you will notice a difference. Study the real coins, their appearance and weight, and you'll be ready to distinguish real silver coins from something less.

Weight is key for both gold and silver coins; they *feel* heavy. It's important to know the weight of the coin(s) that you are interested in, and this information is easy to find on the Internet.

Also, as you begin to shop around, you need to know the difference between the spot price and the premium. The spot price is the price of a precious metal as tracked by websites such as Kitco and Forex, while

Successful people save in prosperous times so they have a financial cushion in times of recession.

—BRIAN TRACY

the premium is the price charged by the dealer in addition to the spot price. The premium changes based on supply and demand. For example, if there is more of a demand for Gold Eagles, it will have a higher premium than a Krugerrand although both coins contain the exact same gold content.

Here is some information about specific silver coins that may be helpful:

Silver Rounds: Look for .999 and 1 troy ounce on the coin. The advantage to these coins is that they have a cheaper premium. The downside is that they are less recognizable than other silver coins.

Silver Eagle: Look for the date on the obverse (front) and look for "1 oz. fine silver—One Dollar" on the reverse (back). Silver Eagles are U.S. currency and very recognizable, but they come with a high premium. All pure 1-ounce silver coins should weigh 31.1 grams, or 1 ounce.

Silver Currency: also known as 90% silver. The advantage to these coins is that they are U.S. currency, have a low premium, and are very recognizable. These coins include pre-1965 quarters and dimes. Their main disadvantage is that they are bulky, but then again, so is silver in general. Other silver coins that I like are Silver Maples, Silver Philharmonics, and Perth Mint products.

Common Morgan and Peace Dollars: These are 90% silver and are better known as silver dollars. I like them because they have a face value, and the Morgan dollar, in particular, is easy to recognize. They were originally minted in the late 1870s and contain 90% silver, or .7734 ounces of silver. If you're buying silver for the silver content only, I recommend buying only common-date dollars because they will have a lower premium. 1921 Morgans are very common, as are 1922 Peace Dollars. There are many other common dates, so do some research. Go buy a common silver dollar and have the coin shop "ring" the coin for you. A Morgan or a Peace dollar has a distinctive "ring" to it.

The Survival Mom: What about purchasing gold coins?

Chris: Three common gold coins you'll find in most coin shops are the Gold Eagle, the Krugerrand, and the Maple Leaf. Each has advantages and disadvantages for the buyer.

Gold Eagle: 22K, comes in 1-, ½-, ¼- and ¹⁄₁₀-ounce sizes. Its main advantage is that it's easily recognizable, but these come with very high premiums.

Krugerrand: 22K, usually seen in 1-ounce size. This coin usually has a low premium but isn't as recognizable as an Eagle.

There are people who have money and people who are rich.

—COCO CHANEL

Maple Leaf: 24K, usually seen in 1-ounce size. Again, this coin usually has a low premium, but it's not as recognizable as an Eagle, and it scratches easily.

Other commonly seen gold coins are the Chinese Pandas, Austrian Philharmonics, and Australian Nuggets. Name-brand gold bars are good as well (JM, Engelhard, Sunshine, Credit Suisse, RCM, Perth Mint, and Pamp).

Buy a *Red Book of U.S. Coins*. Get the larger edition, because it includes photos so you can see what the coins look like.

The Survival Mom: Is gold and silver an investment, a form of insurance, or both?

Chris: I recommend buying gold to people who have a large amount of "paper" assets that need to be hedged. If you have all your assets denominated in dollars, euros, etc., and the currencies get devalued, so do your "assets." Gold will keep your purchasing power stable in the event of a currency crisis.

Thus, gold is an *insurance policy* against currency devaluation and general economic malaise. If the economy breaks down, like I said before, I would prefer 90% silver.

The Survival Mom: If there is an economic collapse, what will be used as money?

Chris: Food, bullets, water, cigarettes, and booze (I especially like the airplane-size booze bottles), toilet paper, tools, fingernail clippers, etc. —anything that would be hard to find in the event of a collapse. Even diapers might be used as money. Think creatively!

The Survival Mom: What's the best form of precious metals in a collapse scenario?

Chris: Silver. Those 90% silver dimes, quarters, halves, dollars, Silver Eagles, and silver rounds—in that order—will be especially useful as a currency because they are all easily identifiable. Everyone knows that a 1960 dime, for example, is 90% silver, and it has the denomination right on the face of the coin. Fractional gold in amounts of less than 1 ounce might also be a useful currency.

Chris also recommends Michael Maloney's *Guide to Investing in Precious Metals* as a great place to start your education when it comes to gold and silver.

Bartering

People have always bartered, or traded, with each other for goods and services. I'll bet you've done it yourself more than once.

"Hey, I'll babysit your kids this Friday night if you'll make a birthday cake for my son!"

Does that sound familiar? That's a type of bartering.

Some Survival Moms have realized that a future in which the value of the dollar is down and their incomes aren't exactly booming might be a time in which bartering becomes the preferred currency. They have stocked up on everyday necessities that could become difficult to find and, therefore, more valuable. After all, a mom with a 3-month-old baby might be more than happy to trade a month of piano lessons or 8 boxes of brownie mixes for 48 disposable diapers!

Preferred items for barter are common products and services we take for granted every day, yet without them, life is more difficult and a little less enjoyable. Before going crazy and stocking up on masses of items for barter, be sure you have your own necessities covered first: water and food for at least 3 months and vital supplies and tools that your family needs.

Top items for barter

Here are some items considered to be useful for bartering.

cosmetics

cigarettes

feminine protection

coffee

matches

duct tape

batteries

herbs and spices

salt

firewood

bleach

eggs

toilet paper

baby formula

diapers

flashlights

food

candy/chocolate

toothbrushes and toothpaste

hand sanitizer

services/skills

What Is an Economic Collapse, and How Can I Prepare for One?

As far back as the 1940s, economic seers have been warning us of a coming collapse of the American dollar and our economy. I remember seeing doom-and-gloom books such as *The Coming Currency Collapse* by Jerome F. Smith (1980) and *Death of the Dollar* by William F. Rickenbacker (1986) and rolling my eyes. They might as well have been predicting a Category 5 hurricane on a cloudless April day, because back in the '80s, there were very few storm clouds swirling over our economy. Sure, there were short-term recessions and a bubble or two burst, but overall we were all living high on the hog.

Then along came the subprime mortgage crisis of 2007 and the crash of 2008. I saw our retirement savings dip by thousands of dollars seemingly overnight. At the same time, home foreclosures were sky-rocketing and unemployment rates soared to heights foreign to my generation. What was happening, and would things ever return to normal?

Well-known financial experts, such as Harry Dent and Peter Schiff, have been making dire economic predictions for some time, including a major stock-market crash and a collapse of the healthy, thriving economy we have known all our lives. By definition, an economic collapse is when the economy of a nation experiences a severe depression and high levels of bankruptcy and unemployment. The national fiat currency—in our case, the dollar—is devalued, and banks are in crisis.

> *There's no use talking about the problem unless you talk about the solution.*
>
> *—BETTY WILLIAMS*

A possible scenario for America is what happened in Argentina back in 1999 and continued through 2002. Argentina had amassed an enormous amount of debt, and when the country was unable to pay it back, its fiat currency, the austral, collapsed. It had very little value anymore, and citizens who had saved and invested their money in the austral found themselves living in poverty. Sometimes the rate of inflation would hit 200% in a *month*! Imagine a haircut that costs $25 on April 1 costing $75 just 30 days later! Apply that rate of inflation to all goods and services, and you get an idea of what life was like for most Argentineans. To make matters worse, unemployment increased and wages fell. People living on fixed incomes were hit the hardest.

For more than a decade, the citizens of Argentina faced repeated devaluations of their currency and severe banking crises. Naturally, people with money withdrew it and exchanged it for dollars. This caused runs on banks, and soon people were unable to withdraw more than $250 at a time from their own accounts. Protests, riots, and increased crime and violence turned this once-prosperous nation into a third-world country. At one point, in 2002, more than half of the population was living below poverty levels.

Argentina has been making a slow but steady comeback, but the collapse of the economy, of the currency, and of life as they knew it took a dramatic toll on those living through this crisis. It's a story that should make all of us think: "What if that comes to America? How could my family survive?"

Our economy may or may not collapse completely. If it does, it could happen suddenly or over a longer period of time. What matters

Who can I believe?

When I hear conflicting information about the health of our economy, I do what makes sense to me. I listen to different sides of the story but ultimately depend on what my eyes, ears, and common sense tell me.

- Are more businesses shutting down or starting up?
- Are they doing any hiring?
- Are restaurant prices increasing while serving sizes are decreasing?
- What about the prices of the basics: food, fuel, and power?
- Are empty store and office spaces filling up, or are they still vacant?
- Am I still seeing "For Sale! Bank Owned Property!" signs in front of houses in decent neighborhoods?
- How easy is it to buy or sell a house in my neighborhood?

Too many people are swayed by a single happy headline, even when the evidence around them points to the opposite truth. If the headlines prove to be true, they will be backed up by what you already know.

Mini-Glossary

Quantitative Easing (QE): issuing or printing new money without backing. The influx of "new" money is usually intended to stimulate the economy. Today, the money can be generated electronically and not necessarily printed on paper.

Premium: a fee attached to the purchase of something, including precious metals.

Fiat currency: money in the form or coins and paper that has value only because government regulation has established that value.

most is what we do *today* to get our own finances in order, make smart money decisions from this point forward, stock up on the necessities of life, and learn how to become more self-reliant. It just so happens that this book contains information to do all that and more!

It's Time for the Big-Girl Panties

I doubt there's another mom out there who loves to live for the moment more than I do. I hate sitting down to pay the bills, I hate comparing the prices of laundry detergents to make sure I'm buying the cheapest one, and I hate going to a restaurant and looking for the least expensive item on the menu. Our world is changing, though, and it's time to be a grown-up. There are still good times ahead, but I need to see the world as it is, not through rose-colored glasses.

Several years ago a friend passed along this quote to me: "Being a grown-up means doing what you need to do when you need to do it." I hate that quote because most of the time I don't want to be a grown-up! I want to be a big kid—a kid with a driver's license, a car, and a credit card! But living in a world of immaturity and denial isn't going to help my family survive during tough times. My husband needs a wife and a partner to face hard times with, and my kids depend on both of us to make difficult decisions and do difficult things when we'd rather close our eyes and pretend the world was prettier, softer, and kinder.

Financial survival isn't easy, and I hate to be the one to deliver the news, but it's time to put on those big-girl panties. Money in savings plus no doubt equals a family that's better prepared for the future.

We can tell our values by looking at our checkbook stubs.

—GLORIA STEINEM

☑ Teach financial responsibility by example. Talk about the family's budget and help your kids understand that buying one thing may mean not being able to afford something else. One of the greatest lessons they can learn is the postponement of gratification. If they've just gotta have the latest toy, let them wait for it until they earn enough money or until "it's in the family budget."

☑ If you have a family business or decide to start one, get your kids involved at the very start. This will help develop an entrepreneurial attitude, one that says, "I can be my own employer!"

☑ Have your kids sit right next to you when you do comparison shopping. Talk about quality versus bargain prices and features that are nice but not necessary and help your kids learn to do the same.

☑ When your kids have money, and before it's spent, discuss their options. Would they rather spend it all now and have nothing later, spend some and save some, save it toward the purchase of something expensive that is their heart's desire, or save some to use as spending money during an upcoming vacation? All of these options are dizzying, but kids need to learn that spending fast isn't their only option!

☑ Talk about your donations to charities, church, or other worthy causes. When a disaster happens somewhere, be sure they know you are donating money to help the victims. Foster an attitude of generosity and empathy toward those who are less fortunate.

The Prepared Family

Family Preparedness Plan: **Financial Survival**

Our family's financial grade: A B C D F

To have a grade of A, we need to: _____

_____

_____

_____

Savings Goal #1: **Monthly expenses**

Based on these numbers, we need to save $_____ to cover one month's expenses.

We need to save $_____ to cover _____ months.

	Creditor	*Monthly payment*
Monthly bills:	_____	_____
	_____	_____
	_____	_____
	_____	_____
	_____	_____
	_____	_____

	Expense	*Monthly amount*
Necessary expenses:	_____	_____
	_____	_____
	_____	_____
	_____	_____
	_____	_____
	_____	_____
	_____	_____

Miscellaneous expenses:	_____	_____
	_____	_____
	_____	_____
	_____	_____
	_____	_____
	_____	_____

Savings Goal #2: Upcoming, major expenses (list and prioritize)

Expense	Amount
_____	_____
_____	_____
_____	_____
_____	_____
_____	_____
_____	_____
_____	_____

Financial mistakes we've made that we don't ever want to make again:

_____

_____

_____

The Top Five Smart Things we've done with our money:

1. _____
2. _____
3. _____
4. _____
5. _____

Possible streams of additional income:

1. _____
2. _____
3. _____
4. _____
5. _____

CHAPTER 10

It Takes a Compound

I never bought into the idea that it takes a village to raise a child. I could just see my own two kids running wild through the village, terrorizing the elders and accidentally setting fire to the community eating hall. They needed two dedicated, focused parents, and that's what they got.

On the other hand, life would be far more difficult without the support of our families and circle of friends. Just writing this book required me to rely on friends and family to take my kids to music lessons; to open their homes to my kids at five in the morning; to worry when my son's cough lingered for more than a day or two; and to concern themselves with whether my daughter had something to wear to a birthday party. Their love and generosity helped make this book a reality.

We know from history and ancient texts that humans have always lived in groups. Whether it was a tribe, a band, a clan, or a village, humans have always clustered together for protection, friendship, food, and shared skills. I'll bet another reason moms, especially, appreciated the tribe was free child care—a bonus in any community!

Now many modern homes and neighborhoods are designed to isolate us from each other, cities promote anonymity, and families are scattered from one coast to the other. A lot of us have to build our own communities—even if it's just a small group of friends—to provide and ensure our safety and well-being in difficult times. The fact is, no Survival Mom can survive on her own, without supportive people in

It's not denial. I'm just selective about the reality I accept.

—BILL WATTERSON

her life. During a disaster or a worst-case scenario such as an EMP or war, the Lone Wolf will likely be the first casualty.

Here's a question for you: When, or if, that time comes, will you have others to rely on, and if so, who will they be?

|||||||||||||||||||||||||||||||||||||||||||||||||||||||||||||||||||||||||||||||||||||||||||||||||||||||||||||||||||||||||||

Sometimes OpSec Works Against Us

Some of us feel sheepish when we buy extra food at the grocery store. We invent elaborate tales to justify our purchase to the cashier, because, after all, what *normal* person buys this much food?

"What about all this tuna? My husband's platoon from 'Nam is staying with us over the holidays."

"My church has asked us to take in the entire African Children's Choir. That's a lot of mouths to feed!"

If we're sensitive to what a cashier thinks about our food purchases, it's even more difficult to tell others that we have freeze-dried food or that the family has an evacuation plan in case of a hurricane or a terrorist attack.

What would the neighbors think?!

Along with that understandable reticence, as Survival Moms, we're also concerned about security. There are many reasons we don't want everybody and their dogs to know what we're stocking up on or discussing in the privacy of our homes. OpSec (Operational Security) is a smart practice, but it can also work against us when it keeps us from connecting with others and forming relationships that could help us through a difficult time.

It's not possible for any one person or family to have *all* of the skills, knowledge, equipment, food, supplies, and real estate to survive 100% on their own. I know some pretty tough military guys, and not one of them could stay awake 24/7 to protect his home if it came right down to it. Even the toughest among us need to depend on others.

So, to connect with others, we need to first find those who are like-minded (I hate that word—it brings to mind robots, but it's a helpful term). To do that, we have to sift through all of the people who think we're nuts.

Two Stigmas a Survival Mom Has to Deal With

I sometimes cringe when someone refers to me as The Survivalist Mom, not because I have anything against survivalists, but because I know that some equate this term with being crazy. Unfortunately, somewhere along the way survivalists got a really bad reputation. They're portrayed as wild-eyed, woman-hungry, crazy men who rarely bathe, stockpile guns, and spend hours sharpening their knife collections—sort of like in an Idaho-based *Deliverance*. Be honest, that's what comes to mind when you think "survivalist," doesn't it?

Okay, there was that Kari Swenson episode in Montana (look it up), but really, it was an aberration. All of the survivalists I've ever known just want to be left alone to enjoy nature, their families, and life the way they believe God intended it. I have no problem with that.

The second stigma has more to do with the perspective of the person questioning your point of view and causing you to feel defensive about something that is perfectly rational. Chances are, the person who stares at you and then slowly backs away when you bring up the likelihood of hyperinflation or mention that you've started stocking up on food is suffering from normalcy bias. I'll bet a lot of your friends and relatives suffer from it, which explains why *they* think *you're* the crazy one!

Normalcy bias: Why everyone but you is crazy

Human bodies don't normally fly through the air, but one winter night that's exactly what I witnessed while waiting for a red light to turn green.

I was sitting in my Tahoe at an intersection not far from home when I heard the loud rumble of a truck engine. I couldn't quite believe my eyes when a green pickup veered around me, raced into the intersection, and plowed into a white sedan. While my mind was registering this violent accident, I saw a scarecrow fly through the air. I took a few deep breaths, tried to remember the details of how the accident happened, and waited to give my eyewitness account to the police who appeared on the scene within minutes.

My mind replayed the scene, always with that scarecrow flying out of the truck and into the adjacent field. It wasn't until half an hour later, when I saw EMTs trying to revive a young man, that I realized what I had actually seen was this man's body being ejected from the front seat. Even now when I remember the accident, I don't see a human. Instead, the image of a scarecrow is imprinted in my brain—because humans don't fly through the air!

What I experienced was an example of normalcy bias, a survival mechanism our brains are equipped with that can place us in grave danger when we're faced with something traumatic. Simply put, it causes our brains to insist that all is okay and that everything will return to normal. For most of us who have never faced true peril, normalcy bias tells us that nothing bad will ever happen. "This is America!" some people insist when I tell them about the possibility of a deeper Great Depression or hyperinflation. Incredibly, the most obvious warning signs are ignored.

We simply *expect* life to go on as it always has, and our brains are wired to accept that and nothing else. A driver attempts to cross a flooded river. Thousands of New Orleans residents faced with a deadly hurricane refuse to leave the city, and city officials don't even have written contingency plans for dealing with a large-scale disaster. One survivor from 9/11 tells of going blind as she saw dozens of human bodies hitting the ground outside the Twin Towers. Our brains can accommodate billions of bits of information each day, but, apparently, some things are too terrible to comprehend.

If you want to test your memory, try to recall what you were worrying about one year ago today.

—E. JOSEPH COSSMAN

Survivalists, Preppers, and Survival Moms

Over the past few years, an increasing number of people around the world have identified themselves as "preppers." They are neo-survivalists who, for the most part, live in cities and suburbs. They have much in common with their survivalist counterparts; in their desire to live more self-reliant lives, preppers recognize the uncertainty of the future and take active steps to prepare for it. Their wish is to maintain a normal life for their families by being proactive, and they do this in any number of ways, from stocking up on extra food to learning how to grow and preserve their own food to using alternative sources of energy, and sometimes even to moving to more rural locations in order to maximize their independence.

Tom Martin, co-founder and director of the American Preppers Network, says, "Anyone can be a prepper. Just the act of preparing for anything makes you a prepper."

If you're a Survival Mom, you are probably a prepper as well—just another mom who wants her family to be prepared and well cared for, no matter what happens.

Those of us who believe in preparedness, whether beginners or veterans, know the frustration of trying to convince loved ones that the future is not at all secure. However, the normalcy bias isn't something we can debate. It's not based on logic or rational thought. It's the brain doing its best to help its human owner deal with terrifying events and possibilities, as well as with escalating situations whose logical, final outcomes can't be accepted.

Comments like "life will get back to normal" and "there's no need to worry" are a dead giveaway that normalcy bias has claimed yet another victim.

In fact, it's often the case that a bad situation will blow over, but normalcy bias continues to deny reality, even when the funnel cloud is headed for your backyard.

So, it's not really the fault of your friends and family who just aren't on board with the idea of an uncertain future and the need to plan and prepare for it. In my experience, debates and loud discussions do very little to dissuade them. I can give you four good reasons to give up when you realize you're dealing with someone happy in her own little world.

1. She'll think you're crazy anyway. You can talk and talk and talk, but from her perspective, what's *really* crazy is stocking up on groceries and saving every possible penny. To her, it's more important to take another expensive vacation and outfit her kids in the very latest fashions. Hey, we're still living in the 1990s, right?

2. Some people choose to remain uninformed. One friend of mine put her hands over her ears when she had heard enough of my speech about the decline of our economy. Another makes a point to *never* pay attention to the news. These folks tell themselves they're too busy to pay attention to what's going on, and, at any rate, the problems of the world are too confusing. They can watch hours of Gerald Celente interviews and then leave saying, "Weren't we going to run by that Hummer dealership?" There's no point in wasting your breath.

3. Think OpSec, Operational Security. There's that OpSec term again. How many people do you really want to know about your stash of ammo and firearms? In times of plenty, it's hard to believe that someone would want to steal your extra blankets, food, or other supplies, but looting is common after disasters. It's better to err on the side of caution and be careful about what you say and to whom

it's said. If you don't want your kids blabbing to all of the neighbors, either keep information from them or train them in OpSec, too.

4. There are more pleasant things to talk about. Let's face it, we're not exactly wearing rose-colored glasses, and we can easily become downright depressed about the state of the world and discouraged by all of the preparedness still to be done. Why *not* spend a pleasant afternoon chatting about the latest shows on TV or about the best lineup for Fantasy Football? After all, those buckets of wheat will still be there when you get home.

Where Does a Community Start?

Start with those closest to you—your immediate family. If you're married and your husband is on board, that's ideal.

If he just isn't seeing things your way and you're convinced of the need to prepare, remember the first rule of preparedness: "Do your best where you are, with what you have." He may not be on board, but there's a great deal you can do on your own, such as creating a food-storage plan, packing emergency kits, and learning helpful and practical skills. Of course, you could always use your trump card: "It's a woman thing. You wouldn't understand."

A genuine crisis is all it will take for him to realize that you were right and he was wrong.

Your kids will be the next ones to incorporate into your plans. An important piece of preparedness is self-reliance. Explain to the kids that Mom and Dad have decided it's important to be a little more like Ma and Pa Ingalls of *Little House on the Prairie*. A family viewing of the series is a perfect time for pointing out how the Ingalls family was ready to survive on their own. Their independence, hard work, and family cohesiveness is pretty impressive. (By the way, I prefer the 2005 Little House mini-series starring Cameron Bancroft and Erin Cottrell.)

Your family unit, however small, is the absolute most important community and is the foundation for other connections and relationships. Beyond that first circle, parents, grandparents, and other extended family members may have similar concerns and would be willing to have conversations and begin making plans. You'll never know until you ask.

Top ways to become survival-savvy

- Join a survival- or preparedness-related Internet group.
- Do a Google search for "survival blogs," and you'll have more reading material than you can handle.
- Look for meet-up groups that are centered on survival and preparedness topics, such as gardening, backyard chickens, wilderness survival, or simply preparedness.
- Search online for free, downloadable survival manuals.
- Survival forums abound, and the old-timers are always willing to help out the newbies.

- "We're thinking of getting some backyard chickens. Have you ever thought of that?"
- "Have you thought of starting a garden of your own?"
- "I'm learning how to can my own vegetables. Would you like to learn with me?"

Very quickly, you'll know if you have an ally or not. If they look at you askance, zip your lips and ask who they think is the best *American Idol* winner.

I know of families who have recently moved closer to each other for the purpose of being nearby in troublesome times, and last year a cousin I rarely see sent me an e-mail and said: "I sincerely mean it when I say I am going to use your blog to begin taking active steps in preparing

Is your spouse survival-minded or a skeptic?

Does your marriage ever feel like a rowboat with you and your spouse paddling in opposite directions? It's impossible to reach a mutual goal if your goals aren't mutual! My husband and I are polar opposites in many ways, but when it comes to preparedness, we have the same mind-set. We're both worried just enough about the future to agree that taking steps to become more self-reliant and better prepared makes a lot of sense.

How about you and your significant other? Is one of you convinced it's past time to prepare and the other more than a bit skeptical? If your spouse or significant other is a skeptic, I have a few suggestions for coaxing that sweetheart of yours on board.

First, understand that almost every man in the world is concerned with the security of his loved ones. The instinct to protect runs deep in the male psyche. Whether it's the desire to protect his family from crime, economic hardship, or just a flat tire, most men are naturally wired that way. If, or when, he decides that preparedness is a top priority, don't be surprised if his first instinct is to go to the closest gun store and buy the biggest, bad-ass firearm he sees—even if he's never shot a gun in his life.

If the topic of preparedness seems to be completely closed with him, it's probably because your guy is fearful of the future and afraid that he may not be able to protect and provide for his own. It's actually very touching when you think about it. Therefore, you'll have far more luck winning him over with calm, matter-of-fact words than by launching into a hysterical appeal. Most men admire strong women—women who take the initiative. They also tend to be appreciative of a just-the-facts approach. They dread emotional conversations. If you present him with a plan in writing, so much the better. Your plan could be a list of ways your family could cut back on expenses. I don't know a single dad who would be opposed to that! Have some sort of plan in mind, whether it's getting ready for an ice storm or stocking up on extra canned food.

Watch for conversation openings when a friend or a family member loses a job or finds himself in severe economic difficulty. Even if your own income is secure, ask your man, "Have you thought about what we would do if *you* lost your job?" If this opens up a meaningful conversation—as opposed to, "Don't say that kind of thing! I have a job, and I'm not gonna lose it!"—then you can begin with what should be the first preparedness step for any family: preparing for a possible loss of income.

Current events offer the perfect opportunity to, again, talk about what-ifs.

"What if it were our house in the pathway of a wildfire?"

"Those families in Oklahoma have been out of power for 2 weeks. What would we do if that happened to us?"

Watching events unfold on TV provides great lessons in preparedness versus the head-in-the-sand approach.

Once you've caught his attention and he seems open to the idea of preparedness, introduce him to this book and The Survival Mom blog. Don't be surprised if survival becomes his newest hobby and obsession. After all, so much of it appeals to men: the gun part, the protection part, and the opportunity to wear camo.

It's okay to begin this journey solo! Setting a small goal of having a month's worth of groceries on hand is something you, as the mom, would most likely be in charge of anyway. Tuck away a few extra dollars here and there, read aloud books to your kids that underscore the need for being self-sufficient, and learn all you can about survival and practical skills. When your significant other comes to his senses, he'll be amazed at what His Woman has accomplished. Trust me. He'll be bragging about you to his friends the first chance he gets.

What men worry about . . .

- Going bald
- Losing their job
- Losing their woman
- Paying the bills
- Having moobs (man boobs)
- Their kids
- Erectile dysfunction
- Prostate exams

my family for what I hope never comes. I am way overdue in my preparations!" And here I thought I was the only nut on the family tree!

As you can probably guess, there are also plenty of Survival Moms whose parents and siblings think they're crazy for wanting to plan ahead, and some of those family members live in the middle of hurricane country and Tornado Alley!

5 creative ways to teach preparedness to your child

Children fear what they don't understand. When a difficult concept such as preparedness is presented in a creative way at their level, it helps them feel reassured and satisfied. Here are five creative ways to teach this concept to your children in ways that will reinforce important concepts and include a lot of fun along the way:

- Teach practical skills. Kids should know how to cook, clean, and scrub the kitchen floor! Learning how to mend ripped jeans or do laundry isn't child abuse. They're real-life skills that teach independence and instill a healthy work ethic. Older children can be taught target shooting, how to put up a tent, and how to start a campfire. I'm all in favor of plentiful playtime, but children also need to learn skills and knowledge that are truly worth learning. Don't worry, they'll have fun and love every minute of it.

- Children naturally love learning about animals, and there's no better source for examples of preparedness than the animals they're already familiar with. Bears, squirrels, and other forest animals get ready for the winter, and geese begin a long trek south when they sense that cold weather is near. Did you know that prairie dogs purposely mound up the earth around the entrances to their homes so rain doesn't flood their burrows? My own children love *The Burgess Book of Animals*, which uses entertaining stories to teach facts about dozens of animals.

- Keep an eye on current events. Don't focus on details that might terrify your kids, but if the Weather Channel is reporting on an approaching hurricane, for example, talk about the steps families in those areas should be taking.

- Participate in activities that teach or reinforce preparedness. Scout programs and 4-H are ideal for children to learn some terrific practical skills and socialize with other like-minded kids. You just can't beat that combination.

- Utilize the suggestions for The Prepared Family at the end of each chapter in this book.

Extending Your Network

The scenes we saw after Hurricane Katrina were horrific, but those that are probably most memorable—the crowds milling around the Superdome, for example—don't tell the full story of the aftermath. In countless areas, neighbors banded together to ensure their neighborhood's safety and to help each other rebuild. There is not too much drama there, so it didn't make the six o'clock news.

It's a sad fact of modern American life that millions of us have no idea who our neighbors are. You might be just fine with that, but if you'd like to begin connecting with those around you, begin establishing something called *territoriality,* which is another word for old-fashioned neighborliness—you know, like in the old episodes of *The Andy Griffith Show* when Aunt Bea would peek out the window to keep an eye on a stranger walking down the street. Here are a few tips to get you started:

- Get to know the neighbors around you, especially those on either side of your home.
- When new neighbors move in, greet them promptly with a basket of fresh fruit or a homemade treat.
- At holidays, take small gifts to your neighbors.
- Invite them into your home to establish trust.
- Offer to help with tasks such as raking leaves or pulling weeds, especially if the neighbor is elderly or overwhelmed with managing a house full of kids.
- Small courtesies go a long way. Carry a newspaper up to their front door, or pick up stray trash that has blown into their yard.

> *The family is a haven in a heartless world.*
> —CHRISTOPHER LASCH

As trust develops, not only are you enlarging your circle of trusted friends, but also neighbors watching out for each other are a criminal's worst nightmare. The bonus is that you can begin finding out which neighbors are doctors or nurses and which are in law enforcement or the military, either active or retired. If any neighbors are LDS (Mormon), they might know a thing or two about food storage and will probably be willing to give you advice. If you're lucky, you'll have at least a neighbor or two who have the greenest of thumbs and are willing to trade some of their fresh-grown produce for something you or your family can offer.

You just might find out that you live near a family whose hobby is geocaching, fly fishing, or some other skill you've wanted to learn. A neighbor who knows how to make homemade preserves and can food is definitely someone you want to get to know—even if it means dog-sitting her four Chihuahuas!

If you live in an area prone to natural disasters or extreme weather, your neighbors will have stories to tell about how they survived, or maybe almost didn't, which will help you know better how to prepare for those events. They may even know a few "secret" ways out of town in case of a worst-case scenario or even have an extra well on their property they're willing to share.

Revealing your own preparedness efforts and planning will be up to you. It's a good idea not to tell anyone *everything*, but that's just good advice anyway. I'd rather my neighbors didn't know about all of my former marriages and the fact that I'm wanted in four states. (Just kidding. I've only been married once.) Apply the same level of smartness to the food you have stored, any firearms you own, etc.

Not all neighbors will take kindly to a gesture of friendship. If you think they might be running a crack house or a prostitution ring, my advice is to stay away! Once, my sister had to set up a hidden camera to monitor a particular family whose kids were vandalizing her neighborhood. I know those types of neighbors exist, and you have my pity. You just have to work with the willing.

TheSurvivalMom.com

Meet other Survival Moms just like you on my blog, www.thesurvivalmom.com.

IIIIIIIIIIIIIIIIIIIIIIIIIIIIIIIIIIIIIIIIIIIIIIIIIIIIIIIIIIIIIIIIIIIIIIIIIIIIIIIIIIIIIIIIIIIIIIIIIIIIIIIIIIIIIIIIIIII

Where Are All the Other Survival Moms?

Birds of a feather flock together, and sooner or later Survival Moms will find each other. It's our commonalities that draw us together, so it makes sense that if you're doing Survival Mom "things," you'll meet up with your counterparts. Survival Moms tend to hang out:

1. Around produce co-ops, organic or traditional. They may be looking to buy large quantities of fruit or veggies to dehydrate or can.

2. In classes that promote self-reliance. Sometimes you can find these classes at local LDS (Mormon) churches, organic farms, county

extension offices, yarn stores, etc. If there's a particular skill you'd like to learn, find an organization that teaches or promotes it and find out if they offer classes or have regular meetings—*or* offer to teach one yourself.

3. Community events sponsored by police and fire departments.

4. In meet-up groups. If there isn't one already established in an area that interests you, start one yourself.

5. At church. Church activities are designed to promote friendships, and some churches are very much on board with preparedness.

6. In online e-mail groups. Yahoo Groups has something for everyone.

7. In community-minded groups such as CERT classes or neighborhood watch groups. If there's a meeting for disaster planning in your area, you can bet that you'll find other Survival Moms in attendance.

8. With other homeschool families (if you homeschool).

You may find others with your same point of view just by asking simple questions like, "Have you ever thought about stocking up on a little extra food?" I asked that question of one friend, and boy, did I get an earful! Not only did she tell me about all of the boxes of ramen noodles she has stashed behind her couch but went on to say they were prepared to filter the water in their pool for drinking if they ever became desperate.

If you overhear someone talking about her backyard chickens, that's a red flag, as is an expressed interest in learning canning or any of the other heirloom skills that were part of everyday life for our grandmas and great-grandmas. Moms all over the country are wising up to the necessity to be prepared, so keep your eyes and ears open.

I think you may be surprised at how many of your nearest and dearest are worried about the future, watching the news and trying to figure out what to do next. That really seems to be the stumbling block for a lot of people. Once they get over the fear and denial, they usually don't have a clue that there's anything they *can* do!

A lot of food storage and survival supply companies offer discounts on large orders. As your circle of Survival Mom friends grows, check into placing orders together with companies like Walton Feed and Azure Standard. If a discount isn't offered, just sharing the shipping charges will be a huge bonus.

Can generosity hurt?

In desperate times, handing out extra food and water could clue others into how much you have stored. A better plan is to either donate items to a church or a charity and direct needy people to those organizations or arrange to meet the needy person or family at a location several miles from your home. Is this being paranoid? Maybe, but you know what I say about desperate people.

Are you a single mom?

A single parent is one of the hardest-working people on earth. If you also have the heart of a Survival Mom, you're my hero. There may not be a spouse in the house, but you can nevertheless instill important attitudes in your children, along with teaching them practical skills and nurturing a can-do, self-reliant point of view. The Internet was designed with you in mind, with simply dozens of other moms ready to chat and advise 24 hours a day. If, for now, your Survival Mom friends are all on the Internet, that's okay. Strong friendships that eventually become real-life relationships can begin online. I ought to know. In 1994, I met my future husband in an AOL chat room!

I'm not suggesting you start trolling the survival forums looking for a man, but I'll let you in on a little secret: There are *lots* of single survival-minded guys out there who would love nothing more than to meet a woman on their same wavelength. If your avatar is a photo of you at the shooting range, you're gonna have a mighty full dance card!

Be sure to send me an invitation to the wedding!

Are you single with no kids?

Hey, I was in my 30s when I got married ("Finally!" is what I believe I heard my parents say as they walked me down the aisle). Single life can be awesome, and as with the empty-nesters, your road to survival and preparedness is pretty easy, but your challenge will be con-necting with others who are like-minded and supportive. Check out meet-up groups that get together to discuss topics like gardening, raising chickens in the city, or living off the grid. There are plenty of city-dwellers interested in those topics and desirous of linking up with others.

You actually have advantages over married or attached Survival Moms. If you live alone, there's no one to say, "Do we really need another bucket of wheat?" If you decide to take a handgun class, the only person you need to consult is yourself, and if you decide to chuck it all and move up to Montana, only your mom is going to complain.

I was single when I started my first side business. It became a huge success, but it would have been impossible for me to accomplish what I did if there had been a marriage, or especially kids, to juggle. If you have the heart of a Survival Mom, the only thing standing in your way is whatever *you* place there.

IIIIIIIIIIIIIIIIIIIIIIIIIIIIIIIIIIIIIIIIIIIIIIIIIIIIIIIIIIIIIIIIIIIIIIIIIIIIIIIIIIIIIIIIIIIIIIIIIIII

Online Connections Count!

The Internet is one of God's greatest gifts to humanity! I really mean that. We're able to instantly access directions and information on any subject we can imagine, but we can also access other people who share our interests. The Survival Mom Blog Ring features blogs by women who live on homesteads, single moms, grandmas, and moms who live

Are your kids grown and gone?

Okay, so I have a dear friend who has been on a Survival Mom tear all year long. She has her water barrel (filled), loads of stored food and buckets of lentils for her famous soup, and she manages to hold on to her sense of humor. She confided to me that her daughter is coming for a visit but, "She's really coming to check up on me and see if I've lost my mind." In her case, her kids aren't exactly on board.

If your kids are grown and you have an empty nest, well, you only need to worry about those who are still actually living in the nest. That's a big plus. There's less to buy, less to store, and less to do. One or two people can definitely live on less. If your home is free and clear and you're debt free, or nearly so, you're actually in a very good position to make some giant strides toward preparedness.

My retired friends Butch and Judy just recently decided they wanted to be better prepared for the future, and they have jumped right in, learning something new about food storage or solar generators every day. A favorite quote of mine is, "You'll never be younger than you are right this minute," so why not make the most of it?

You have decades of information to share with younger people. I know that I would welcome more grandparents to my Survival Mom compound! If you garden, can catch, clean, and cook fish, know how to make jams and jellies, and can rock a baby to sleep, you're quite a catch! You've spent a lifetime learning, observing, and doing. Please! Share your knowledge, skills, and wisdom with the rest of us! A lot of us are playing catch-up.

Most of the grandparents I know want to stock up on enough food, diapers, and other supplies in order to take care of their kids and grandkids. They tell me, "When times get hard, guess who's going to show up at my front door?" They have a point.

smack dab in the middle of big cities. You can connect with thousands of other moms on forums, websites, Facebook, blogs, and even online webinars. They're there to advise, commiserate, laugh with, and befriend. They may not be able to watch your kids when you and hubby have a date night, but they can become the next best thing.

Online friends are great for one other reason: The Internet has a way of dissolving boundaries between people. Age, race, location, or education—none of that matters online. Even though I'm more of a city girl, I'm friends with homesteaders and moms half my age. In real life, we tend to hang out with others who are almost exactly like us. When it comes to preparedness and survival, that's not the smartest strategy. City-based soccer moms need to learn from moms who live on farms, ranches, and in tiny towns that boast, "Population 524." If we want to get back to our roots, the easiest way to do that is to learn from someone who is already there, even if we never leave the city.

No Grandma Left Behind

In 1995, I was in Chicago during one of its deadliest heat waves ever. Of the 700-plus people who died, most were elderly. I remember thinking, "Why didn't their families or neighbors check on them and help?"

Who in *your* life is elderly, sickly, and/or disabled and might need some help in a catastrophe? A game plan needs to be put in order right away to provide a sense of security for everyone involved. You want to make sure that *your* grandma is looked after, no matter what might happen.

Note: To make my job as a writer easier, I'm going to refer to the elderly person in your life as "Grandma"—no offense to Grandpa, Aunt Beryl, or your neighbor Zelda!

A bad neighbor is a misfortune, as much as a good one is a great blessing.

—HESIOD

1. What medications is Grandma taking? Is it possible to get an additional 30-day supply? A reserve of life-saving medications should be a top priority. If something needs to be kept refrigerated, that should be noted and planned for.

2. Make a list of each medication, the dosage, the doctor who prescribed it, and the name, address, and phone number of the pharmacy. Give a copy to Grandma and another family member, or two, and keep a copy for yourself. This would be a good thing to have in your Grab-n-Go Binder.

3. What doctors does she see on a regular basis? Make a list of their names, specialties, addresses, email addresses, and fax and phone numbers. While you're at it, make a copy of her Medicare and health insurance cards, in case she's ever incapacitated and you're the one making medical decisions. Again, give her a copy and keep one in your Grab-n-Go Binder.

4. Does Grandma have someone designated with power of attorney? If so, that document should be readily available and up to date.

5. What routine could be established so you're certain of her well-being each morning? With a neighbor, it could be a specific window blind being opened each morning. Alternatively, a morning phone call at a certain time each day could provide that reassurance.

6. Is there medical equipment she relies on? In an evacuation situation, would that equipment fit in your or her vehicle? Help her make a plan for evacuation that includes assistance from family members in the area.

7. If Grandma is a neighbor or a family friend, make a point of meeting her family members, even if it's just in a phone conversation. Get their names, addresses, and phone numbers because in an emergency, it might be important for you to know whom to contact.

8. Put together a simple emergency kit for her, including one she can keep in her vehicle, if she drives. Be sure to add items unique to her needs, such as a list of her doctors and medications, an extra pair of eyeglasses, and a sweater. (This last suggestion is based on the stereotypical Grandma who *always* wears a sweater!)

9. If Grandma has a pet, talk with her about how she'll care for it in an evacuation situation or some other emergency.

10. Electrical outages can be frightening to anybody. Make sure that Grandma not only has flashlights and extra batteries on hand, but that she also knows exactly where to find them.

11. None of us would want to leave behind cherished photos and heirlooms. Help Grandma put these together in one container that can be packed up quickly. Make sure other family members know its whereabouts. Particularly valuable items should be kept in a safe deposit box or in a heavy-duty home safe.

12. Put yourself in Grandma's place. In a crisis situation with events changing by the moment, what would *you* need for reassurance? When my grandmother became ill shortly before her death, it seemed like even the smallest changes in her routine were monumental to her. (I'm kind of like that *now*!) What else can you think of that will not only give her a sense of security but also a plan of action?

The best time to make friends is before you need them.

—*ETHEL BARRYMORE*

Survival Moms tend to be very busy with multiple irons in the fire. Having an elderly family member can add to the stress of our everyday lives, and much more so during a disaster or an emergency of some sort. By all means, include other concerned people in your planning. Nobody's Grandma or Grandpa should be forgotten and left behind in a crisis.

I'd Like to Teach the World to Sing in Perfect Harmony

Whatever.

The fact of the matter is that most of the world isn't interested in joining hands and singing kum-bah-ya with you. It's possible that despite all your good intentions and reaching out, you'll be met with unpleasant people, difficult decisions to make and tough circumstances.

After the Japanese earthquake and tsunami of 2011, the world was amazed at the continued civility in Japan. We were shocked to see lines of desperate people, people who had lost everything, stand patiently in line to get a few items of food and some water.

It was a contrast that embarrassed me as an American, when I remembered the scenes of looting following championship basketball games, some of our own natural disasters, and even controversial court decisions. My first thought is always, "Who *are* these people and where do they come from?" I don't know if those types of responses are innate in the American culture, but I've seen enough to realize that there are plenty of bad people out there, and if I'm smart, I'll avoid where they hang out and watch for them where *I* hang out.

Speaking of incivility and violence, every now and then I hear the comment, "I've got a .45, and that's all the preparation I'm going to need." Interpreted for those who scarcely know what a .45 is (it's a caliber of handgun), these people are openly communicating that they will steal, at gunpoint, food, water, heat, and whatever *they* need in order to survive. It's an ignorant statement and point of view, but I think we always need to keep in mind that not everyone is as nice and polite as we are. Plan, prepare, and live accordingly.

It really pays to have a group of trusted friends you can count on. If they're former Navy SEALS and come with CIA connections, so much the better.

> Our greatest weakness lies in giving up. The most certain way to succeed is always to try just one more time.
>
> —THOMAS EDISON

☑ Teach kids what is okay to share and what isn't. The more casual you can be about choices your family is making related to preparedness, the easier it will be for your kids to accept it.

☑ Set an example of being a good neighbor by looking for ways to help out neighbors and get to know new ones. Every Christmas, the kids and I make several different types of Christmas goodies and deliver them on holiday plates to our neighbors. Small acts of kindness can go a long way toward forming friendships and establishing strong bonds within your community.

- With permission, rake the leaves in a neighbor's front yard.

- Make it a habit to be out and about in your neighborhood, along with the kids. Point out to them elderly neighbors who might be in need of a hand and look for opportunities to be of help.

- Order a "secret pizza" for a family in need of encouragement. Dial up your favorite pizza place, pre-pay for the meal, and arrange for delivery by five o'clock or so. Then, swear the kids to secrecy!

- As a family, put together an emergency kit for someone unable or unlikely to do it themselves. You'll reinforce the importance of being prepared for emergencies, and the kids will turn their focus to the needs of another person.

The Prepared Family

Family Preparedness Plan: **Making Connections**

When it comes to a preparedness mind-set, who is in *my* compound?

☐ Spouse/Significant Other ☐ Other relatives

☐ Siblings ☐ Parents

☐ Children ☐ Close friends

I want to connect with other like-minded Survival Moms and families.

☐ Yes

☐ No

My level of comfort when it comes to talking about and sharing my family's preparedness efforts is:

0 · **10**

(Loose lips sink ships.) *(I don't care who knows.)*

If or when I'm ready, I could probably meet other preparing families here: _____

_____

_____

When it comes to survival and preparedness in our family, I see myself as being primarily responsible for this: _____

_____

_____

_____

My spouse's or significant other's responsibilities are: _____

_____

_____

_____

Practical skills I want my children to learn are: _____

_____

_____

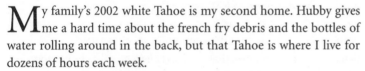

CHAPTER 11

Preparedness on the Go: Evacuation Basics

My family's 2002 white Tahoe is my second home. Hubby gives me a hard time about the french fry debris and the bottles of water rolling around in the back, but that Tahoe is where I live for dozens of hours each week.

One of the most satisfying experiences I've ever had with that vehicle was a trip I took to Lake Tahoe with the kids. That's right: Hubby had to stay at home. As we packed up, I admit to feeling a fairly high level of panic at the thought of driving some 2,000 miles without him next to me. If a tire went flat, there was no way I could change it on a vehicle of that size. What if an EMP happened while we were gone and we could never get home? And this was my biggest fear of all: Could I handle such a long drive all by myself *and* keep the kids entertained and out of trouble?

Just 50 miles later, my fears had completely eased. The kids and I were having the time of our lives! Beneath the suitcases, bike helmets, skateboards, and blankets, I had packed a first-aid kit, a Vehicle Emergency Kit, plenty of water, and lots of food. We were as prepared as a mom and her two young kids could be. We went on to have a memorable, amazing 3-week vacation. The extra preparation, and hourly phone calls to Dad while we were on the road, brought a great deal of peace to my mind. The GPS didn't hurt, either.

Why Is Away-from-Home Preparedness So Important?

Life brings with it the unexpected. Sometimes these surprises are fun, but sometimes they bring danger. A flat tire in town isn't usually considered a crisis, but the same event occurring a thousand miles from home on Interstate 80 out in the middle of Wyoming is a whole different story. Winter storms sometimes roll in without giving forecasters a clue as to their severity. A family stuck miles from home amid blocked roads and 10-foot-high snowdrifts is in for the adventure of their lives—if they survive!

If you're a mom, chances are that you put a lot of miles on your vehicle of choice and are away from home many hours each week. You may run a dozen errands a day or have a part-time or a full-time job. Think about how much time you spend away from home, overall, and it probably adds up to at least several hours each week, not counting family road trips. It makes a lot of sense that your home away from home, your vehicle, should be equipped for all sorts of emergencies. Since there's no guarantee that all of your family will be home, together, when the next big crisis hits, make sure every vehicle in the family is ready.

||||||||||||||||||||||||||||||||||||||||||||||||||||||||||||||||||||||||||||||||||||||||||||||||||||||||

A Ready Car, a Ready Family

Road Survival Rule #1

Don't ever forget this one: A half-full tank of gas is an empty tank of gas. Try to never let the tank in your car get below half full.

A car that's ready to take on a long trip of any kind is a good thing, but if you're ever stranded far from home, you need something else. That something else often goes by the name of a 72-Hour Kit. Seventy-two hours, for those of you who were never exactly math-major material, is the equivalent of 3 days. My problem with "72" is that no one ever knows what to expect in a crisis, especially how long it will last. If you pack an emergency kit for just 72 hours and the situation ends up lasting for 72 days, you are in deep trouble! The best solution is to have a plan for various contingencies and then pack your kits accordingly. For example, I have enough food in my Vehicle Emergency Kit to last for 3 days, but I keep about a dozen #10 cans of freeze-dried

Every vehicle equipped for almost anything

The first obvious step is to make sure that your car, truck, or van itself is ready. Driving around with bald tires and the oil light flashing is no way to get through life! Some emergencies require a hasty evacuation. If your vehicle is always ready to go, you'll be able to hit the highway long before the rest of the crowd. Here's a checklist to help you get your car ready for anything:

- Stay up to date with routine maintenance:
  - Oil changes
  - Air filter changes
  - Tire rotation and maintenance of proper tire pressure
  - Regular tune-ups
- Maintain the proper levels of important fluids:
  - Brake fluid
  - Antifreeze
  - Oil
  - Power-steering fluid
  - Transmission fluid
  - Windshield washer fluid
- Have extra parts and supplies on hand:
  - Wiper blades
  - Air and oil filters
  - Bulbs for headlamps and brake lights

- Store a tankful of extra fuel in a safe place and rotate.
- Attempt to keep fuel tank no less than half full.
- Keep spare tires properly inflated and ensure that you have all of the necessary tools for changing a tire.
  - Use a Sharpie to write the correct PSI for your tires on the front cover of your vehicle's manual.
  - Keep at least one air-pressure gauge in your vehicle.
  - Flat-tire repair kit
- Have good road maps for your state and each surrounding state.
- Store emergency supplies:
  - Blankets
  - Walking shoes and extra socks
  - Cash
  - Well-equipped Vehicle Emergency Kit (see pages 250–252)
  - Sturdy work gloves
  - Road flare
  - Jumper cables

A healthy car brings a lot of peace of mind. Just as we moms should never ignore health warning signals, we should also take seriously things like dashboard warning lights and the sound of gears grinding. Ignore *those* at your peril!

meals stored close to our back door. If we even have a hunch that a crisis may be long-term, we can grab that extra food and be ready.

Plenty of survival experts argue that 72 hours will pass all too quickly and your family may be better off with even more supplies. I agree, but then, I'm the woman with close to 300 rolls of toilet paper stored in her bonus room!

One of the first questions I
often get from newbies to
the survival/preparedness
scene is, "Where should
I buy my MREs?" An MRE
is a military Meal Ready to
Eat. I think everyone
should try at least one for
the experience. They can
be helpful as a temporary
source of nutrition in an
evacuation or a similar
crisis. However, MREs aren't
exactly known for their
fiber content, giving way
to a few unflattering
nicknames, such as
"Meals Refusing to Exit."

Your emergency kits should be equipped well enough so that you or even your entire family would be able to survive in relative comfort, whether stranded or in the middle of an evacuation. If you have multiple kits—think "layers"—you'll do quite well.

Below and on pages 251–252 are the basics for a well-equipped Vehicle Emergency Kit. Customize as needed

Believe it or not, all of this will fit into a moderately small space, and you probably have most of these items, or at least their equivalents, around the house. When I put our kit together, I was actually shocked by how quickly it came together. I added a few things over time, but the kit was ready in 1 day.

I keep several 2-liter bottles filled with water in my vehicle at all times. Thus, they would not be something I would have to add to my emergency kit. Collapsible containers are good for water storage. Make sure you buy good quality, though.

Because I have an SUV, I use an opaque, under-the-bed storage box to hold our kit. Take a look at the size of your car trunk or how much room you have in the back of the minivan and use a container that fits just right.

One scenario that should be considered and planned for is the need to leave your vehicle behind and walk to a more secure or comfortable location. I've included nylon bags and backpacks on my list just for

Vehicle Emergency Kit Checklist

Make a copy of this list, check off what you include in your kit, and then place it on top of everything in the kit as an inventory.

Sanitation

- ☐ Rolls of toilet paper with cardboard center removed and the roll flattened
- ☐ Hand sanitizer
- ☐ Toothbrush/toothpaste or a packet of those little single-use tooth-scrubbers
- ☐ Plastic tablecloth
- ☐ A few plastic grocery bags
- ☐ Trash bags to line potty
- ☐ Baby wipes
- ☐ Liquid soap, double-bagged
- ☐ Dental floss
- ☐ Porta-potty, stored separate from the kit
- ☐ Clorox wipes
- ☐ Feminine protection
- ☐ Small box of tissues
- ☐ Ziploc bags
- ☐ A pair of underwear per person

Sustenance

- [ ] Energy bars (high-calorie)
- [ ] Almonds
- [ ] V8 juice
- [ ] Canned pasta
- [ ] Gatorade mix
- [ ] Plastic utensils/metal cup
- [ ] Cocoa mix
- [ ] Peanut butter
- [ ] Jerky
- [ ] Dried fruit/canned fruit
- [ ] Applesauce/fruit cups
- [ ] Rice cakes
- [ ] Pilot bread/Triscuits
- [ ] Hard candies
- [ ] Tuna packs
- [ ] Dry cereal
- [ ] Jam/jelly cups
- [ ] Trail mix (no chocolate)
- [ ] Shelled sunflower seeds
- [ ] Freeze-dried meals
- [ ] Can opener

Survival

- [ ] Water
- [ ] Water filter
- [ ] Purification tablets
- [ ] Flashlight(s) (LED uses less battery power)
- [ ] Rain ponchos
- [ ] Emergency radio
- [ ] Heavy-duty trash bags
- [ ] Emergency blanket
- [ ] Duct tape
- [ ] Fleece blankets
- [ ] Tarp
- [ ] Paracord
- [ ] Multipurpose knife
- [ ] Headlamp(s)
- [ ] Batteries

- [ ] Hand and foot warmers
- [ ] Work gloves
- [ ] Small, sturdy shovel
- [ ] Fire starters
- [ ] Waterproof matches
- [ ] Multi-tool
- [ ] Binoculars
- [ ] Light sticks
- [ ] Maps
- [ ] High-quality first-aid kit
- [ ] Bandanna
- [ ] Small pair of scissors
- [ ] Collapsible nylon bags
- [ ] Shoelaces
- [ ] Walking shoes
- [ ] Floppy cotton hat
- [ ] Sunblock
- [ ] Medications
- [ ] Face mask
- [ ] Bug repellent
- [ ] Moleskin
- [ ] Long-sleeve shirt
- [ ] A pair of socks for each person
- [ ] Wind-up weather radio
- [ ] Survival and first-aid manuals
- [ ] Medium-size backpack(s)
- [ ] Compass
- [ ] A few coffee filters (to use to filter out particles in water)

Security

- [ ] Whistle
- [ ] Cash, including coins
- [ ] Disposable camera (to photograph storm damage, perps, etc.)
- [ ] Pepper spray/Taser
- [ ] Emergency phone numbers

continued on page 252

Sanity

☐ Deck of cards
☐ Foam earplugs
☐ Book(s) on CD and paperbacks
☐ Bible
☐ Small journal and pen or pencil
☐ Chapstick
☐ Battery-powered fan

Note: If you keep small, related items together in Ziploc bags of various sizes, the bags can later serve other purposes.

Be safe *and* legal

If you choose to keep a firearm in your vehicle, know the law in your state and follow it. The safest place for a handgun is a small gun safe designed to fit beneath the driver's seat.

that purpose. You'll be able to load these up with the most important items from your Vehicle Emergency Kit and continue on foot.

Before going on a road trip, I'll add a 5-gallon bucket, a snap-on toilet lid, several heavy-duty black trash bags, and a small bag of kitty litter, just in case the bucket has to serve as an emergency toilet.

When you put together a Vehicle Emergency Kit for your hubby, I suggest assembling all of the kit's contents, laying them out on a table and then having the man in your life pack his own kit. If you do it for him, he'll have no idea where to find things, and if he's ever surrounded by a pack of zombies and has to fumble through his kit, you're going to have one very angry man on your hands by the time he gets home!

Know how to use everything!

Make absolutely sure that you know how to use each item that you pack in your kits. Do you actually know how to navigate using a compass? Can you use a flint striker to start a fire? Are you familiar with all of the little tools on that multi-tool? If you're thinking that you'll somehow know how to use all your equipment under duress, think again!

Emergency Kits for the Home

By now, your vehicle should be well on its way to becoming the envy of Survival Moms everywhere. If you're ever stuck out in the boonies or just across town, you'll be equipped to survive.

Now let's talk about setting up similar kits for your home. Every year thousands of Americans are forced to leave the comfort of their homes because it's no longer the safest place to be. Vicious storms, earthquakes, wildfires, and hurricanes can transform the most stable family into a pitiful group of refugees in a matter of minutes. Are you ready to hit the road if you absolutely have to?

It's one thing to throw a few necessities in a bag and run, but it's quite another to do that while the adrenaline is pumping, the kids are crying, and hubby is yelling, "Honey, come ON!" If you think you can do that and remember everything that needs to be packed, you're a stronger woman than I am. Even with weeks of advance prep time, I've forgotten to pack essentials like socks or toothpaste for vacations!

Who Needs an Emergency Kit?

Everyone in your family needs his or her own emergency kit—and that includes pets! These kits don't need to take up much room; in fact, a good place to keep them is inside by the garage door, or an outside door nearest to your vehicles, or in your safe room. I prefer the safe room location because the supplies will be there in case we're ever locked in during a home invasion or some other critical event.

There are three categories of family emergency kits: individual kits, the family kit, and specialty kits.

Individual Kits

Your kids will probably love the idea of having their very own emergency kit, although you might want to call it something friendlier, like a Getaway Bag. Avoid terms like "Run-for-Your-Life Kit" or "We're-All-Gonna-Die Kit"!

Individual emergency kits are specific to the person. The contents can be packed in any type of bag, preferably something you already have on hand or can pick up at a garage sale. Some people prefer medium-size duffle bags, and one gal has hers packed in a plastic bin.

What about those ready-made kits?

I have mixed feelings about the kits sold by just about every emergency and survival website. On one hand, they're a no-brainer. You hand over your debit or credit card information, and a kit is on its way. There's a price to be paid for this convenience, however. You may find that some of the contents are of less than high quality. When you put your own kit together, not only will it be customized to your needs, but also you can shop around to make sure you are getting quality supplies that will do what they're supposed to do when your survival is depending on them.

Something with shoulder straps or at least a handle will make carrying easier if you have to hoof it.

An Individual Kit should have two changes of clothing. Think of layers when planning the clothing for each Individual Kit and try to select items that aren't bulky. In a nutshell, here is a list of clothing items that would be suitable for most people and situations:

☐ Two short-sleeved, cotton T-shirts. One should be brightly colored to help family members locate each other.

☐ One long-sleeved, light-colored, cotton shirt

☐ Two pairs of lightweight pants

☐ One pair of shorts—useful for swimming and as pajamas

☐ Three pairs of underwear

☐ An extra bra or two

☐ Three pairs of socks

☐ A lightweight jacket, waterproof if your climate demands it

☐ Shoes—comfortable and practical

☐ A floppy hat and/or wool cap, depending on the season

Your kits should contain clothing suitable for your climate and typical weather conditions. I suppose you *could* worry about color-coordinated outfits and accessories if you really want the added stress, but comfort and packability are far more important factors. Also, since there really is a lot involved with this whole "preparedness" thing, save money by using clothing you already have or can purchase very inexpensively. Secondhand stores are your friends!

A few items that should also be in every kit are:

☐ Individual water bottle, to be refilled as needed

☐ Several packages of high-calorie snacks

☐ Gum and/or candy

☐ Headlamp with extra batteries

☐ Small individual toiletry bag with toothbrush, small toothpaste, a few hand wipes, and comb or hairbrush

☐ $40–50 in cash. In case the family gets separated, I want my kids to have money for food, phone calls, bribes, or whatever. A Visa gift card would be another good choice, just not as versatile as cash.

☐ Contact information for parents and trusted relatives and friends

Your kids' kits should be lightweight enough for them to carry in a backpack. Even a preschooler can wear a backpack for a good, long

An emergency kit by any other name . . . is still an emergency kit!

Survival Moms have all sorts of creative names for their kits. Some, such as "Disaster Bag," are straightforward. Others are cute and meant to obscure the kit's true purpose. Here's a selection for you to choose from, if you feel the need to be creative:

- EPK (Emergency Preparedness Kit)
- Disaster Bag
- What-If Bag
- GOOD-e Bag or GOODie Bag (Get Out of Dodge Bag)
- Go Bag
- To-Go Bag
- Scramble Pack
- Get-Home Bag
- Survival Bag
- BOB (as in, "Go get BOB," also known as Bug Out Bag)

Last-minute add-ons

Make a list of must-haves for your emergency kits that can only be added at the very last minute. These might include prescription medication, an inhaler, over-the-counter meds for any current sicknesses or allergies, a firearm and ammo, cash, and maybe some fresh produce to keep everyone regular! If you're in an area that experiences extreme winter weather, add bulky items like gloves, mittens, or heavy jackets at the last minute.

while if it's the right size and isn't too heavy. Heck, there are even dog backpacks! In a dire situation, *no one* gets a free ride! Sorry, Fido!

Speaking of kids, include a few items to provide comfort and entertainment, such as a favorite toy or a lovie of some sort. Other than taking into consideration the size and weight of an item, I would suggest giving your children plenty of leeway when they make their comfort item choice. A puzzle book, a pad of paper, and colored pencils can help keep older kids occupied, and a small bag of hard candy can provide a much-needed treat in a stressful situation. Audio books, along with an iPod, take up very little room for the hours of entertainment they provide.

Even the very best-equipped emergency kit won't do you much good if you fall victim to theft or violence. Parents should include in their own kits *something* that will help provide protection for the family. My husband's choice is a 9mm Glock handgun with a couple of extra, loaded magazines. I always have pepper spray, and one of my last-minute add-ons would be my own handgun.

And what about comfort items for Mom or Dad? A small knitting or stitchery kit doesn't take much room, and a book or an MP3 player will provide hours of stress-free entertainment.

Repack these individual kits every 6 months. Kids grow, seasons change, and stuff spills. Moms gain and lose weight!

When your Individual Kits are complete, decide where they will be kept and then hold a family meeting to discuss what the kits are for and the fact that they *are not to be touched* until Mom or Dad gives permission.

The Family Kit

The Family Kit is meant to complement the Individual Kits and the Vehicle Emergency Kit. It will contain everything else needed by the family as a whole that *isn't already packed in other kits*. Be sure to keep inventories for every kit you put together to avoid redundancy, unless you need more than one of an item. You may end up dividing this kit into more than one container. In fact, one Survival Mom uses a plastic garbage can on wheels, and another friend packs blankets and inflatable pillows in a 5-gallon bucket that can double as the ubiquitous emergency toilet. The idea of using different types and sizes of containers is a good one. You never know when you'll need to repurpose that duffel bag or rolling ice chest.

Be sure not to overpack. There's no need for everyone in the family to have a hatchet, for example, unless you're a family of firefighters! However, make sure your kit contains supplies for staying warm and dry, heating up food and water, and being safe. Remember, you can live for 3 weeks without much food, but once you get cold and wet, all bets are off, and you'll be miserable.

Some other items for the Family Kit include:

☐ Paper towels
☐ Over-the-counter meds, such as Benadryl, pain relievers, cough medicine, and hydrocortisone cream
☐ Small plastic or metal plates or bowls
☐ Laundry soap (store away from food!)
☐ Small spray bottle of anti-bacterial cleaner/disinfectant. Store in a leakproof container, away from food.
☐ Plastic tablecloth that can double as ground cover but would also improve the sanitariness of a road-stop picnic table.
☐ Multivitamins, both adult and child formulas
☐ Set of nesting pots for cooking.
☐ Plastic utensils.

Consider vests as an option!

My very good friend Debbie suggests using hiking or fisherman's vests with lots and lots of pockets in place of backpacks, especially for kids. The pockets can hold many small items, making a backpack unnecessary or lightening its load.

INSTANT SURVIVAL TIP

Once each kit is packed, place a flashlight in an outside pocket or on top of all contents to make it easier to find what you need when it's dark outside. Then, slap a piece of masking tape on the front of the kit and mark it with the date it was packed.

This kit will contain the majority of your food. You know what your family will eat and if there are any food allergies, so plan accordingly. If you pack food that must be warmed up, make sure you include a dependable cooking method, along with enough fuel to last for a few weeks. As a backup, I purchased a couple of Nuwick candles and a folding stove; other moms prefer a small, propane cook stove. I figure that a warm meal is far more satisfying and comforting than eating cold ravioli 3 days in a row.

To avoid rampant snacking and food theft, it's best to devise written daily meal plans. Pack food according to these plans and then stick with the plan. If there are snacks available in the Vehicle and Individual Kits, there's no reason to dig into these meals.

Since the Family Kit will contain food, it's important to check it once a month for spoilage, pests, and expiration dates, and remember to keep it stored in a cool, dry location.

Suggested on-the-road breakfasts

- Individual packets of instant oatmeal or cream of wheat
- Individual servings of granola in Ziploc bags, along with 2 tablespoons dehydrated milk (reconstitute with ⅓ cup of water for ready-to-eat cereal)
- Granola or cereal bars
- Include a serving of canned, dehydrated, or freeze-dried fruit for a more satisfying and nutritious breakfast.
- Add a serving of a high-Vitamin C drink, such as Tang, to each breakfast.

The breakfast breakdown in your kit might look something like this for a family of four for 7 days:

- ☐ 35 packets of oatmeal/cereal. (My husband would need two packets in order to get his day going. Take into consideration the nutritional needs of growing kids and the expected level of exertion.)
- ☐ 7 servings of dried apples and peaches
- ☐ 7 servings of Tang in a heavy-duty Ziploc bag

It's vital to take measures to carefully store any food item that could leak, such as fruit cups. I prefer to pack dried foods as much as possible.

It's okay to have more than one . . .

- Pocket knife
- Pair of scissors
- Roll of duct tape
- Fire starter
- Pair of work gloves
- Pair of sunglasses
- Firearm (with magazines)
- Black Sharpie
- Multi-tool

Suggested kit lunches

It's helpful to have one meal that won't require any type of heat or cooking. For planning purposes, I've designated lunch as that meal.

- Canned entrees
- Peanut butter with crackers or pilot bread
- Dried fruit and/or veggies

Once the meals are packed, a family of four might have something that looks like this:

- ☐ 6 cans of SpaghettiOs (2 per meal)
- ☐ 4 MREs (for the novelty and to give Mom a break, since MRE = no prep or cleanup)
- ☐ 6 cans of mini ravioli (2 per meal)
- ☐ 7 packages of cheese and crackers
- ☐ 7 cups of pudding and/or tapioca

Suggested kit dinners

Assuming you have a way to warm up food, here are some good options:

- Freeze-dried entrees. If you've purchased these in #10 cans, repackage them in Ziploc bags or plastic food-storage containers with lids.
- Canned chili, soup or beef stew
- Canned corn beef hash
- MREs are okay for meals once or twice a week
- Pudding and fruit cups

A family of four would have these foods on hand for a 7-day emergency:

- ☐ 16 servings of the freeze-dried entrée of your choice (4 meals)
- ☐ 4 containers of End-of-the-World Mac 'n Cheese (2 meals)
- ☐ 2 cans of a hearty soup, such as Progresso's Chicken Corn Chowder or another favorite flavor (1 meal)
- ☐ 14 pieces of pilot bread or other sturdy cracker
- ☐ 7 servings of dehydrated fruit
- ☐ 4 packages of cookies
- ☐ 3 chocolate bars

A must-have for your kits

If you will be packing any electronics, I highly recommend a nifty product from Radio Shack—the Enercell Portable Power Bank. Use a USB connection to power this battery and then use it to recharge cell phones, digital cameras, iPods, iPhones, and MP3 players. Once charged, the Enercell's lithium battery loses only 5% of its original charge each month. Charge it, drop it in an emergency kit, and you'll never have to worry about a dead cell phone at a critical moment.

Depending on your particular emergency, you may or may not have access to cooking facilities. Sooner or later, you'll be *craving* a hot meal—that's for sure. Include in your menus foods that can be eaten cold; you'll have the hot meal option when the opportunity presents itself.

Is all this fine dining? No! Dear God, no! However, it's survival. In the midst of a Katrina-size crisis, having these meals pre-planned and ready to go will bring more peace of mind than most of us can imagine.

When a crisis forces you to leave home, supplement your emergency kit meals with fresh produce, milk, cheese, and bread whenever you can: Not only will your packed provisions last longer, but everyone's digestive systems will appreciate the goodness of fresh foods.

Specialty Kits

"Specialty Kit" sounds like something you might find at a cute little boutique, but these kits are unique to special situations within your family.

Pet Emergency Kit

If you have a pet and there's a critical event, you have a real problem on your hands if you haven't planned ahead. Not only could I never leave our pets behind—we have three dogs and two cats—but I also couldn't deal with the weeping, wailing, and gnashing of teeth from my kids. I always say: "Pets aren't 'just like' family. They *are* family." So, even though it's a little more work, a Pet Emergency Kit is a must. Fortunately, most pets have the same basic requirements: food, water, and place to pee and poop. If your kit covers these basics, you're golden.

Do you have pests?

The multilegged kind, that is. Whenever and wherever you have food stored, insects and rodents will likely be a problem. This will affect the food in your emergency kits. I recommend storing meals in individual Ziploc bags or other containers and then placing everything in something sturdier, such as Rubbermaid's ActionPacker.

Here are some general supplies to gather together:

☐ A week's worth of food per pet. Plan on feeding your pets slightly less food than usual, since there's a good chance they won't get to be as active and less food means less poop.
☐ A lightweight water and food bowl. Collapsible bowls are really nice for travel.
☐ A collar and a leash
☐ A pet crate, which can pull double-duty to store the kit until the crate itself is needed.
☐ A small bag of kitty litter. If you're likely to be in close quarters, go ahead and buy the more expensive clumping/deodorizing brand.
☐ A small- or medium-size box for the cat's litter
☐ A copy of your pets' immunization records from the vet

Make sure your pets are up to date with their vaccines and that you have copies of the vaccine records. If you have no other choice but to hand your dog or cat over to a shelter, these records will become invaluable and it will bring peace of mind to know that your beloved animal is in a safe, *temporary* environment. Photos of each pet will also come in handy for identification purposes.

Our cat Daisy could have been the model for Duchess in Disney's *The Aristocats,* but let me tell you: She is plain mean, and I'll never again try to put her in a crate. I just don't have that much blood in my body to spare! Here's a word to the wise: Get your pets accustomed to traveling and being placed in and out of their crates long before you ever have to get out of Dodge.

If you have a reptile, you'll have to decide what to put in its Pet Emergency Kit. One of the most important factors reptiles rely on to survive is heat, which may not be easy to provide on the road. Likewise, fish aren't exactly easy to transport. If you have a large RV and toting a fish tank or a reptile habitat isn't an issue, then pack some of their food, and you're good to go. The rest of us may have to make some hard decisions about whether to leave Nemo or Kaa behind.

Emergency Tool Kit

Your home and garage are probably very well equipped when it comes to having various and necessary tools. When you need a Phillips screwdriver or a hammer, it's probably stored just a few steps away. Leave

Nine-tenths of wisdom is being wise in time.

—THEODORE
ROOSEVELT

home, however, and all those handy tools will be out of reach.

It's a smart idea to put together an Emergency Tool Kit, packed specifically for evacuations or bugging out. A few must-haves are:

☐ Claw hammer. This multipurpose tool can be used for anything from hammering nails to demolition.

☐ Nails and screws, assorted sizes

☐ Set of screwdrivers, both Phillips and straight. There should be different sizes of each type. Larger screwdrivers can be useful for prying and chiseling.

☐ Pair of lineman's pliers, often called by the trade name, Kleins. These are especially useful because they combine the flat surface of regular pliers with a cutting edge. Make sure your pair can cut through steel, in case you need to cut through wire or nails.

☐ Utility knife, a.k.a. box cutter, with extra blades in the handle

☐ Wood saw and hacksaw. The hacksaw can be used to cut through steel, plastic, and wood, but the wood saw is useful for cutting through large branches and small trees.

☐ Crescent wrenches in two sizes: small and medium

The more you care, the stronger you can be.

—JIM ROHN

Once the basics are in place, a few additional tools you might add are files, prybars, box-end and open-end wrenches, and channel locks. Include other tools specialized to whatever disaster scenarios are most likely in your neck of the woods, such as a small axe, a chain saw, or, perhaps, a soldering gun.

Handyman tools are just part of what should be packed. Common tools for simple vehicle repairs, as well as repairs to bicycles, motorcycles, and even wheelchairs, should also be considered.

A final category of tools includes those used by anyone in the household who relies on them for a living. An electrician, a carpenter, a machinist, a mechanic, or a plumber may want to pack his collection of specialized tools. These tools are usually quite expensive, and they might come in handy for earning money while away from home during a long evacuation period.

Before running out and buying a bunch of new tools, take an inventory of what you already have. There's a very good chance you have duplicates that can be packed away in the Emergency Tool Kit, but if you'll be making purchases to complete your tool kit, look for tools that can do more than one job (multiuse) and kits of tools in multiple sizes.

Wilderness Survival Kit

Even if you're not exactly a camping fanatic, there are some very good reasons for having basic camping supplies on hand in a Wilderness Survival Kit. If you find yourself driving long distances on a regular basis, or if your family owns a home or property in the wilderness, do what some of my survivalist friends do: They keep a heavy-duty Rubbermaid ActionPacker in the trunk or by the back door, and it's always filled with everything they might need if they had to rough it in the wilderness for more than just a day or two. Does this describe you? Then, you might want to put together these items in a kit of your own:

☐ Sturdy but lightweight tent. Use either a tent large enough for everyone or multiple smaller tents.

☐ Sleeping mat(s)

☐ Rugged survival knife. KA-BAR is a well-respected brand.

☐ Compact cook stove with fuel

☐ Set of sturdy cooking pans and utensils

☐ Compact sleeping bag(s) suitable for your climate

☐ Fishing gear—if you're into fishing. Look for a good-quality, collapsible fishing rod, or two.

☐ Hunting rifle or shotgun with ammunition

☐ Bug netting—if you live in a tropical climate or just really, really hate bugs

☐ Bear repellent—if you'll be traveling or camping in bear country

☐ A tarp or two

☐ Paracord (rope)

You may not want to store this Wilderness Survival Kit in your vehicle all the time. Some families keep it in a handy place in the garage or, perhaps, by the back door—already packed and ready to go, just not taking up valuable trunk space in the meantime.

Even if you don't use these supplies for camping out, they would be very handy for providing shelter just about anywhere. If your only option is to stop for the night and park in a church or a hotel parking lot, the tent and a sleeping bag would be much more comfortable than trying to get everyone cozy in your car.

The never-fail fire starter

If you have cotton balls and Vaseline around the house somewhere, you have the ingredients for a top-notch fire starter. Infuse several cotton balls with Vaseline and store them in a small container. This simple combination is easy to make, is easy to pack, and makes starting a fire quick and easy. Leon Pantenburg of Survival Common Sense gives it his highest recommendation.

Baby's Emergency Kit

Who doesn't love a baby? Other people in a Red Cross shelter, that's who—if your baby is uncomfortable and on a serious crying jag! If you have a baby, you already have all the supplies needed for your kit. You just need to pull it all together and set it aside for emergencies only. My friend Kendra, who blogs at New Life on a Homestead, helped put together this list:

☐ Supply of diapers for a week. Even if you're a cloth-diaper fanatic, I've gotta be honest: Disposables will make life immeasurably easier in a crisis.

☐ A few cloth diapers and diaper covers, in case the crisis lasts longer than a week and you're unable to buy more disposables. Just be sure you have a plan for sanitizing and laundering them.

☐ Waterproof pants, if you don't have diaper covers

☐ Diaper pins

☐ Diaper rash cream

☐ Baby wipes

☐ Pacifier and backup pacifier

☐ Baby formula. If you breast feed, that may be all you need, but it sure doesn't hurt to have a bit of formula and a bottle, just in case.

☐ Baby-friendly snacks, such as Cheerios

☐ Winter wear in an appropriate size

☐ 7–10 comfortable outfits. One-piece outfits are preferred to even the cutest little two- or three-piece sets. Heck, why not plan on the baby wearing pajamas most of the time?

☐ A portable baby bed, if there's room. The Leachco Nap 'N Pack is preferred by a lot of moms.

☐ Baby sling or carrier

☐ Infant Tylenol or Motrin

☐ Hyland's Teething Gel

☐ Hyland's Earache Drops

☐ Baby chest rub

☐ Nasal aspirator

☐ Saline drops

☐ Baby thermometer

Your eyes need a backup

My eyesight is about 20/1000, so I'm very sensitive about having at least one pair of contacts as my backup. If you or anyone in the family wears contacts or eyeglasses, include a spare pair in your kit, as well as an eyeglasses repair kit.

- ☐ Vaseline
- ☐ Baby-safe bug repellant
- ☐ Baby-safe sunblock
- ☐ Liquid baby vitamins
- ☐ Baby medicine dropper
- ☐ Gas relief drops
- ☐ Tear-free baby wash/shampoo (double-bagged in a Ziploc bag)
- ☐ 1–2 baby blankets
- ☐ Hand sanitizer
- ☐ Sippy cup, if age appropriate
- ☐ A couple of baby toys
- ☐ Small wet bag to keep baby's laundry separate from the rest of the family's

Wet bags aren't just for babies!

The wet bag is a welcome addition to any diaper bag. It's a leakproof, waterproof bag that zips tightly to contain a wet diaper, dirty laundry, or anything else that is damp. Wet bags are a great add-on to any emergency kit, because sooner or later you'll be searching for *something* to hold that wet washrag or sticky T-shirt.

Who said babies were uncomplicated? Once you've collected all of your baby's must-haves, think about storing them in a container that can pull double duty. A 5-gallon bucket with a lid can also serve as a diaper pail. The lid of a plastic bin could also serve as a changing pad, and the bin itself would make a handy baby bathtub.

Special-Needs Emergency Kit

Millions of families have a family member or two with special needs. It might be a child with autism or Down syndrome, an elderly parent or a loved one who is mentally ill or depends on life-saving medical equipment. Their emergency kits will have to be customized not only to their special needs but also to possible contingencies once they're away from home.

Depending on the circumstances, your best plan might be to stay at home for as long as possible. Consulting ahead of time with medical doctors and others involved in the care of your family member with special needs is an absolute must. Just let them know you are preparing for an emergency that might require relocating and ask for their advice. They might be able to provide referrals to out-of-town colleagues and resources or prescribe more portable medical equipment. If you have a chance to network with others in your situation, whether online or in real life, do so; they have walked a hundred miles, or more, in your shoes and may be your best resource.

Another helpful action would be to begin journaling and making lists of the supplies, equipment, medications, dietary requirements, and routines that provide the best possible level of care, and then figuring out how to duplicate those as closely as possible when you and your family are away from home and familiar surroundings. Sometimes when we wake up in the morning, we just *do* without much thinking. Do you know what I mean? Start paying attention to your special-needs family member's best time of day, what keeps him or her calm, and what initiates panic or distress. The more information you can collect, the easier it will be to plan.

In the case of someone who cannot possibly be moved, double down on your plans to shelter in place, no matter what. Truly, there are not that many disasters of Katrina or 9–11 size. Yes, there may be a bit of a gamble when you make the choice to stay put, and there may be some very, very hard choices to make, but there may be no other option.

If you *are* able to move out, make the move early on in the crisis, when the roads are still relatively clear and the crisis hasn't peaked. This will help *you* stay calm, which, in turn, will help make the process go more smoothly. If you've practiced an evacuation and everyone knows the procedure and their responsibilities, so much the better.

Keep in mind that your special-needs person's supplies will likely need to be posted on your Last Minute Add-Ons list.

If your vehicle is in good condition and your emergency kits are ready, it's time to put together that Emergency Exit Plan.

> *Thirty-two percent of Americans have done nothing to prepare for an emergency.*
>
> —THE COUNCIL FOR EXCELLENCE IN GOVERNMENT, 2006

The Emergency Exit Plan

What could be more terrifying than the sudden realization that your home is no longer a safe place? Whether it's because of nearby riots, an oncoming firestorm, or the aftermath of an earthquake, every family should have an evacuation plan in place. Delegating tasks, holding a family meeting, rehearsing the plan, and then posting it will alleviate anxiety and lay the groundwork for a smooth exit. There are six basic steps to make this happen:

1. Make provisions for animals.
2. Pack personal necessities, food, and water.
3. Prepare the house.
4. Pack important documents and a computer.
5. Ensure the vehicle is ready to go.
6. Delegate, post, and rehearse.

1. Make provisions for animals.

Bugging out is difficult enough for the human members of the family, but the excitement, fear, and flurry of activity will be highly stressful for your animals. Once you've made the decision to evacuate, one of the first steps should be to determine how best to care for each animal.

Certainly, cats and dogs will need to be either evacuated with you or transferred to a safer location. Either way, you don't need them underfoot as you rush around, so a first step will be to put them in crates or carriers. Delegate this task to one or two family members, preferably someone whom the animals trust.

Depending on the size of your dogs and cats, you may want to first load their crates into your vehicle and *then* place the animal(s) inside. Collars, leashes, and water and food bowls should be in the crates, along with some food. Dry food should be double-bagged in two large Ziploc bags, and if you use canned food, don't forget the can opener. Add your pet, and you're good to go!

If you're the proud owner of fish, reptiles, rodents, and/or farm animals, consider whether you'll take them along, leave them on their own with a plentiful supply of food and water or transport them to another location. Take care of planning this detail *now* and have a Plan B for their care in case circumstances suddenly change. An evacuation is highly stressful, and the heartbreak of leaving beloved animals behind is something that should be avoided if at all possible. You're the owner, and your animals are relying on you for their safety and well-being.

2. Pack personal necessities, food, and water.

While the designated family member is rounding up the animals, delegate who will be responsible for each of the following:

Any idiot can face a crisis. It's day-to-day living that wears you out.
—ANTON CHEKHOV

- Load your emergency kits. If there are any supplies you may have to get into during the trip, make sure those kits are easily accessible.

- Load firearms and ammunition. Guns are one of the first things vandals look for, and I don't want ours getting into the wrong hands. In a worst-case scenario, we may need them for defense.

- Get cash. I usually keep this in $20 bills or smaller. In case of a widespread electrical outage, ATMs and credit/debit card machines may not be working. Be sure you can pay for hotels, gas, food, and campground fees. A roll of quarters is a good idea if you may be washing clothes at a Laundromat or using pay phones, which, by the way, are often up and running before landlines and cell phone towers are operational. Remember this: In a crisis, CASH IS KING!

- Pack everything else on your Last Minute Add-Ons list.

- Make sure you have some sort of emergency toilet. I don't want my family using the side of the road as a toilet—ever. Enough said.

- If you're expecting to be away for a long time, load some additional food and water, as much as there is room for. Your emergency kits will contain some emergency provisions, but extra food will always come in handy. Collapsible water containers are a good option, since they gradually take up less space as they're emptied.

- Bedding items, such as sleeping bags, blankets, and pillows, will add comfort and reassurance en route and at your destination. How much you can take with you will depend on how much room you have left in your vehicle. I always keep a couple of lightweight blankets rolled up under the backseat, just in case.

- Prepare family heirlooms and valuables, including photos. Decide now, before a crisis hits, what items you absolutely cannot leave behind. Now is the time to transfer irreplaceable photos to CDs. It's much easier to grab a few CDs than armfuls of photo albums or, if you're like me, boxes of loose photos.

3. Prepare the house.

As you drive away from your home, no doubt you'll have feelings of sadness and, perhaps, loss. A written plan to protect your home will

Don't expect kindness or generosity

You may be expecting casual strangers to assist you and your family in a dire situation, and that just might happen. Sadly, it's just as likely, maybe even more so, that it will be an "every man for himself" scenario. One mom who was stranded in a church basement during a blizzard told me about truck drivers who walked in and took anything and everything they wanted. If you encounter kindness, be thankful. However, stay on guard.

increase the chances of having a home to come back to. Remember to delegate, if possible.

The name of your bank could be a life-saver

It's a good idea to keep some funds in a national bank with lots of branches, in case a disaster causes local banks to close. An account with Chase or Bank of America, for example, will make it easier to get a check cashed, withdraw cash, or have an out-of-state check accepted by local businesses if a local branch is nearby.

- First, follow any directions given by city and/or utility officials.

- Turn off gas and water. Make sure you know exactly where the tools are to do this task.

- If there's a possibility of a hard freeze while you'll be gone, take precautions so water pipes don't freeze, such as draining faucets, turning off the inside valves for external faucets, and opening outside faucets to drain.

- Go out to your electrical panel and switch off everything except for the breakers marked for the kitchen and any other room containing equipment or appliances that must be kept running. Do the same with outbuildings.

- Unplug everything in the house except the refrigerator, freezer, and, perhaps, a lamp.

- Shut down and unplug all computers.

- Close and lock all windows and doors. Close blinds and curtains.

- If your emergency requires it, board up the windows or put up your storm shutters.

- Depending on the current weather, turn off the air conditioner or heat or set it at minimal level. (Make sure to leave those breakers on your electrical panel in the "on" position.)

4. Pack important documents and a computer.

Breaker! Breaker!

Are the electrical breakers in your main electrical panel correctly labeled? You'd be surprised by how often they aren't. Now would be a good time to test each breaker and label or relabel, if necessary.

- If you have a portable safe, strong box, or something similar, grab it. If you don't have one, use my checklist in Chapter 6 to assemble all your important papers *now*.

- Pack your Grab-and-Go Binder, containing copies of vital financial and family documents, and your Survival Mom Binder, with printed information helpful in emergencies, such as maps, evacuation routes, etc.

- Use a flash drive to save important business, personal, and financial information from each desktop computer. Make sure to take the flash drive with you!

Consider alternate Bug Out Vehicles

It is really, really difficult to maneuver a truck, a car, or an SUV in a traffic jam, especially if an evacuation is in progress. If possible, consider utilizing bicycles with trailers or motorcycles. You'll be limited to how much you can carry, but fuel likely won't be a problem, easy maneuverability will be a huge bonus, and if you're headed to a location that is already stocked with food and supplies, this may be far better than even your 4WD Hemi pickup.

- Pack the laptop computer, if you have one. Be sure to include the charger.
- Pack external hard drives.

5. Ensure the vehicle is ready to go.

Hopefully, you've been keeping an eye on the weather and news reports and have made sure your vehicle's gas tank is full. In addition to those simple, obvious steps, here are a few more:

- Load extra, filled gas cans, if you have them.
- Check air pressure of tires.
- Be sure you have everything necessary for dealing with a flat tire, including a spare.
- If your vehicle is likely to need it, pack extra engine oil and other fluids.
- Make sure your Vehicle Emergency Kit is packed.

6. Delegate, post, and rehearse.

Now that your plan is finished and your kits are packed, discuss each evacuation step with your family and delegate tasks to family members. Even the youngest will want to be useful, and in a crisis situation, assigned tasks will help defuse feelings of panic and confusion. It's more difficult to become hysterical when you have something to focus on—not impossible, just more difficult!

There's one final step. Will this really work? How much time will it take, and will there be any room for passengers in your vehicle once it's loaded? It's now time for an evacuation drill. This will help refine

> One of life's most painful moments comes when we must admit that we didn't do our homework, that we are not prepared.
>
> —MERLIN OLSEN

Stick together, no matter what

One lesson I've learned from observing mass evacuations around the country from the comfort of my couch is that I never, ever, want to be separated from my family. If officials of some government agency are evacuating you, insist that all members of your family leave together, in the same vehicle. Remember the chaos of Katrina and then ask yourself, "How easy will it be to find my kids or my husband if we get separated?" Reuniting family members isn't anywhere near the top of the list for rescue workers. If communication lines are down, it could be days or weeks before you find each other. Make this a non-negotiable.

Don't scrimp on quality

So, you've bugged out and are surviving—thanks to your emergency kits and planning. How long will that shovel hold out? Will that camp stove hold up to daily use for years? The tools and other supplies and equipment in your kits should be of the highest quality you can afford. Shop on eBay, garage sales, and Craigslist if the retail prices are too expensive for buying new. Your family's lives could, literally, depend on the quality of what you've packed.

your plan and give everyone a real-life rehearsal. Post your final plan around the house and then, when your family members least expect it, start the drill.

You Got Out of Dodge, But Now What?

This may very well be the most important step of preparing for an evacuation. Bugging out or "getting out of Dodge" is a popular conversation topic of many survival- and preparedness-minded people. Some fantasize that they'll bug out to a national park and live off the land or even become squatters out in the wild. Get serious! Really?

Once you leave home, you've become a refugee. History teaches us that refugees are highly vulnerable, especially if there is no ultimate, safe destination. To avoid the dangers that come with leaving your eye of the storm, here are some tips for making the safest emergency exit:

- If you'll need to stay in a hotel, make your reservation early. Hotels may be filled for miles around if you wait too long.
- Decide ahead of time what you will leave behind at home and what you will take.
- If flooding is a possibility, place furniture legs on top of canned goods and cover it with a waterproof tarp.

A Survival Mom's Story
Kathlyn Smith, Texas

Just as mobile homes attract tornadoes, Galveston Island attracts hurricanes. Kathlyn Smith, 59, works there and has experienced three major hurricanes. Divorced for the past 11 years, she survived both Hurricane Rita in 2005 and Hurricane Ike in 2008 on her own. She told me, "If you live on the Gulf Coast for any period of time, you learn to stay prepared for the next storm." She may be single, but she can handle herself in a crisis.

When Hurricane Rita was headed straight for Galveston, Kathlyn made the choice to evacuate. It took her the better part of the day to travel just one hour's distance. Gas stations were quickly emptied, with people fighting over gas at the pumps. Kathlyn says: "You can't predict what others will do when they're under a lot of stress. We heard reports of people pulling guns and robbing others of money and supplies. I kept my pistol loaded and under the front seat, in case I needed it."

The level of stress during an evacuation is nearly unimaginable. Kathlyn remembers having to not only pack her vehicle but also include extra cans of gasoline, as well as the difficulty of getting all of her outdoor furnishings and potted plants into the safety of her garage. She says, "If there is any way to shelter in place and be safe, that would be optimal." Evacuations aren't glamorous!

Sometimes the weather following a disaster becomes a secondary enemy. Kathlyn wasn't able to evacuate as Hurricane Ike rolled in. The traffic jams were just too massive, and she didn't want to risk riding out the storm in her vehicle. However, once the storm rolled through, she faced lengthy power outages, floodwaters in her home, and temperatures that reached 100 degrees and more. She had to leave in order to stay safe and sane. On her trek out of town following Ike, there was so much debris and so many abandoned cars, dead animals, and piles of vegetation on the highways that the only way she could make progress was to follow a caravan of the National Guard vehicles as they slowly cleared the way.

Kathlyn's "fur babies" go with her, no matter what. Watching the fates of abandoned pets following other hurricanes, she has planned ahead for her Yorkies. Their supplies are packed right along her first-aid supplies, freeze-dried meals, and extra cash.

She remembers what it was like being stuck in evacuation traffic with an 18-month-old years earlier and advises other Survival Moms to prepare ahead of time, so when a crisis hits, they won't be panicking in front of the kids. She says, "Let your children know that you have a plan and allow them to help to the degree that they are able."

Not surprisingly, Kathlyn has taken to heart the lessons learned: "If you are leaving, plan to leave early, before a mandatory evacuation is called. Be ready to hit the road. Spend the days prior preparing your home." It's a good bet that future disasters will once again find her and her Yorkies fully prepared.

- A GPS could be a life saver, helping you find alternate routes you may not know about.

- Having enough fuel is vital. Store it safely and have enough to get to your destination. As Survival Mom René told me, "If you don't have enough fuel, your Bug Out Location is pretty much wherever you run out of gas!"

- The importance of planning and preparation cannot be over-emphasized. Once you've left your home, you're a refugee facing unknown dangers.

Even if you have a second home or a planned Bug Out Location, brainstorm other possible safe destinations. Think of locations to the north, south, east, and west of your home. If a devastating storm damages roads and bridges to the north and your home is no longer a safe place, you'll need to head out in another direction with a different destination in mind.

Do you remember the last time you were in a really awful traffic jam? Getting stuck in backed-up traffic is one of the things I dread the most about going downtown to a baseball game. Now imagine what a mass exodus from your neighborhood, town, or city would be like if a disaster of any type hit. Thousands of panicked people hitting the streets and freeways all at once is a disaster waiting to happen. Throw in some winter weather, summer heat, and woefully unprepared motorists, and the result could be a deathtrap.

Before disaster strikes, decide as a family what the markers will be for your trip out of Dodge:

- Will it be 1 day, 2 days, or 3 days before a hurricane is expected?

- How serious will a storm warning need to be before you decide it's safer to go elsewhere, temporarily?

- Will you leave town when you see an increase in civil unrest? How close to your home will the riots and looting have to be for you to get out?

- Will you look for economic indicators, such as an increase in bank closures or signs of hyperinflation?

- Will it be when the power is down for more than 24 or 48 hours? How much longer will it be before your town or city erupts in panic?

- How about events that might signal that martial law is about to be imposed?

Be the smartest family on your block

Evacuate ahead of the crowds. Use your own judgment and trust your instincts. Be ready with packed luggage, pet carriers, food, water, and a plan. If you wait until government officials say, "Go!" you've waited too long. You will almost certainly have to deal with massive crowds of people all headed in the same direction.

- Will it be at the first sign of serious fuel or food shortages?

- Will it be when the water level of a nearby river rises to a certain point? What is that point?

- Will it be when the government appears to be in disarray with no clear leadership?

- How about if all communication lines—phone, cell, and Internet—are down? Will you stay put or get out?

Yes, some of these scenarios are a little dramatic, but hyperinflation and bank closures could trigger riots. A government in chaos might be just the signal that local thugs have been waiting for to start widespread, systematic looting. All of these possible developments will require that you stay tuned in to sources of news, both local and national, in order to stay informed and make wise decisions.

Above all, if you leave, *have a place to go*. Bad things can happen to refugees, and until you get to your destination, you're highly vulnerable.

Pre-Plan Your Routes

A second way to avoid being trapped in an evacuation is to have several pre-planned emergency exits that will get you safely from point A to point B. Ideally, those routes will include detours. It's very likely that your planned route will run into unforeseen obstacles, and you'll have to make swift adjustments to your route.

Right now, could you identify at least three ways to make an emergency exit from your town or city? If you were miles from home and had to evacuate, what route would you take and where would you go? What if you were at work and needed to get home to your family? Do you know several routes you could take in case you hit any roadblocks?

Here are nine steps to help ensure a safe and speedy evacuation:

1. Get a detailed road map of your area and road maps for neighboring states.

2. Determine at least one destination at least 100 miles from your home as your safe place.

3. With your maps and a marker, identify various routes you could take from your home to your destination. Look for possible detours in case you hit a roadblock or standstill traffic. Events such as earthquakes and violent storms quickly result in roadblocks.

4. Using a city map, identify at least three routes you could take from your place of work to your home.

5. Take time to actually travel each route you have plotted out. Watch for potential problem areas, such as water routes that may fill to overflowing in a flood.

6. If roads are unpaved, do you have the correct type of vehicle for them? A stranded vehicle may be the worst-case scenario for you and your family.

7. Label each route you have planned. In an emergency, you can communicate to family members, "We'll be taking Route A," for example.

8. Make more than one copy of your planned emergency exits. Store copies in each vehicle, each workplace, and at home and keep at least one with an out-of-town friend or relative.

9. Make a plan to get additional fuel for your vehicle. In emergencies, gas stations quickly run out of gas. In the event of an electrical outage, gas pumps don't work!

Take the time to plan these emergency exits for you and your family. They might come in handy the next time you're caught in a traffic jam, and in the case of a true emergency, they could be a life saver.

Real difficulties can be overcome. It is only the imaginary ones that are unconquerable.

—THEODORE N. VAIL

What Is a Red Cross Shelter Really Like?

The American Red Cross strives to provide free, temporary emergency shelters that are safe, sanitary, and reasonably comfortable. In order to do this for a large number of people, they have rules and procedures that must be followed so as to not wear out your welcome.

Be ready to fill out a registration form on which you will have to list each person accompanying you, any special needs, and medical concerns. Have a form of personal identification with you to make the process easier. You will be required to sign out each time you leave the shelter and sign in when you return.

You'll be housed with perhaps dozens of other people, maybe more, and it will be your responsibility to keep track of your belongings. If you have valuables with you, it is best to store them in your locked car or carry them on your person at all times. If something is lost, damaged, or stolen, it will be entirely your responsibility.

Your kids are also your sole responsibility. Just because there are other adults in the shelter, and even a nurse, doesn't mean you have built-in babysitters. Children cannot be left unattended. Loud and rowdy kids will make life in the shelter more difficult for everybody. Keeping them occupied and reasonably quiet may be the biggest challenge of all!

Be aware that no weapons of any kind are permitted in Red Cross shelters, except those carried by security personnel. Additionally, no alcohol or illegal drugs are allowed, and persons under the influence will be asked to leave or, possibly, turned over to law enforcement.

If your only option is to take refuge in one of these shelters, here are some guidelines of supplies to bring for making the experience tolerable.

Smooth seas do not make skillful sailors.

—AFRICAN PROVERB

- Water. Bring more than you think you'll need.

- Food, both prepackaged and ready to eat. Snacks and meals will be available at the shelter, but you may want to have more on hand.

- A change of clothes, or two, for each person in the family. Flip-flops would be a good idea for wearing in the communal showers.

- Prescription medications. The Red Cross has nurses who can call in prescriptions, but in a disaster situation, there may not be a pharmacy that can fill them.

- Hygiene kit (washcloth, soap, shampoo/conditioner, brush, razor, feminine items, toilet paper, etc.). The Red Cross hands these out, but they may be limited in a large-scale disaster.

- Important papers (identification, insurance papers, relatives' names and numbers, etc.). Your Grab-n-Go Binder is ideal. Just make absolutely sure you can keep it secure at all times.

- Pillows and blankets. Children, especially, find it easier to sleep if they have their own familiar bedding.

- Eyeglasses and dentures.
- Diapers, formula, wipes, and other baby supplies.
- Flashlight with fresh batteries (that walk to the bathroom can be tricky in the dark!).
- Entertainment for kids (books, crayons, portable video games, etc.).
- A cell phone, so you can call relatives, and a charger. Chances are there's gonna be a line for the phone!
- Do not bring pets, unless they are service animals.

12 difficult truths from a real-life, worst-case scenario

Survival Moms want to be prepared for just about anything, and that includes even the worst-case scenarios. In August 2005, families in the Gulf Coast states were hit with the full power of Hurricane Katrina. Thousands evacuated ahead of the storm and many stayed behind to face the storm on their own, but all of them faced hardships that lasted for months and even years.

That experience taught the survivors some pretty tough lessons about security and survival:

1. You're going to need a lot more supplies than you think you will need. Your emergency may end up lasting weeks or months, not days. A so-called 72-Hour Kit is not exactly something you can count on in a large-scale emergency.

2. Have enough money with you, in small bills, to last at least 2 weeks and preferably longer. In a large enough crisis, banks can be destroyed by hurricanes or face closure in an economic collapse. Consider hotel costs, fuel, medical care, food, and other supplies to determine how much cash you should have saved and on hand.

3. A government shelter should be your last resort. You may discover that your constitutional rights don't apply. You'll be under the authority of whoever runs that particular camp or shelter and may not be able to leave—even if you want to.

4. If you have your emergency kits packed, that's great, but be sure to check them periodically for dead batteries, leaky containers of liquid, shoes and clothes that are too small, missing items, and spoiled food.

5. It's foolish to pack luxury items. Remember the scene from *Little House on the Prairie* that showed boxes of books, beautiful furniture, and even an organ abandoned on the shores of a river? If you overpack, your luxury items may face the same fate, except they may be abandoned along a highway somewhere.

6. If you have property or a second home, be careful about whom you invite to stay with you and make sure they do not bring others along with them. Similarly, don't tag along with another family unless the home- or landowner has invited you.

7. Rescue workers, including law enforcement, may ignore your civil rights in the form of unlawful searches and confiscation of legal belongings, such as firearms, and you may have no recourse.

8. Expect chaos. The only way to prepare for it is to prepare for it now.

9. Your world may turn upside down and may never, ever, return to normal. It's very likely that you and other family members will experience depression and even post-traumatic stress disorder. This can happen to *anyone* who has lived through a harrowing event. Recognize warning signs, such as feeling physically and mentally drained, having difficulty making decisions, and feeling more lonely, sad, tired, or numb than usual. Be willing to see a doctor or counselor.

10. Lack of communication will be particularly distressing, especially if you do not know where your loved ones are. Regular updates on TV and radio may not be available, and you may feel as though you are living in a vacuum, not knowing what is going on in the outside world. Getting an amateur radio license and investing in a basic ham radio will get you in touch with others outside the crisis zone.

11. If you appear to be well-prepared, expect to be a target of those who are not. It's an ugly truth and is one reason for prepared families and neighborhoods to band together. OpSec may never be more important.

12. One stupid slip-up could be fatal. An overtired family might stop for the night at a park, and what might be perfectly safe in normal times might result in theft or something more violent. Never allow yourself to become so tired that your judgment begins to lapse.

The power of a text message

If the phone lines are ever down and cell phone service is sketchy, a text message might get through when a phone call can't. What's the explanation? It takes just a blip of time for a text message to transmit.

The family evacuation drill

Before the drill:

1. Survey each room. What, if anything, should be included in an emergency evacuation—family photos, the wedding album, or the kids' schoolbooks? If you determine ahead of time that nothing in a certain room is worth packing, you won't waste valuable time searching through drawers or shelves and trying to make on-the-spot decisions under duress.

2. Make a master list of what must not be left behind and then begin gathering those items into one or two locations. Make it a point always to return those items to their assigned spots.

3. If you have a safe, decide whether you will empty the safe out and take everything with you or pack only certain essentials. Decide this now, not in the heat and panic of the moment when a real emergency strikes.

4. Pack Individual Emergency Kits for each member of the family according to the checklists in this chapter. The kits should include a jacket appropriate to the current season and additional outerwear for cold weather, if appropriate. See checklist on page 254.

5. Pack the Family Kit with enough nonperishable food to last 7 days, a first-aid kit that includes important medications, a way to heat water and food, a portable water filter, maps, and any other items to see you through at least 7 days. Review list on pages 256–258.

6. Do you have cases of water bottles ready to grab? Where is the water you will pack with you?

7. Don't forget your pets. Determine now if they will go or stay and then prepare accordingly. Our turtle stays—sorry, Mona!—but the cats and dogs go.

8. How will you prepare your house? Who will be in charge of making sure that every door and window is locked? Who will turn off the gas, water, and/or electricity, if need be?

9. Check out your Bug Out Vehicle. Do you have at least a can or two of extra fuel and motor oil? Are you prepared to change a tire if necessary? Do you have a Vehicle Emergency Kit, including road flares, a jumper cable, and a flat-tire repair kit? Is that vehicle 100% ready to get on the road and go as far as you need it to go?

10. Where will you go? Once you're in your vehicle, along with all your carefully planned and packed supplies, now what?

Once you have your plans and preparations in order and have determined who does what, it's time for the drill. Yell out, "Evacuate! Evacuate!" Set a timer and see if you're able to evacuate in one hour.

☐ Animals and their supplies packed

☐ Individual Kits packed

☐ Family Kit packed

☐ Any other Specialized Kit and supplies packed

☐ Family heirlooms and valuables packed using a previously written checklist

☐ Water and food packed

☐ House shut down for the duration

Evaluate the results:

1. What was your actual time, or did you have to call it quits after 3 hours?

2. Who remembered their assigned tasks? Who forgot theirs?

3. If your 30-minute goal wasn't met, what can be done to speed up the process?

4. Was there anything of importance you forgot to include?

The Prepared Family

☑ It's important not to alarm kids, but it's even more important that they know about evacuation plans. Present two or three realistic but not overly alarming possibilities, such as a power outage that lasts for more than a couple of days or an earthquake, if you live in earthquake country. Calmly talk about why it is sometimes safer to leave home for a while. Be prepared for questions such as, "What if we come back and our house is gone?" or "Will we have to live in this other place forever?"

☑ Have the kids pack their own emergency kits. If they're old enough, give them a checklist to follow and then double-check what they've packed. If your kids are younger, have them pick out clothing items or a favorite storybook or two.

☑ Schedule one day of eating meals according to your Bug Out Menu. Let everyone know that these are the sorts of meals they can expect if the family ever needs to evacuate. Not only will they get used to the idea, but it will also give *you* information about which foods are popular and which you should probably not pack, after all.

☑ Review your Emergency Exit Evacuation Plan as a family. Allow kids to practice their roles and tasks. Set a timer and see how quickly everything and everyone can be loaded into the car. See guidelines on the next page.

☑ Schedule a camping trip to try out any new equipment you have. Teach older kids how to start a campfire using starters other than a match or a lighter. Teach everyone how to manage a campfire safely.

Family Preparedness Plan: Preparedness on the Go

1. Equip each vehicle for emergencies.

☐ Vehicle #1: _____

- Vehicle Emergency Kit, see pages 250–252
- Up-to-date maintenance
- Spare tire in good condition
- Stashed tire-changing equipment
- Road maps of our state, other states optional
- Roadside Emergency Kit
- Sturdy, comfortable walking shoes for everyone
- Other _____

☐ Vehicle #2: _____

- Vehicle Emergency Kit, see pages 250–252
- Up-to-date maintenance
- Spare tire in good condition
- Stashed tire-changing equipment
- Road maps of our state, other states optional
- Roadside Emergency Kit
- Sturdy, comfortable walking shoes for everyone
- Other _____

☐ Additional vehicle: _____

- Vehicle Emergency Kit, see pages 250–252
- Up-to-date maintenance
- Spare tire in good condition
- Stashed tire-changing equipment
- Road maps of our state, other states optional
- Roadside Emergency Kit
- Sturdy, comfortable walking shoes for everyone
- Other _____

☐ Extra fuel and necessary fluids

2. Individual Kits packed for each member of the family

See checklist on page 254.

- ☐ Mom
- ☐ _____
- ☐ _____
- ☐ _____
- ☐ _____
- ☐ _____

3. Family Kit

- ☐ Emergency toilet supplies
- ☐ Paper towels
- ☐ Over-the-counter medications and first-aid kit
- ☐ Small plastic or metal plates, bowls, and utensils
- ☐ Metal pot with lid for cooking
- ☐ Laundry soap, stored away from food
- ☐ Anti-bacterial cleaner
- ☐ Plastic tablecloth
- ☐ Method for cooking (e.g., rocket stove, propane stove)
- ☐ Other _____

4. On-the-road menus—store ingredients for each meal in airtight and pestproof packaging.

- ☐ Breakfasts: Meal _____
  - Meal _____
  - Meal _____
- ☐ Lunches: Meal _____
  - Meal _____
  - Meal _____
- ☐ Dinners: Meal _____
  - Meal _____
  - Meal _____
- ☐ Snacks: _____
  - _____
  - _____
  - _____

5. Last-minute add-ons

☐ _____

☐ _____

☐ _____

☐ _____

☐ _____

☐ _____

☐ _____

☐ _____

☐ _____

6. Specialty Kits

See lists on pages 259–264.

☐ Pets ☐ Baby

☐ Tools ☐ Special needs

☐ Wilderness/outdoor survival

7. Our Emergency Exit Plan

☐ Provisions for animals

- Pet _____
- Pet _____
- Pet _____
- Other _____
- Other _____

☐ Evacuation delegations

- Pets
- Load kits
- Load firearms and ammo
- Cash
- Grab-n-Go Binder
- Survival Mom Binder
- Safe or lockbox
- Last-minute add-ons

- Emergency toilet and supplies
- Water for at least 7 days, longer if you anticipate a lengthy evacuation
- Additional food if a long evacuation is likely
- Bedding for each person
- Family heirlooms and valuables
- Prepare the house and property
    - ☐ Turn off gas, water, and electricity as directed by city officials or weather conditions
    - ☐ Unplug everything except refrigerator and freezer, including computers, stereo, and TVs
    - ☐ Close and lock all windows and doors
    - ☐ Other _____
    - ☐ Other _____
    - ☐ Other _____
- Pack important electronics
    - ☐ Computers (which ones?)
    - ☐ Flash drives, external hard drives
    - ☐ Other _____
    - ☐ Other _____

☐ Exit routes
- Route #1: _____
    - ☐ Map marked with route
    - ☐ Destination: _____
- Route #2: _____
    - ☐ Map marked with route
    - ☐ Destination: _____
- Route #3: _____
    - ☐ Map marked with route
    - ☐ Destination: _____

8. Additional copies of the Grab-n-Go Binder stored with:

☐ Family member _____

☐ Friend _____

☐ Other _____

CHAPTER 12

Survival Mom to Survival Mom

I became a mom for the first time when I was 39. My old body took it hard. About 7 months into the pregnancy, I was detailing to my mother all of my aches and pains: It was hard to walk, I had heartburn 24/7, and sometimes there was so much pressure it felt like the baby was going to fall out at any moment. My mom looked at me quizzically and said, "I don't remember it ever being like that for me." No wonder. She was just 18 when I was born. There's a big difference between the body of a teenager and that of an almost-middle-aged woman.

When my daughter was born, however, every ounce of pain, every discomfort, and even the episiotomy was worth it. I bet you felt the same way when your kids were born.

Sometimes I wonder: If I were still single or if we didn't have kids, would I bother with food storage? Would it ever occur to me to keep a first-aid kit in the car, and would there always be blankets shoved under the backseat? For me, I prepare because I love. I can't control tomorrow, and I can't control what happens with the world banking system, tectonic plates, or the politics of our country. But I *can* have a hot meal for my family on most nights, and I can keep a supply of soft blankets and pillows for cuddling. When soup is on sale for 79 cents a can, I can buy extras, just in case, because my husband and I are the only people I fully trust to care for my family's future.

There must be billions of examples of moms setting aside their own wants and needs for the sake of their children. The Survival Mom gene is an ancient one—it is part of your DNA at the moment your first baby is born. Worries for the future are somehow embedded in that gene; I don't know of a single mom who doesn't fret about what the future holds for her kids.

Paranoia Can Be Your Friend

In the early days of the 2007 recession and the burst of the housing bubble, I had a gut feeling that this downturn was different—an uncomfortable feeling that the worst was yet to come and that my family was nowhere near ready to face it. The next logical step was, then, figuring out what to do next. I may not look like it, but I'm a woman of action. Inaction makes about as much sense to me as standing on train tracks and watching the oncoming headlights of the locomotive.

Have you had one of those eyes-wide-open, "OMG what are we going to do" moments? Did it come when your husband announced that he had been laid off or maybe when you saw what your retirement fund is worth now? Do you get that feeling when listening to the nightly news? Maybe your area is prone to hurricanes, and the prediction for the next catastrophic season has just been announced. Sometimes what I learn scares me, and it takes a while to process the information and regain my equilibrium. But a little bit of anger can be energizing when it's channeled into something constructive, and turning paranoia into something productive is a smart way to handle emotions and thoughts that keep you awake at night.

Be grateful for whatever wakes you up and causes you to think, "I have a family to take care of, no matter what happens." A little paranoia can be your friend.

When the world says, "Give up," Hope whispers, "Try one more time."

—AUTHOR UNKNOWN

Freeze, Fight, Flee, or Feed?

My husband and I have a pretty equitable marriage. Neither of us were youngsters when we got married, and there have been only a few times we've had serious disagreements about what I wanted to do. One of those came in the early days of my survival research. I had discovered one particular website that left me frozen with fear, day after day. Unwittingly, I had stumbled into the realm of the Doomers.

My virgin ears had never heard of Peak Oil or an EMP before. I hadn't realized we were doomed unless we lived in a compound up in Idaho. My husband came home one day to find me researching properties that offered space for guard towers and came with underground bunkers. Piles of dirty laundry surrounded me, and there was no dinner in sight. That was the day he took a drastic step: He forbade me from ever going to that particular website again. It was feeding my fears and introducing terrifying new ones to my fertile imagination. My initial reaction to these terrifying possibilities was to freeze.

Some moms freeze forever, never taking actions that might equip them and their families to deal with the future. Others get angry—angry at the messenger, angry at the message, and angry at the family dog. How *dare* someone or something threaten their status quo and the mapped-out life they have planned for the next 40 years?

Others flee and take a plunge right into the Denial River for a nice, long swim. After all, bad things never happen to good people, right?

What about me? After I thawed out, I suddenly had a craving for a chocolate malt—an extra large one. For some reason, my brain screams, "Feed!" when it senses danger.

In such a crazy world, how can a Survival Mom sleep at night?

1. You know the importance of water, how to store it, and how to purify it. That's way more knowledge than your sister-in-law has.

2. You can cook rice and beans five different ways without your family realizing they've been eating the same two ingredients night after night.

3. You've learned how to grind wheat and make homemade bread.

4. Freeze-dried foods are nothing to fear, and you have a nice little collection of them.

5. Your financial situation may not be perfect, but you know what you need to do and how to do it.

6. Your kids understand that a prepared family is a smart family, and they've finally stopped looting your food-storage pantry.

7. If the "S" ever hits the fan, you know your family is ready for just about anything.

8. You've figured out where you want your safe-ish room to be, and you've started equipping it, just in case.

Mini-Glossary

Peak Oil: The notion that oilfield production has peaked or will peak in the near future, ultimately dooming the world to complete societal collapse.

Doomers: An affectionate term for those who believe in the imminent collapse of the world as we know it.

Plate Tectonics: Some Doomers believe that the actual plates on which our continents and seas sit will soon shift, causing unimaginable trauma to our planet.

Change before you have to.

—JACK WELCH

9. After years of procrastination, you've taken steps to protect yourself and your family. You may not be a black belt or a sharpshooter yet, but you're getting there.

10. There are thousands and thousands of other Survival Moms out there. You're not alone.

And that's the key, isn't it?

You're not alone. From the minute you picked up this book, you weren't alone anymore. You're one of thousands of Survival Moms.

For millennia, women have come alongside each other to support, encourage, teach, and comfort. We've watched each other's kids, shared recipes, consoled each other after a bad breakup, and answered, honestly, the question, "Do I look fat in this?"

It's no different now. Yes, our world is rapidly changing, but the heart of a mom, the heart of a woman, is the same as it's always been, except now we may be sitting in Starbucks over a Mocha Frappuccino talking about the price of silver and whether it is a good time to invest in precious metals. On Friday nights, we may decide to attend Ladies' Night at the shooting range instead of Ladies' Night at the local sports bar. The heart hasn't changed; only our priorities and the focus of our attention have changed. After all, we only want what our mothers, grandmothers, and great-grandmothers wanted: a secure future for our families.

If you can't sleep, then get up and do something instead of lying there and worrying. It's the worry that gets you, not the loss of sleep.

—DALE CARNEGIE

||||||||||||||||||||||||||||||||||||||||||||||||||||||||||||||||||||||||||||||||||||||||||||||||||||||||||||||||||||||

You Have Everything You Need

You have the heart, a purpose, a plan, and now plenty of information to move forward. You always had a Survival Mom inside you, but now you can wear the badge on the outside, loud and proud.

When it seems like the world has come to an end and you realize that it's The End of the World As We Know It, you can look down at your kids or grandkids and sincerely say, "We're going to be okay." You're a Survival Mom.

Are you a Survival Mom?

Share your story at www.thesurvivalmom.com or drop me an e-mail: mystory@thesurvivalmom.com.

Survival Mom Extras

My book would have been nearly twice as long if I had included everything I wanted to! I managed to sneak in these few extra pages. I hope they're helpful!

Here's what you will find in this appendix:

Online Resources:
- Free downloads from my blog
- If you're shopping online . . .

All-natural recipes:
- Make your own seitan, or wheat meat
- Andrea's Soda & Vinegar Hair Treatment
- Homemade Budget Baby Wipes

Bonus tips:
- Survive a tornado!
- Survive a hurricane!
- Survive an earthquake!
- Survive a flood!

- When all is lost, start here!
- The Survival Mom's End of the World Shopping Guide

Lists I know you'll appreciate:
- 21 more Baby Steps for getting started
- 33 books every Survival Mom should read
- Fun survival literature for kids
- Common freeze-dried and dehydrated foods
- Skill-of-the-Month Club
- Where to learn new skills

Online Resources

Free Resources on TheSurvivalMom.com

You can download all of these for free at www.thesurvivalmom.com:

- Dehydrated Dinners—step-by-step instructions
- Emergency Exits
- Handy No-Cook Foods
- Prep Your Vehicle for an Emergency
- Reconstituting Dehydrated Foods
- Safe Plastics for Storage
- Survival Moms on the Go
- Vehicle Emergency Kit Checklist
- Vehicle Emergency Kit 2
- Wheat Storage Worksheet
- Wilderness Survival Kit for Every Kid
- Plus much more!

If You're Shopping Online . . .

Some of these companies offer discounts to the readers of this book. Companies with an asterisk (*) by their name pay me a small commission.

Chapter 2: Survival Begins with Water

SteriPEN, www.steripen.com

Berkey water filters, www.theberkeyguy.com and www.readymaderesources.com

Cal-Shock 65, www.inyopools.com

Potable Aqua tablets, www.readymaderesources.com

WAPI, www.sunoven.com

Lehman's, www.lehmans.com

Chemisan and the GottaGo Toilet, www.chemisan.com

Diva Cup, www.divacup.com

Glad Rags, www.gladrags.com

Luna Pads, www.lunapads.com

Water BOB, www.waterbob.com

Chapter 4: The First Steps of Food Storage

Cheese waxing supplies, www.thecheesemaker.com and www.blendedwaxes.com

Excalibur food dehydrator, www.excaliburdehydrator.com

* Freeze Dry Guy, www.survivalmom.fdguy.com

Azure Standard (organic foods), www.azurestandard.com

Honeyville Grain, www.honeyvillegrain.com

Ready Made Resources, www.readymaderesources.com

* Shelf Reliance's THRIVE foods, www.survivalmom.shelfreliance.com

* Shirley J. foods, www.shirleyj.com/5018

Walton Feed, www.waltonfeed.com

Chapter 5: Increase Your Food Storage Savvy

Dried whole milk, www.kingarthurflour.com and www.americanspice.com

Gamma Seal lids, www.readymaderesources.com

* Gluten-free food-storage products, www.survivalmom.fdguy.com

Nestle Nido Instant Dry Whole Milk, www.nestlenido.com

Celtic sea salt, www.readymaderesources.com

Coconut oil, www.tropicaltraditions.com

Organic natural supplements, www.rawsourceorganics.com

Sorbent Systems, www.sorbentsystems.com

TATTLER Reusable Canning Lids, www.reusablecanninglids.com

WonderMill grain mills, www.thewondermill.com

Chapter 6: Your Home Base

Free encryption software, www.truecrypt.com

Chapter 7: The Unplugged Home

The Cobb Stove, www.cobb.com.au

FlashLantern, www.flashlantern.com (use coupon code TSM10 for a 10% discount)

Faraday bags, www.techprotect.com (use coupon code Tech10SM for 10% off)

The Global Sun Oven, www.sunoven.com

* Eco-Zoom Rocket Stove, www.ecozoomstove.com/survivalmom

StoveTec Rocket Stove, www.stovetec.net

Volcano Grills, www.volcanogrills.com

Chapter 8: The Essentials for Safety and Security

Eddie Eagle GunSafe Program, www.nrahq.org/safety/eddie

Flashbang bra holster, www.flashbangholster.com

Sure-Board, www.sureboard.com

Security window film, www.solutions.3m.com and www.shattergard.com

Chapter 9: Survival Finances

Dave Ramsey, www.daveramsey.com

Clickbooth, www.clickbooth.com

E-Junkie, www.e-junkie.com

Commission Junction, www.cj.com

LinkShare, www.linkshare.com

Online financial calculator, www.helpsavemydollars.com

Chapter 11: Preparedness on the Go

Enercell Portable Power Bank, www.radioshack.com

* Freeze-dried pet food, www.survivalmom.fdguy.com

MREs (Meals Ready to Eat), www.readymaderesources.com and www.thereadystore.com

Nuwick candles, www.waltonfeed.com

Safety Tats, www.safetytat.com

Amateur radio information, www.arrl.org

Leachco Nap-n-Pack, www.leachco.com

All-Natural Recipes

Seitan, or Wheat Meat

If you've ever eaten a vegetarian hot dog or other "meatless" entrée, you've almost certainly eaten seitan. Seitan, sometimes called wheat meat, is made of gluten, the protein component found in wheat. The easiest recipe I've found for making seitan was passed along to me by Stephanie Petersen, owner of Chef Tess Bakeresse.

This is a great way to use a part of your stored wheat to provide a meat substitute in your meals. Unfortunately, if you are on a gluten-free diet, this stuff is not for you.

1 package (6½ ounces) or 1½ cups Vital Wheat Gluten powder

1 cup highly seasoned stock or
1 tablespoon MSG-free, low-sodium bouillon plus 1 cup stock

You will also need:

1–2 feet heavy aluminum foil (Don't use the cheap stuff. It won't work as well.)

Oil or pan spray to keep the seitan from sticking to the foil (easy-release foil works wonders!)

4-quart Crock-Pot or a solar oven

1 quart of water

1. Combine the stock with the gluten powder. Mix together for about 2 minutes, until a gummy mass is made and all dry ingredients are moistened.

2. Take 1 cup of the mixture and place on 1½ feet of aluminum foil that has been sprayed with a nonstick coating or oil.

3. Fold the foil over the gluten dough and shape into a tight roll. Twist the ends of the foil to seal. It will look like a hamburger chub. This is called a force meat. It is wonderfully effective in producing a very firm texture similar to meat.

4. You can bake the chubs in the oven on a sheet pan at 250 degrees for 3 hours or immerse in a 4-quart Crock-Pot full of water. Cook in the Crock-Pot, or slow cooker, for 2–3 hours.

5. The seitan can also be cooked in a solar oven. Fill a dark-colored pot with water, immerse the seitan, cover, and cook for 3–4 hours.

When the seitan is finished, it can be utilized in a variety of ways and in all different types of recipes. It can be sliced, breaded, and chopped. Additional seasonings can be added to the dough to provide a more flavorful "meat" in Italian and Mexican recipes. Experiment with different combinations of spices and herbs and enjoy this meatless option.

Seitan nutritional information:

Serving: ⅓ cup (30g)

Calories: 160

Protein: 23g

Carbohydrate: 11g

Total Fat: 0.5g

Fiber: 2g

Andrea's Soda & Vinegar Hair Treatment

For clean, soft, and tangle-free hair, use this all-natural recipe:

Shampoo

To 1 cup of warm water, add 2 tablespoons of baking soda and stir until the soda is dissolved. Massage the solution into wet hair and allow to set for 1 or 2 minutes. Rinse well.

Conditioner

Mix together 1 cup warm water and 2 tablespoons of apple cider vinegar. Work the solution through wet hair and rinse.

Homemade Budget Baby Wipes

Here's a great recipe for making your own baby wipes and maybe saving a dollar or two:

- **2 tablespoons baby wash**

- **2 tablespoons mineral oil**

- **2–4 cups of warm water**

- **½ roll of soft paper towels** (Viva Select-a-Size is a good choice.)

Separate and place the paper towel sheets into a sturdy container. Mix the water, oil, and soap and pour over the towels to saturate. Cover tightly with a lid.

Bonus Tips

Thanks to my Facebook friends for many of these tips!

Survive a tornado!

1. Buy a home with a storm cellar. Sorry if this sounds obvious, but if you have the option, go for the house with the cellar and then reinforce the cellar entrance with steel doors.

2. Make sure you have up-to-date homeowner's insurance. This holds true for preparing for any natural disaster.

3. Check the FEMA website for helpful information regarding tornado preparedness.

4. Have at least 3 days' (72 hours') worth of food and water stored in a cellar, an interior closet, or another safe place.

5. Know where the nearest shelters are and make sure your kids know their locations, too.

6. Stay tuned in to local news, either TV or radio. After the storm passes, old-fashioned rabbit-ears (TV antenna) might help you get local channels if your cable is down.

7. Know all of the safest or safe-ish locations to shelter; e.g., a bathtub or a closet. You may be visiting friends, out shopping, or at the park when a tornado hits. Know how to be as safe as possible wherever you are.

8. Have flashlights, oil lamps, and other sources of light. Extra batteries are a must.

9. Have an emergency, hand-crank radio.

10. Have a cell phone charger. During tornado season, always have your phone charged. An Enercell from Radio Shack would be a good idea. Keep it fully charged in your emergency kits.

11. Some TV stations offer free weather warnings via text messages. Check the websites of your local TV and news/talk radio stations to see if they are offering this service. Police and fire departments may also offer this service.

12. Have family drills so everyone knows what to do and where to go. Have an occasional drill in the middle of the night. Who says tornadoes only strike during convenient daylight hours?

13. Put on sturdy shoes as soon as a siren goes off. A tornado produces enormous amounts of debris, including broken glass, nails, metal, and wood. The last thing you need is a foot injury that would keep you sidelined.

14. Know how to safely shut off your electric service, gas line, and water.

15. Keep a small refrigerator/freezer in the basement or your shelter.

16. A local map will help you keep track of weather alerts.

17. Talk with old-timers and find out how they have weathered past tornado seasons.

18. If your kids have friends with whom they spend a lot of time, find out what those families have planned in case of a tornado—or in case of any other emergency, for that matter.

19. Keep the tank of your car filled with gas. You may need to evacuate to a safer location.

20. If you have an underground shelter, keep in mind that these shelters can get buried under debris. Make sure a neighbor knows where your shelter is and will check on it following a tornado.

21. Know what the sky looks like during tornado weather. This will help you stay a step ahead if danger is on the way.

22. If your area is experiencing tornado weather, have everyone sleep in the same room at night to make an evacuation quicker and easier.

23. Keep a few tools in your shelter for dealing with debris and making repairs following a tornado.

24. Bicycle helmets can protect heads from falling debris. Keep one for each person in your storm cellar or shelter.

Survive a hurricane!

1. Keep cash on hand. You'll probably have to pay for those Red Cross doughnuts!

2. A good chainsaw is a worthwhile investment for dealing with fallen trees and large branches.

3. Have your emergency kits ready at all times.

4. If you decide to weather out the storm, consider joining forces with another family if their home is in a safer location. A few extra sets of hands can come in handy. Just be sure to plan ahead and have enough food and supplies for the larger group.

5. Buy extra tarps and rope. You may need them to cover broken windows, missing outer walls, or as a makeshift roof.

6. Keep the gas tanks in your vehicles filled. There *will* be fuel shortages once the hurricane passes.

7. If you decide to evacuate, take with you extra bedding and pillows or sleeping bags, in case a traffic jam forces you to spend long hours in the car.

8. If you live in hurricane country, a generator is a must, along with extra fuel that is stored safely.

9. Have a few cans of insect spray on hand. Hot, muggy weather is made worse by swarms of mosquitoes and other insects.

10. With no electricity for air conditioning, you'll probably be spending a lot of time outside. Have an extra tarp and some rope handy to provide shade.

11. Have all your preparedness measures taken care of no less than 3 days in advance of the storm's arrival. After that, the gas stations and stores will be swamped by the multitudes that didn't plan ahead.

12. Even if you have a planned exit route or two, you still need a detailed road map of your city and state in order to quickly find other safe routes.

13. Make sure your insurance policies are up to date. Meet with your agent to discuss adequate hurricane coverage, as well as coverage for family heirlooms and other valuables.

14. Any form of transportation is better than none. If streets are impassable or your vehicle has been damaged, bicycles are a great option.

15. Hurricanes often spawn tornadoes. Be sure to read "Survive a Tornado!" in this section.

16. Be prepared for looters following a hurricane. The best defense is a group of neighbors joining together to communicate the message that looters will not be welcome.

17. Weather conditions following a hurricane are typically hot and humid and may be dangerous for babies, toddlers, the elderly, and those with health issues. You may have to temporarily evacuate to a location that has electrical power in order to remain healthy.

18. Stock up on camping supplies, even if you're not a camper. You just might end up spending the night in your tent and cooking in a Dutch oven over a campfire until power is restored and your home is livable again.

19. Beware of complacency and overconfidence if a hurricane turns out to be a dud. The next one just might be another Katrina. Continue to plan and prepare accordingly.

20. Following a hurricane, sanitation is likely to become a problem. Prepare an emergency toilet and waste disposal system ahead of time.

21. Remember, when bad weather hits, pets get scared, too. Have pet carriers and leashes handy in case you need to make a quick getaway. Terrified pets will run away, so have a plan to keep them contained and with you.

Survive an earthquake!

1. Keep inexpensive hard hats handy to protect your head, and your children's heads, from falling items, including anything hanging on your walls and sitting on shelves. When the earth shakes, everything shakes!

2. Get in the habit of keeping a pair of shoes next to each bed. Cuts and splinters in the feet are one of the most common post-earthquake injuries.

3. I recommend a pair of Crocs-style shoes as emergency shoes, especially if they have a furry or padded liner. They're quick to slip on, oversized—so it takes a while for kids to outgrow them—and wide enough to allow for a pair of heavy socks.

4. Keep a pair of eyeglasses in a secured spot near your bed. If a quake occurs in the middle of the night, you'll need to see where you're going.

5. Packed emergency kits are a necessity, since a quake can leave you homeless in a matter of minutes.

6. Teach your kids the Red Cross earthquake survival technique: "Drop, Cover, and Hold On." This is safer than standing in a doorway, which may or may not have structural integrity.

7. Learn and teach "Drop, Cover, and Hold On" even if you don't live in earthquake country.

8. Inspect your home for construction and repair issues that will only worsen with an earthquake, such as a cracked foundation or a damaged roof. Take care of repairs now, if possible.

9. Cut down tree branches that are near power lines. In an earthquake, these branches often fall on the power lines, causing them to snap.

10. Know how to shut off the water and gas supplies into your home and where the shut-off valves are located. Make sure to have the correct tools on hand to do the job.

11. Keep an LED flashlight or a headlamp in a secure spot next to every bed.

12. Keep a spare set of keys by your bed, in case your other set is inaccessible or can't be found due to fallen debris.

13. Have a lanyard that holds a simple photo I.D., including the address and phone number, for each member of the family. Keep each person's lanyard by his or her bed, either in a drawer or hanging from a bedpost. Instruct kids to put theirs on in case of an earthquake or another emergency.

14. For very young children, buy a set of safety tattoos that you can quickly apply to an arm or a leg to help I.D. an injured or lost kid. Check out www.safetytat.com.

15. Stay calm. A terrified parent is going to send the kids right over the edge.

16. Every framed photo and mirror on the wall presents a danger. If they fall off, the glass will shatter. Consider removing glass from all of the frames or replacing it with Plexiglas.

17. Broken gas lines and power lines can cause fires. Keep at least two or three fire extinguishers in the house. Know where they are and how to use them.

18. Know where the shut-off valve is for your neighbor's natural gas line and how to turn off the neighbor's electrical panel. If their house goes up in flames, chances are yours will, too.

19. A supply of dust face masks can help you breathe if the air is filled with smoke, dust, and other airborne particles. If you don't have a dust mask, tie a T-shirt or another piece of fabric over your nose and mouth.

20. Keep a basic emergency kit at work to help you survive the quake and assist you with the basic supplies you'll need to get home.

21. Teach your kids to tap on anything within reach if they are ever trapped underneath furniture or other debris.

22. Bolt all tall pieces of furniture to the wall. It ain't feng shui. It's survival!

Survive a flood!

1. Know what is upstream from you if you live in a flood plain or near a river. You should know the names of any dams or reservoirs and determine if they pose a hazard to your home.

2. Buy a self-inflatable boat. If the water rises higher or more quickly than you expect, this may be your best escape transportation. Store a patch kit with the boat, just in case.

3. Be aware that floodwaters force small animals and snakes out of their underground homes. Know which poisonous snakes are in your area and how to identify them.

4. Again, be ready for a fast evacuation with emergency kits packed and escape routes planned.

5. Be prepared to move everything possible to the attic or the second floor of your home.

6. Don't underestimate the power of moving water. Just 6 inches of moving water is enough to make you lose your footing.

7. The most reliable and timely news will be from local news stations. Tune in to them, rather than to the big national networks.

8. Keep a few tools in your attic if you're planning on using it as your "higher ground" location. In case you need to break through the roof from the inside, you'll need an axe or a hatchet. A claw hammer to remove nails and a hacksaw will also come in handy.

9. Floodwaters can overrun water treatment plants. Have plenty of stored water, as detailed in Chapter 2, and at least two ways to purify water from other sources.

10. If you must wade through water, be sure to wear a pair of shoes with sturdy soles. Glass, sharp metal, and other dangerous debris will be lurking at the bottom of that muddy water.

11. Make sure you know alternate evacuation routes or routes home in case of damaged bridges.

12. If you're moving into an area that is prone to flooding, buy a house on high ground. Sounds obvious, but in the excitement of choosing a new home, it's easy to ignore practical safety issues.

13. That meandering little stream that crosses your property or runs through a nearby park can become a roaring monster within a short period of time. Keep that in mind, especially if your kids are outdoors playing.

14. Talk with your insurance agent about buying flood insurance. It might turn out to be the best money you've spent in a long time.

15. What loose items are in your front- or back-yard that might float away in flood waters? Be aware of them and plan to secure them inside.

16. If furniture cannot be easily moved, buy individual blocks of wood or use cans of paint to elevate it off the floor.

17. Food that has come into contact with flood-waters, including canned food, will have to be thrown away. Store as much of your food as possible at least 12 inches off the ground.

18. Never try to drive on a road that appears to be flooded. The road may have been washed away or weakened beneath the water, leaving a death trap for unwary drivers.

19. Take photographs of the water damage for insurance purposes and then begin cleaning up immediately.

20. Mold is likely to grow on anything porous that has been wet for more than 48 hours. It's important to begin the cleanup and drying process as soon as possible.

21. Keep track of cleanup expenses and save receipts for your insurance claims.

22. Backflow valves or plugs can be installed in drains, toilets, sinks, and anything else that connects to the sewer system. They will prevent floodwaters from entering your home from those outlets.

23. A sandbag placed in each toilet will help prevent sewage from backing up into your home.

When all is lost, start here!

Your home's been flattened, your car isn't running, your food storage has been swept away, and you have only the clothes on your back. How do you begin picking up the pieces?

1. You need help! Check to see if a relative or a friend can provide temporary housing for your family. This is no time to be proud. You need help, and your true friends will be more than willing to do anything they can to help.

2. If help from your loved ones isn't a possibility, approach a local church or charity for help.

3. If a Red Cross or FEMA shelter isn't an option, you'll have to stay in a hotel or a tent. If you're a timeshare owner, this might be a good time to use up some of those banked weeks!

4. Move quickly if you need a hotel or a rental car. It will be a matter of hours before other desperate people have the same idea!

5. If you have pets, begin looking for them if they have become lost during the crisis.

6. Access your important documents in your Grab-n-Go Binder, or the one you have stored with a trusted friend, and begin to contact your insurance companies.

7. Use your cell phone or digital camera to begin documenting the damage to your home, vehicle, and property. E-mail the photos to yourself, so you'll have easy access to them in the future and will be able to forward them to your insurance agent.

8. Quickly access any funds you have in your banking account(s). Remember, in an emergency "Cash is King!" If the power is out, chances are that your debit and credit cards will be useless, and vendors may not be willing to accept checks.

9. Use my End of the World Shopping Guide (next page) once you have cash and transportation and can begin shopping for necessities.

10. In the first few days following the disaster, delegate tasks among teenage and adult family members in order to maximize the window of opportunity you have for taking quick action.

11. Try to get into a routine of sorts as soon as possible to establish a sense of normalcy. Get the family outdoors, if possible—for walks around the neighborhood, bike rides, or anything physical that will help tire out worried kids and release endorphins that will lift your spirits. You'll probably be a lot more physically active without the previous creature comforts you owned. The exercise will build endurance and physical strength.

12. Get your hands on books and activities to keep your kids busy and focused on something other than their current reality. Find a fun read-aloud that the whole family can enjoy and become immersed in.

13. If it seems that you'll be homeless for a long period of time, begin looking for a long-term rental and jobs. Your employment and education records should be in your Grab-n-Go Binder, making this step a bit easier.

14. Now, more than ever, spend time with people who lift you up and always seem to see the silver lining behind every cloud.

The Survival Mom's End of the World Shopping Guide

Use this shopping guide for stocking up on important survival essentials either before a disaster or afterward. A warehouse store, such as Costco or Sam's Club, will have most or all of these items. This list is also helpful as a guide for stocking up on nonedible supplies.

Electronics

Batteries

Rechargeable batteries and charger

Pre-paid phone cards

Walkie-talkies

Spare USB drive

Home goods

Space-saver bags

Plastic storage bins

Backpack/duffel bag(s)

Portable heater

Portable fan/air conditioner

Blankets

Towels

Storage shelving

Hand truck

Fire extinguisher(s)

Solar-powered lights

Brita water pitcher and filters

Lightbulbs (multiple sizes, including floodlights)

Auto supplies and tools

Flashlights

Work gloves

Hand tools

Vehicle Emergency Kit

Wiper blades

Tarps

Generator

Motor oil

Extension cord(s)

Car battery

Blue (garage) paper towels

Microfiber towels

Rope

Duct tape

Office supplies

Binders

Paper

Printer ink

Page protectors

Writing pads

Pencils

Sharpies

Blank CDs/DVDs for copying data

Kitchen goods

Cooking burner

FoodSaver system

FoodSaver bags

Canning jars and lids

Cast iron pots

Food dehydrator

Plastic food-storage containers

Outdoor supplies

Sleeping bags

Propane tanks

Lighters

Lanterns

Two-way radio

Cold-weather gear

Camelback/water backpack

Cold-weather gloves for all

Grill

Fire pit/outdoor heater

Cleaning supplies

Lysol wipes, spray, or liquid cleaner

Dish soap

Bleach

Laundry detergent

Drano/drain cleaner

Vinegar

Paper goods

Toilet paper (one roll per person per week)

Facial tissue

Disposable gloves (check sizes)

Ziploc bags in different sizes

Trash bags in different sizes, including the big, black contractor bags

Plastic spoons/forks/knives

Paper plates (not foam)

Paper cups

Aluminum foil

Plastic wrap

Pet supplies

Kitty litter

Food

Treats

Rawhide bones

Personal supplies

Feminine hygiene products

Cheap nonprescription
eyeglasses (in case glasses
are lost)

Liquid hand soap

Shower gel

Shampoo/conditioner

Baby shampoo/baby skin
lotion

Bar soap

Hand sanitizer

Lotion

Shavers

Shaving cream

Antiperspirant/deodorant

Toothbrushes

Toothpaste

Dental floss (good for more
than just teeth)

Fluoride rinse

Condoms

Pregnancy test

Flushable wipes

Baby wipes

Baby formula

Diapers

Nutritionals/vitamins

Multivitamins

Medical and first-aid supplies

First-aid kit

Advil (adult and child)

Tylenol (adult and child)

Motrin (adult and child)

Aleve

Nyquil

Dayquil

Zicam (adult and child)

Robitussin (adult and child)

Prilosec

Pepto-Bismol

Cough drops

Afrin

Claritin (adult and child)

Benadryl (adult and child)

Mucinex (adult and child)

Delsym

Zyrtec

Imodium

Tums

Hydrocortisone cream

Airborne (adult and child)

GasEx/Beano

Alcohol

Alcohol swabs

Neosporin

Hydrogen peroxide

Fiber product like Metamucil

Epsom salts

Contact lens solutions and
cleaner

Bandages/Band-Aids

Cotton balls/cotton pads

Nitrile gloves (check sizes)

Blood pressure monitor

Clothing and other goods

Blankets

Towels

Socks

Underwear

Camisoles (for layering)

Shoes/boots

Extra clothing (pants, shirts,
etc.)

Coats/jackets/blanket pajamas

Sanity savers (books, CDs,
puzzles, etc.)

Lists I know you'll appreciate:

21 More Baby Steps for Getting Started

- Make an evacuation plan for your home, hold a family meeting, and conduct a drill.
- Learn how to use a solar oven.
- Take a first-aid or CPR class.
- Take a basic firearm class or an advanced class, if you already know the basics of shooting.
- Choose a family hobby that is preparedness-oriented.
- Learn how to start a fire using three different techniques.
- Go through your monthly expenses line by line to see which expenses can be either eliminated or decreased.
- Find the shut-off valve for your home's water and gas systems.
- Try a new variety of freeze-dried food to see how your family likes it.
- Learn how to bake bread from scratch.
- Start an herb garden and dehydrate your own herbs.
- Go camping. Sleep in a tent, not an RV.
- Plant three vegetables that your family enjoys eating.
- Declutter one room in your house to make space for your food and supply storage.
- Get an annual physical.
- Make a family plan to gather everyone together in the event of an emergency occurring while everyone is away from home.
- Buy $25 worth of "junk silver" each month. Buy more, if you can afford it.
- Read a preparedness-related book every month.
- Find someone with a preparedness skill you'd like to learn and schedule time for a lesson or two; e.g., fishing, carpentry, or knitting.
- Take a class to learn orienteering.
- Sign up for a local CERT class.

33 Books Every Survival Mom Should Read

Wake up, people! Books for motivating you to prepare

Alas, Babylon by Pat Frank

American Apocalypse by Nova

Lights Out by David Crawford

Lucifer's Hammer by Larry Niven

One Second After by William Forstchen

Patriots by James Wesley Rawles

The Walk by Lee Goldberg

Mental preparedness

Deep Survival: Who Lives, Who Dies, and Why by Laurence Gonzalez

The Gift of Fear by Gavin de Becker

The Survivors Club: The Secrets and Science That Could Save Your Life by Ben Sherwood

The Unthinkable: Who Survives When Disaster Strikes—and Why by Amanda Ripley

Wilderness and outdoor survival

The Boy's Book of Outdoor Survival by Chris McNab

Bug Out: The Complete Plan for Escaping a Catastrophic Disaster Before It's Too Late by Scott B. Williams

Survive! Essential Skills and Tactics to Get You Out of Anywhere—Alive by Les Stroud

Will to Live by Les Stroud

TEOTWAWKI survival

Crisis Preparedness Handbook by Jack A. Spigarelli

The Backyard Homestead edited by Carleen Madigan

The Encyclopedia of Country Living by Carla Emery

Gardening When It Counts by Steve Solomon

How to Survive the End of the World as We Know It by James Wesley Rawles

The Modern Survival Manual by Fernando Aguirre

Prescription for Herbal Healing by Phyllis A. Balch

Square Foot Gardening by Mel Bartholomew

When All Hell Breaks Loose by Cody Lundin

When There Is No Doctor by David Werner

Where There Is No Dentist by Murray Dickson

Food storage

Ball Complete Book of Home Preserving by Judi Kingry

Cooking with Home Storage by Peggy Layton & Vicki Tate

Dinner Is in the Jar by Kathy Clark

Food Storage 101 by Peggy Layton

Food Storage Made Easy, e-book at www.foodstoragemadeeasy.com

Mary Bell's Complete Dehydrator Cookbook by Mary Bell

The Complete Idiot's Guide to Food Preserving by Karen K. Brees

Fun Survival Literature for Kids

Many of the fiction titles are great as read-alouds even if they are written for older kids. Some of my favorites are:

Fiction

The Cay by Theodore Taylor

The Courage of Sarah Noble by Alice Dalgliesh

Dakota Dugout by Ann Turner

Farmer Boy by Laura Ingalls Wilder (particularly good for an example of self-sufficient living)

Fly Away Home by Eve Bunting

Hatchet by Gary Paulsen

Homeplace by Anne Shelby

Island of the Blue Dolphins by Scott O'Dell

Little Blog on the Prairie by Cathleen Davitt Bell

Little House on the Prairie series by Laura Ingalls Wilder

Meet Kirsten, an American Girl by Janet Beeler Shaw

Meet Kit, an American Girl by Valerie Tripp

The Misadventures of Maude March by Audrey Couloumbis

My First Little House Books series for ages 4–8 by Laura Ingalls Wilder

My Side of the Mountain by Jean Craighead George

Nine for California by Sonia Levitin

Potato: A Tale from the Great Depression by Kathy Lied

Sarah Whitcher's Story by Elizabeth Yates

Tight Times by Barbara Shook Hazen

The Sign of the Beaver by Elizabeth George Speare

When I Was Young in the Mountains by Cynthia Rylant

Yonder by Tony Johnston

Nonfiction

A Kid's Herb Book by Leslie Tierra

The American Boy's Handy Book by Daniel Carter Beard

The Boy's Book of Outdoor Survival by Chris McNab

The Field and Forest Handy Book by Daniel Carter Beard

Survivor Kid: A Practical Guide to Wilderness Survival by Denise Long

Common Freeze-Dried and Dehydrated Foods

Fruit

Apples: chips, dices, or slices

Apricots

Bananas: chips or slices

Blackberries

Blueberries

Grapes

Mandarin oranges

Mangoes

Peach slices

Pears

Pineapple

Raspberries

Strawberries

Vegetables

Asparagus

Broccoli

Carrots: dices

Cauliflower

Celery

Corn

Green beans

Green onions

Mixed vegetables

Mushrooms

Onions

Peas

Peppers

Potatoes: chunks, dices, flakes, hash browns, or slices

Spinach

Sweet potatoes

Tomato powder

Zucchini

Baking ingredients

Butter powder

Cheese: freeze-dried or powder

Eggs: powdered egg white and whole eggs or freeze-dried scrambled eggs

Milk

Shortening powder

Sour cream

Skill-of-the-Month Club

There are just too many skills to learn, and even great-great-grandma couldn't do everything. What has worked for me and many other Survival Moms is to designate a skill to learn each month. On The Survival Mom blog, we call it "The Skill of the Month." Here's a sample schedule:

January   Learn how to grind wheat and bake bread from scratch. Expand your repertoire by making sourdough bread, English muffins, tortillas, and whole wheat crackers!

February   Learn how to sprout seeds. Wheat berries, radish seeds, Mung beans and alfalfa all work just fine.

March   Write out an evacuation plan for your family. Include at least three routes out of town, if possible, and assemble 72-Hour Kits. See Chapter 11 for details.

April   Plant an herb garden or expand the selection of herbs you already grow.

May   Before the hot temperatures hit, learn how to cook using a solar cooker. You won't be heating up your kitchen, and you'll use only the sun's energy.

June   It's Dutch oven month! Learn how to cook a main dish, a side dish, and a dessert in your Dutch oven!

July   Take the kids geocaching. It combines hiking and navigating with hidden treasures. Kids and adults love this hobby.

August   Go camping, primitive style. A tent is allowed, but an RV isn't! Start fire from scratch. Look for edible plants. Determine to rough it for at least two or three nights.

September   Sign up for a Red Cross class. The kids are back in school, and now it's your turn!

October   Research how to start a compost pile and then do it. It takes a few months to develop the best compost, so your spring garden has something to look forward to!

November   Take up either crochet or knitting. With some practice, you have time to create a few gifts in time for the holidays!

December   Make homemade laundry detergent and cleaning solutions and try them for a month.

Now, fill out your own Skill-of-the-Month schedule to keep yourself motivated and on track.

January _____
_____

February _____
_____

March _____
_____

April _____
_____

May _____
_____

June _____
_____

July _____
_____

August _____
_____

September _____
_____

October _____
_____

November _____
_____

December _____
_____

Where to Learn New Skills

There are so many free and inexpensive resources to support you. Here are just a few that will provide training, supplies, and reference materials:

- Public and university libraries, both for checking out books and occasional book sales
- YouTube videos
- Websites and blogs
- Family members, friends, and neighbors
- Senior citizen centers
- Community centers
- County and university extension offices
- 4-H Club
- YMCA classes
- Game and Fish departments
- City Parks and Recreation departments
- Hobby clubs
- Specialty retail stores, such as Cabela's or Home Depot
- Public domain books, available for free online
- Garage and estate sales
- Craigslist, eBay, and Freecycle
- Online courses and webinars

If you find yourself returning to the same store time after time as you buy supplies for your hobby or project, ask the manager if the store offers classes. Sometimes the training is there just for the asking.

Heartfelt Thanks

No Survival Mom is an island, and I'm no exception. The truth is that many, many people helped me from the very beginning—before the book was even a concept—to the end, with friends scrambling to test the final versions of recipes!

Gary Morris, my agent, first discovered my blog and sent me an e-mail that changed my world. "Have you ever thought about a book?" was his subject line. I never deleted that e-mail. Thanks, Gary, for everything.

Cindy DiTiberio, Lisa Zuniga, and the team at HarperOne kept me on track and coached me through the many questions I had. As a first-time author, I'm sure I tried their patience.

Numerous people, including all my Facebook friends, freely shared many of the tips found in this book. They were a constant source of creative tips and real-life experiences. All I had to do was ask, and they answered. Thanks so much, everybody!

Expert advice came from:

- Dave Turner and Patrice Blank, dedicated medical professionals
- Marta Waddell, gardening expert
- Kevin Bock and Scott Gamm shared their financial expertise.
- Alan Erickson knows more about generators than I ever will and happily shared his knowledge.
- Doug Babcock of Cygnus Security Consulting and Brian Baker of Baker Security Group

- Chrystalyn Trimble for her Super Rice recipe and for her assistance with my food storage chapters.
- Chris Slife of Howling Coyote Silver
- Podcaster Bob Mayne of the *Handgun World Show* and *Today's Survival Show* is also a home security expert. Thanks, Bob!

Anna Biava, Alan Martindale, Holly Cooley, Leon Pantenburg, Lucas Mayeur, and Rob Hanus all provided expert advice, going above and beyond my expectations.

And thanks to all Survival Moms who shared their stories with me. I wasn't able to use all of these stories in this book, but your spirit and courage inspired me.

Giving credit where it's due

Chapter 2:
Composting information,
http://www.motherearthnews.com/Organic-Gardening/2006-10-01/Compost-Made-Easy.aspx

"No burn" list, http://www.epa.gov

Well tips, http://www.healthunit.org/water/infosheet/pathogens.htm

Sanitizer recipe, http://www.ocfs.state.ny.us/main/childcare/assets/Bleach%20Sanitizing%20Solution%20%28rev%20APR%202009%29.pdf

Chapter 5:
Dry ice packing instructions,
http://www.providentliving.org/content/display/0,11666,2257-1-1147-1,00.html

Chapter 7:
Kelly McCann, http://www.themodernsurvivalist.com/?p=912

Chapter 8:
Home security statistics, http://household-tips.thefuntimesguide.com-2010/05/security_systems_for_home.php

Chapter 11:
Hurricane Katrina experiences,
http://bayourenaissanceman.blogspot.com/2008/08/lessons-learned-from-hurricanes-katrina.html

On the personal side were friends and family who not only believed in this book and in me, but also demonstrated it in so many ways.

The co-op moms—Debbie Jones, Debbie Montano, Linda Blinn, and Jolene Berger—deserve an especially big thank-you for giving me a free ride this school year and providing an amazing educational experience for my kids.

My good friend, Diana DelPrincipe, was a surrogate mom like none other during the busy weeks when this book was my only focus and I was far from home, and Debbie Tennant treated my kids so well that I worried they might not want to come home!

Thanks for taking me in and showing me so much hospitality, Janice Marley and Byron and Lisa Wise.

Alyssa Wise provided timely and expert research assistance.

My family has always believed in me, even when I scarcely believed in myself. Thank you!

Finally, my own awesome threesome deserves the biggest thanks of all for their never-ending love, patience, and encouragement. My husband, Stephen, never gave up hope and belief that I could write a book. My kids, Olivia and Andrew, had their world upended for weeks at a time, eating ravioli and macaroni and cheese day after day. I love you more than I'll ever be able to express.

Soli Deo Gloria,

— *Lisa*

Index